D1569049

OXFORD MODERN LANGUAGES
AND LITERATURE MONOGRAPHS

THE THEATRE
AND ITS CRITICS IN
SEVENTEENTH-
CENTURY FRANCE

HENRY PHILLIPS

OXFORD UNIVERSITY PRESS
1980

Oxford University Press, Walton Street, Oxford OX2 6DP

OXFORD LONDON GLASGOW
NEW YORK TORONTO MELBOURNE WELLINGTON
KUALA LUMPUR SINGAPORE JAKARTA HONG KONG TOKYO
DELHI BOMBAY CALCUTTA MADRAS KARACHI
NAIROBI DAR ES SALAAM CAPE TOWN

Published in the United States by
Oxford University Press, New York

British Library Cataloguing in Publication Data

Phillips, J. Henry
    The theatre and its critics in seventeenth century France.
    — (Oxford modern languages and literature).
    1. Theatre and society — France.
    2. Dramatic criticism — France — History — 17th century
    I. Title   II. Series
    792'.0944   PN2049   79–41801

    ISBN 0-19-815535-2

Set by Hope Services, Abingdon
and printed in Great Britain by
Camelot Press

ACKNOWLEDGEMENTS

This book is a slightly amended version of my doctoral thesis submitted for approval by the Faculty of Modern and Mediaeval Languages and Literature in the University of Oxford. Accordingly I should like to record my thanks to my examiners, Dr M. Gerard-Davis and Professor H.T. Barnwell, for their helpful suggestions and criticisms. I owe too a debt of gratitude to Professor Jacques Morel of the Sorbonne for his constant interest in my work and to both him and his wife for the great hospitality shown to me while researching in Paris during the academic year 1969–70. My task in producing the book was made easier by the kind co-operation of the various secretaries, past and present, of the French Department in the University of Aberdeen, and by the invaluable help given by my colleague, Dr Philip Ford, in reading and correcting the proofs. But the greatest debt is due to the supervisor of my thesis, Dr Denys Potts of Keble College, Oxford, whose great scholarship and sensitivity, constant encouragement, and everlasting patience saw me to the end both of the thesis and of the study in its present form.

CONTENTS

INTRODUCTION

The subject of this book is the difference of opinion between, on the one hand, theologians and religious moralists who sought to prove that the public theatre in France in the seventeenth century, its actors, and the plays they performed, led inevitably to the moral disintegration of the individual and society, and, on the other hand, dramatic theorists and playwrights who advocated the theatre as a means of maintaining and improving moral standards. The book examines the dramatic theorists' conception of moral instruction and their proposals for achieving it in the theatre, and also the arguments in condemnation of drama, advanced by religious moralists. The main focus of attention is the dramatic experience, by which I mean the experience undergone not only by the spectator, but also by the actor, during the actual performance of a play. Hence the book is concerned with the legitimacy of particular subjects, the suitability of certain kinds of play (notably comedy and religious tragedy), and the use and abuse of various literary devices to guide and manipulate the spectator's response. The views expressed by religious moralists inevitably lead on to a discussion of the effects a play has outside the theatre: they hold that the everyday conduct of the individual spectator is affected by what he sees on the stage, and discuss whether any form of official control could effectively check this adverse influence.

The emphasis of this book is thus on theory and I have adopted a thematic rather than historical approach. The choice of such an approach can be justified in a number of ways. Firstly, it avoids needless repetition and focuses much closer attention on the issues involved. The chronological method, adhered to by many previous commentators on the *querelle du théâtre*, has resulted in overgeneralization and a tendency to see the controversy in the seventeenth

century as simply a prelude to that in the eighteenth century.[1]
Secondly, the religious moralists demonstrate a remarkable
unity of outlook in their condemnation of theatre. It is
important to understand that opposition to drama came from
all sections of the Church, and from Protestants as well as
Catholics. Many of the Catholic opponents were certainly
Jansenists or at least sympathizers (Nicole, Conti, Voisin,
Coustel, Varet). The Oratorians were represented in strength
(Lamy, Senault, Lejeune, Lebrun), but so were the Capuchins
(Yves de Paris, Héliodore de Paris) and the Jesuits (Bourdaloue,
La Colombière, Cheminais de Montaigu). Two other major
figures, Bossuet and Fénelon, contributed to the dispute,
as did the Protestants, André Rivet and Philippe Vincent.
The wide range of theologians and moralists represented in
the *querelle* certainly seems to indicate that moral rigorism
had, by the end of the century, made its mark on the whole
spectrum of the Catholic Church.

To a certain extent, such widely differing authors share,
in questions of morals, a common fund of source material in
the works of the early Fathers (although on more centrally
doctrinal issues the Protestants did not accept their validity).
Tertullian, Clement of Alexandria, St. Cyprian, and others
are all quoted at some time or another as authorities for the
moralists' own arguments. The only time, however, that I
specifically refer to a writer's sources is when reproducing
a quotation or when a problem concerning sources is
mentioned by the moralist or dramatic theorist himself, as in
the case of Aristotle or St. Thomas Aquinas. Otherwise I have
not undertaken to elucidate any unacknowledged source.

Dramatic theorists, with a few dissenting voices of greater
or lesser significance, also show a unity of outlook on the
question of moral instruction in drama. The most controversial
statements of unorthodoxy are of course those of Corneille's
Discours and *Examens*. Whether other playwrights are
sincere or not in their adherence to the orthodox line, as for
example Molière in the preface and *Placets* at the head of
Le Tartuffe, is open to question. They too, however, share a

---

[1] I refer particularly to the works of M. Barras, M. Moffat, and L. Bourquin.
In recent years articles by M. Fumaroli, J. Dubu, and J.-M. Piemme have done
much to bring many interesting features of the *querelle* into sharper focus.

common fund of arguments derived from the works of Aristotle, Horace, and their various commentators.

A purely thematic study is not, however, without its dangers. One possible objection is that theories on a single subject can change over the years along with the different historical conditions in which they are elaborated. This problem is perhaps less crucial for dramatic theorists, whose polemical debates are mostly concentrated in the years 1628-60, than for religious moralists whose works range over a longer period. But, apart from the obvious nuances which separate one writer from another, there was a remarkable consistency in the attitudes expressed by religious moralists throughout the century. Moreover, the themes themselves remained constant, although certain arguments may have received more attention than others at a particular moment in time. A good example of this is the role of magistrates in dealing with the public theatre, which becomes a major issue in the *affaire Caffaro* of 1694. The subject had in fact been mentioned briefly by J.-P. Camus in 1632 and by Yves de Paris in 1656, and was dealt with at greater length by Héliodore de Paris in 1685.

However, given the theoretical bias of this study, it is important that the reader should be able to relate the issues examined to the broader context of both seventeenth-century drama and spirituality. This is particularly so in view of the fact that the century which saw the most brilliant single period of theatrical activity in French history, encouraged by the most powerful people in the land, should at the same time have been the target of a sustained and unrelenting attack from all quarters of the French Churches. This seemingly paradoxical situation cannot fully be understood without some explanation of the state of the theatre and its development in the seventeenth century. Equally, the attitudes of theologians and religious moralists must be understood in the light of the evolution of French spirituality and, on one specific issue, the ecclesiastical politics of the time.

The development of theatre was perhaps the most distinctive feature of cultural history in seventeenth-century France. By the mid-1630s there were three troupes with permanent premises in Paris, two French and one Italian, to which Molière's would be added in 1658. But the beginnings of the Paris theatre were not auspicious; it was, in the early years of the century, considered even by many contemporaries to be a somewhat insalubrious institution where the plays were often crude in content and style. While John Lough rightly warns against the simplistic view of the audiences at this time as overwhelmingly plebeian,[2] it is generally accepted that a new and more refined generation of playwrights (among them Rayssiguier, Du Ryer, Auvray, and d'Ouville) brought into the theatres a more, but not exclusively, sensitive and sophisticated public. An equally crucial factor was the patronage of nobles and statesmen, the greatest of whom was Cardinal Richelieu. He is an important figure in the *querelle* because he is credited by many seventeenth-century writers with almost single-handedly raising the status of the theatre from its degenerate beginnings, and his name is often quoted in polemical works as a guarantee of the theatre's social and moral acceptability. His interest took several forms: he commissioned the *Comédie des Tuileries* in 1635;[3] he had a theatre constructed in his palace; and, most important of all, he was undoubtedly the inspiration behind Louis XIII's edict of 1641 which absolved actors from the charge of infamy inherited from Roman law.

After Richelieu's death, patronage from the highest quarters continued, firstly with Mazarin, and then with Louis XIV. The latter gave weighty subsidies to all the Paris theatres (including the Italians) and personally reorganized the French troupes in Paris after Molière's death, eventually creating the Comédie-Française in 1680. The king was also a major impresario, commissioning works from Molière, for example, which were performed in the spectacular surroundings of Fontainebleau and Versailles. Indeed in 1694 Thomas Caffaro provided his detractors

[2] Lough, J., *Paris Theatre Audiences in the Seventeenth and Eighteenth Centuries*, Oxford, 1957, pp. 12–22.

[3] The *Comédie des Tuileries* was written by five authors, Boisrobert, Colletet, Corneille, L'Estoile, and Rotrou, who were each assigned an act. Richelieu himself supplied the idea.

with a difficult problem when he used royal tolerance of the theatre as an argument for its respectability. But Louis's influence was in some ways limited. The great protector of Molière could do little to mitigate the Church's treatment of the comic playwright at his death in 1673. Certainly the king's intercession allowed Molière's widow to give him a Christian burial, but it was a small compromise, not a rehabilitation.

But theatrical conditions were far from uniformly ideal. It is amazing to think that in the seventeenth century itself not one building had been designed specifically for the sort of plays performed and written during this period. The Hôtel de Bourgogne had been constructed a century earlier primarily for the performance of mystery plays, and the Hôtel du Marais, albeit rebuilt in 1644, was a converted *jeu de paume* (this type of building was often used as a theatre in seventeenth-century France). Given that the audience in the pit stood for the whole of the performance, it is not surprising that theatres were often the scene of rowdyism and for this reason still considered a potential source of social disorder. These circumstances, however, did not prevent the French theatre from providing an extra-ordinary range of plays and dramatic forms, from the pastoral, comedy, and farce to tragedy and the *pièces à machines* with their magnificent and literally spell-binding effects. As for the subjects of plays, the tragedies of the first half of the century were principally concerned with political themes, while comedy and pastoral heavily emphasized the love interest. This, to the chagrin not only of religious moralists, was later to dominate the more serious genres as well.

One important development in what were apparently disadvantageous conditions was the growing interest during the 1630s and 1640s in the techniques of the illusionist theatre or of the so-called Italian order.[4] Theorists like Chapelain and d'Aubignac were keen to demonstrate the superiority of this form of theatrical presentation where the

---

[4] T. Lawrenson's *The French Stage in the Seventeenth Century*, Manchester, 1957, is indispensable for the history of staging in our period.

perspective set plays a crucial role. They were conscious too
that such an arrangement of the stage imposed certain
restrictions on the form of plays and it ïs in this context
that the ever-misunderstood rules were elaborated. They
must therefore be seen rather as aesthetic imperatives
deriving from the dramatic illusion than as arbitrary
impositions of Aristotelian doctrine.[5] Indeed, the *Poetics*,
in its definition of tragedy as the imitation of an action, is
a key work for the French illusionist theorists (heavily
influenced by their sixteenth-century Italian counterparts)
who also emphasize the Aristotelian idea of verisimilitude
(not the same as truth which sometimes lacks credibility)
as controlling what can be seen and believed on the stage.
Certainly, Donald Stone has shown in his work on French
humanist tragedy of the previous century that preoccupation
with *vraisemblance* was not new to French dramatic theory.
But, as he points out, the humanists' source for *vraisemblance* was not necessarily the *Poetics* but rather the
rhetorical notion of appropriateness.[6] In any case they were
not concerned with the illusionist theatre which gives the
debate a radically new orientation in the seventeenth century.
The theorists of our period stress yet another feature of
vraisemblance where the latter possesses more than just a
technical function, and comes to play an important part
in determining the moral orientation of a play.

Dramatic theorists of the seventeenth century were of
course deeply convinced of the moral usefulness of theatre,
where instruction is the aim and pleasure the means.[7] Clearly,
in their emphasis on moral instruction the writers of this
period were following a long-standing tradition which
regarded didacticism as an essential part of any branch of

[5] It is interesting to read Rémy Saisselin's remark that 'The conventions of
French classical tragedy are not solely to be explained in terms of pedants elabor-
ating rules against nature and reason, but on the contrary may be seen as making
excellent sense on the basis of certain assumptions concerning the visible and the
imagined', *The Rule of Reason and the Ruses of the Heart: A Philosophical
Dictionary of Classical French Criticism, Critics and Aesthetic Issues*, Cleveland,
1970, p. 217.

[6] Stone, D., *French Humanist Tragedy*, Manchester, 1974, pp. 157 seq.

[7] A provocative view challenging orthodox assumptions about classical theorists'
adherence to didacticism is found in Arsène Soreil's *Introduction à l'histoire de
l'esthétique française*, Brussels, 1955, pp. 37 seq.

poetry.[8] However, the renewed emphasis on moral instruction in the theatre in the 1630s and 1640s was a direct result of the theorists' realization that the ultimate means of persuasion was to be found in the illusionist theatre where the moral message can be reckoned all the stronger for the audience's being convinced, like witnesses at a real event, by what is happening on the stage. Chapelain went further and made catharsis dependent on the audience's level of belief in the action.[9] Another explanation for the increasing importance of moral instruction in theorists' writings is offered by Jean-Marie Piemme who argues that such a defensive stand is necessary for the complete rehabilitation of the theatre as a worthy institution in society and as a means of parrying the hostility shown towards the theatre by the Church.[10]

However, the magnificence and professed moral purpose of a theatre patronized by the rich and powerful did not impress a growing body of opinion within the Church which held that the theatre, plays and players alike, exercised a morally harmful influence on the individual and on society. There are firstly a number of general reasons which may account for the hostility of theologians and religious moralists during the seventeenth century. From Plato down to our own times there has always been a strong tradition of official suspicion of imaginative literature. Some political regimes are obviously more susceptible to this than others, but throughout the centuries most societies have deemed it necessary to operate some form of censorship of the arts, in modern times widening its brief to cover films and television. Censorship is often justified on the grounds that certain types of literature or even certain episodes and expressions in individual works undermine the moral values which maintain social stability. In this sense, the theatre can be assimilated with other forms of imaginative literature and has no special status among them.

[8] See Stone, *French Humanist Tragedy*, pp. 19 seq.
[9] Stone makes a similar observation in *French Humanist Tragedy*, p. 191. T. J. Reiss is also conscious of the relation of *vraisemblance* to moral instruction, *Toward Dramatic Illusion: Theatrical Technique and Meaning*, New Haven and London, 1971, p. 141.
[10] 'L'Utile dulci ou la convergence des nécessités . . .', *Revue d'histoire du théâtre*, vol. 2, 1969, pp. 118-33.

In the seventeenth century, drama did not constitute an entirely separate category but was a branch of poetry, often called 'la poésie représentative', possessing features common to other forms of imaginative fiction. In the context of the *querelle*, drama and the novel are often spoken of in the same breath: Bernard Lamy tells us in the *Avertissement* to his *Nouvelles réflexions sur l'art poétique* (Paris, 1678) that he intends to describe the rules of epic and dramatic poetry, 'lesquelles sont aussi communes à ces Histoires Poëtiques qu'on appelle Romans'; another moralist, Frain du Tremblay, asserts that 'les Comedies et les Romans sont quasi la même chose, et qu'ils ne different presque que dans le style'.[11] In fact many religious moralists are equally concerned with what they regard as the morally harmful effects of novels, especially for young women, when they can be read in private and secretly, thus allowing for all sorts of uncontrolled fantasizing.

There are several other ways in which the theatre may be accommodated within a more general perspective, not necessarily limited to the arts. Here two aspects of rhetoric are particularly relevant: the manipulation of emotion to persuade of falsehood (a problem related to politics and the lawcourts); and the ornamentation of truth, where a love of ornamentation can take precedence over a love of truth, both for the writer and for the reader or listener. Even the pulpit is not exempt from this last tendency. Many preachers and moralists complain that sermons are too often appreciated for their manner of delivery rather than for their content, and warn against pandering to consumer reaction. Might they not become too much like actors? The essential point is, of course, that we run the risk of being persuaded of harmful ideas when our minds are concentrated elsewhere, when our critical sense is thus impaired. One is also reminded of Catholic suspicion of Protestant hymn-singing, where music is akin to rhetorical ornamentation. It is not therefore surprising that religious moralists were so sensitive to certain aspects of secular spectacle, opera included.

---

[11]   Frain du Tremblay, J., *Nouveaux Essais de morale*, Paris, 1691, p. 151.

But it cannot be denied that the theatre attracts attention for reasons deriving from its specific nature as an art form. It is a public spectacle attracting large numbers of people, and as such a possible threat to public order. It is moreover a cult institution where attention is focused on individuals of some personal attraction, many actors and playwrights achieving great personal followings throughout the century. The most important consideration from our point of view is that Horace's dictum about what one sees having far greater impact than what one reads was taken at its face value by theorists and moralists alike. For the latter this makes drama by far the most dangerous branch of literature. The *querelle du théâtre* is also more interesting because religious moralists were dealing with problems which had never arisen in quite the same way before. The early decades of the seventeenth century in France see for the first time a permanent theatre of almost wholly secular inspiration, performing continuously throughout the year.

It would seem appropriate to concentrate our attention, then, on the reasons for the stage controversy more peculiar to the ecclesiastical and spiritual matters of our period. One aspect of the Church's reaction to the theatre has been brilliantly exposed by Jean Dubu in a series of articles on the use bishops made of the diocesan ritual in dealing with actors. The ritual specifies, among other matters of liturgy and parish organization, certain categories of people who, unless certain conditions are fulfilled, are refused the sacraments (and who are, as a consquence, debarred from acting as godparents or from receiving a Christian burial).[12] The seventeenth-century Church used as a model the ritual published by Pope Paul V in 1614. The turning-point in its history in France came in 1641 when Louis XIII published the edict which absolved actors from the charge of infamy. The tradition of the Church, dating from the early years of its history under the Roman Empire, held that those who

---

[12] Interesting here is the fact that Louis XIV and Henriette d'Angleterre were godparents to Molière's first-born. Georges Mongrédien, on the other hand, gives us an example of an actress whose right to the status of godmother was challenged by a priest, *La Vie quotidienne des comédiens au temps de Molière*, Paris, 1966, pp. 18-19.

were *infames* in law were in an irregular position in the
eyes of the Church and were debarred from taking holy
orders. The 1641 edict now allowed, therefore, this possibility
to actors. Many bishops saw this as an unwarranted and
unconstitutional interference by the State in ecclesiastical
affairs and they reacted by publishing rituals with the insertion
of actors among those refused the sacraments, unless they
publicly renounced their profession. The Pauline ritual
gave no authority for this. None the less some bishops
continued using the Pope's name in their own titles. The
first ritual to change (rituals were altered always on the
instigation of the bishop) was that of Châlons in 1645
(Châlons's bishop until 1681 was Vialart, whose association
with Port-Royal is well known), although actors were
mentioned in connection with the refusal of Christian burial
in *sacerdotalia* (instructions for the advice of priests) as early
as 1601. The process gathered momentum until its climax
in the ritual of Metz (1713), the first to abandon the model
of the Pauline ritual, which excluded anyone who had
contributed to performances and their preparation, from
actors to candle-snuffers. Two facts are worthy of mention:
Bossuet, whose *Maximes et réflexions sur le théâtre* so
heavily condemned the public theatre, especially the plays
and person of Molière, never altered his ritual; the Church's
treatment of Molière as he lay dying was on the other hand
made possible by the alteration of the Paris ritual (originally
published along Pauline lines) by Archbishop Jean-François
de Gondy in 1654, and was almost certainly a signal for a
more consistently harsh attitude toward actors until the
end of the century and beyond.

   The prolongation of this movement some time after the
death of Richelieu, the main target of the bishop's wrath
at the time of the edict itself, shows the need to account
for the Church's attitude in broader terms. There is no
question that from around 1640, significantly the date of
publication of Cornelius Jansen's *Augustinus*, a more general
climate of moral austerity found its expression in the works
of many theologians, preachers, and religious moralists.
Imbued with the reforming spirit of the Counter-Reformation
they undertook a domestic crusade against all forms of

behaviour, both in and outside the Church, which they saw as
prejudicial to the pursuit of an authentic Christian life.
Theatre-going was one such form of behaviour. The more
conciliatory spirit of St. Francis of Sales, who found no
necessary moral danger in plays, and the more positive view
of play-acting taken by St. Thomas Aquinas, still highly
regarded in the seventeenth century despite a general decline
in speculative theology, gave way, although not exclusively,
to the less compromising attitude of rigorist spirituality.
The reaction of the bishops to the 1641 edict can be seen as
a manifestation of their frustration that the Tridentine spirit
had not passed into French law. Consequently they seized
upon the ritual in order to institutionalize the reformist
spirit in at least one activity they regarded as harmful to
moral standards. It was therefore no accident or arbitrary fit
of pique that prompted prominent reformist bishops like
Nicolas Pavillon of Aleth, a figure almost venerated at Port-
Royal, to change their rituals.[13] Nor is it surprising that
characters like Nicole, Senault, Lamy or Bossuet should
have added their voice to the debate about the morally
subversive character of the theatrical experience, especially
when they saw prominent laymen, who should have set
an example to their fellow Christians, submit to this experience with such regularity. The *querelle du théâtre* in
seventeenth-century France is thus a good illustration of a
particular spiritual mentality applied to a specific area
of social life.

Let us now look more closely at the actual chronology
of the debate which, as seen in the case of the *sacerdotalia*,
began much earlier than the edict of 1641. In terms of
printed works, however, it appears that the *querelle* falls
into two convenient halves. The major works of the dramatic
theorists form a group covering the years 1628-60 (that is
to say the works of Chapelain, La Mesnardière, d'Aubignac,
and Corneille's 1660 edition including the *Discours* and the
Examens). During this time we also have the *querelle du Cid*,
in which Richelieu involved his newly created *Académie*. On

[13] For this particular case, see J. Dubu, 'L'Église catholique et la condemnation
du théâtre en France', *Quaderni francesi*, vol. I, 1970, pp. 319-49, pp. 327-8.

the other hand the majority of the printed works against the
theatre (setting aside the rituals which enter into no polemical
detail of any substance) appear after 1660. But clearly the
picture is a little more complex than pure convenience will
allow.

Already in 1603 a Mlle de Beaulieu felt moved to write
her *Première atteinte contre ceux qui accusent les comédies*,
and in 1608 Jean de Savaron published his *Traité contre les
masques*. The 1630s seem to be the period when defensive
statements about the theatre became more frequent, and
this at the time of its growing prestige. In 1632 Gougenot
and Scudéry felt under sufficient pressure to defend actors
in two plays bearing the same title, *La Comédie des comédiens*,
although the motives of Scudéry, ever one to jump on a
bandwagon, may have been less generously inspired. While
Corneille's *Illusion comique* (1635), with its direct and
presumably tolerated reference to the king's support of
theatre, appears to show an upward turn in the official
status of the institution, the subject of the play itself speaks
volumes for the need to convince the bourgeois fathers of
present and future actors that their sons' profession is worthwhile. Guez de Balzac too intimates that the theatre's
reputation has improved when he writes to the actor Mondory
in 1636 that his stature has been enough to reconcile the
theatre with 'les ***', which, if he is referring to the Church,
could not have been more wrong. But, whatever the real
situation, these two examples do serve to illustrate the
optimism of those who cared about the position of theatre
in society. It is sad to record, then, that in 1657 Quinault is
still trying to convince the bougeois public about actors in
La Comédie sans comédie, and that Chappuzeau feels obliged
to give us his *Théâtre françois*, the only work of substance
by a layman in defence of the actor in the seventeenth
century, which was published in 1674, significantly the year
after Molière's death.

The first major work against the theatre in our period was
the Protestant André Rivet's *Instruction chrestienne touchant
les spectacles* (1639) which prompted Scudéry's *Apologie
du théâtre* in the same year. The other major anti-theatrical
work before 1660 was by another Protestant, Philippe

Vincent, and entitled *Traité des théâtres* (1647). Among Catholic writers in the 1640s Suffren and Senault both include passages in their works condemning the theatre. Senault is an interesting case: in *De l'usage des passions* his attitude towards drama is much more conciliatory (but not adulatory) than in *Le Monarque, ou les devoirs du souverain* (1661), where the king is advised to shun plays altogether. Is this another sign of more cautious attitudes when Richelieu had a direct hand in theatrical affairs? In any case, Senault never altered the reference to drama in the six editions of *De l'usage des passions* issued after the publication of *Le Monarque* up to his death in 1672.

The 1660s represent the first concentrated period of polemical debate in the seventeenth century, in which Molière's name was to figure prominently and often. In 1662, among pedantic arguments inspired by petty jealousies, *L'École des femmes* came under fire for alleged obscenity and blasphemy. *Le Tartuffe* was a target of sustained attack from its first performance in 1664, and *Dom Juan* (1665) earned its bevy of detractors who took issue with the playwright for the parody of divine judgement in the Commandeur and the cause of religion being upheld by a garrulous fool. Racine became personally embroiled with his former mentors at Port-Royal during the *querelle des Imaginaires* (1665-7), sparked off by the tragedian's reaction to a derogatory reference to playwrights by Nicole in his *Première Visionnaire*, which was anyway directed at Desmarets de Saint-Sorlin and had nothing whatever to do with the stage controversy.[14] Nicole did, however, write in 1667 a more detailed attack on theatre in his *Traité de la comédie*.[15] This period is distinguished by three other works which in fact constitute one single controversy. In 1666 the Prince de Conti, newly converted to piety (he had at one time been a patron of Molière), wrote his *Traité de la comédie et des spectacles* to which he appended a selection of quotations on the subject of drama from the patristic authorities.

[14] A full discussion of this incident is found in Raymond Picard, *La Carrière de Jean Racine*, Paris, 1961, Partie I, chap. 3, pp. 119-25.
[15] The introduction to G. Couton's edition gives a full explanation of the problems concerned with the dating of this work.

L'Abbé d'Aubignac replied in the same year with his *Dissertation sur la condamnation des théâtres*, seeking to discount the relevance of the early Church's condemnation of the theatre of his own time. Such was deemed the Abbé's impertinence that Joseph de Voisin, a supporter of Conti, took five years to amass the erudite arguments of his *Défense du traitté de Monseigneur le Prince de Conti touchant la comédie* . . . , which put d'Aubignac's learning completely in the shade. I have concentrated here on the major works in the debate during the 1660s. Needless to say, many other works touching on all sorts of subjects and countless sermons refer almost as a matter of course to the pernicious effects of drama in society.

In terms of published works which deal specifically with some aspect of drama, or with some aspect of imaginative literature in which drama earns a substantial mention, the next decade of the seventeenth century is relatively peaceful. The most important works of this period are Bernard Lamy's *Nouvelles réflexions sur l'art poétique* (1678), Chappuzeau's *Théâtre françois* (1674), and a virulent pamphlet, hitherto ignored in previous works on the *querelle*, written by an anonymous missionary around 1673.

The debate gained new momentum, however, with a series of works in the 1680s by Héliodore de Paris, another unjustly neglected author, J.-B. Thiers, and Dom Gabriel Gerberon. But the most bitter and by far the most interesting dispute of the whole period was that initiated by the unfortunate Thomas Caffaro in 1694, the author of an anonymous letter which appeared at the head of a collection of Boursault's plays, explaining that no moral danger arose for spectators and actors alike in the pursuit of drama. The letter was soon traced to Caffaro (Boursault's son was a Theatine monk like Caffaro) who was humiliated by the archbishop of Paris and by Bossuet in a letter written before the publication of his *Maximes et réflexions sur le théâtre*. Caffaro's religious status and his attempt to reinterpret radically or reject altogether the relevance of tradition to the seventeenth-century French theatre were enough to bring down on his head a series of thunderous and vituperative replies from representatives of all sections of the Catholic Church, from

Coustel, a former tutor at Port-Royal, Lebrun, an Oratorian, to doctors of the Sorbonne and Bossuet himself. Our discussion of the *querelle* closes in chronological terms in 1695 when the religious theatre again became a matter of controversy with the performance of l'Abbé Boyer's *Judith*.

One interesting feature emerges from this brief outline of the stage controversy. The dispute was at its height during two periods which are interesting in other ways. The 1660s witnessed a particularly crucial stage in the persecution of Port-Royal. As shown above, many of the participants in the *querelle* in those years were Jansenists or their sympathizers. Even the controversy over *Le Tartuffe* can be attributed, in part at least, to the sensitivity of the Jansenist clergy of Paris. But what more general significance the Jansenist contribution had can only really be assessed once a study of the broader range of moralists' attitudes during this period has been undertaken. The second great period of the *querelle* is less difficult to interpret. From 1680 onwards there was a renewal of more general polemical activity, directed at both Jansenists and Protestants (the revocation of the Edict of Nantes coming in 1685). But this period was also marked (the two points are not unrelated) by Louis XIV's renunciation of dissoluteness and his adoption of a more pious image. All this had profound consequences for the king's official patronage of the public theatre, to the extent of discussing the closure of the Paris theatres.[16] The growing moral austerity of his reign after 1680 was more than matched by a regeneration of the Church's hostility to drama, and the all-embracing exclusion of theatrical personnel from the sacraments in the ritual of Metz (1713) was a fitting conclusion to the debate in Louis's lifetime.

Before moving on to analyse the purely theoretical aspects of the *querelle* it may be useful to ask what impact the Church's attitude had in practice. The circumstances in which Molière died have already been mentioned, but his was not the only case of harassment of actors by the Church. Baron, on his first deathbed, Brécourt, and others were all forced to renounce their profession in the presence of witnesses before

---

[16] See Dubu, 'L'Église catholique et la Condamnation du théâtre . . .', p. 337.

they were offered the last rites (Baron, after his recovery, went back to the stage). Molière's troupe after his death and the troupe at the Hôtel du Marais (both of which were amalgamated at the king's command in 1673) had to move their theatre from more than one parish. The impact of the Church's attitude on the public at large is more difficult to assess in any detail. John Lough's albeit tentative figures for audiences at the Comédie-Française from 1680 suggest, if anything, an increase in people attending the theatre over a single year.[17] The documentation of incidents like that of Anne of Austria asking for guidance from the Sorbonne on the desirability or otherwise of attending theatrical performances (her confessor disturbed the mind that the Sorbonne put at rest) is unfortunately rare. Did the general public care for actors and the fate that possibly awaited them at their death? We are for the moment left with La Bruyère's caustic comment in *Les Caractères* that: 'La condition des comédiens était infâme chez les Romains et honorable chez les Grecs: qu'est-elle chez nous? On pense d'eux comme les Romains, on vit avec eux comme des Grecs' (*Des Jugements*, no. 15).

[17] *Paris Theatre Audiences*, pp. 272-3.

I

DRAMA AND MORAL INSTRUCTION

A suitable starting-point is an examination of the dramatic theorists' claim that drama's prime aim is to instruct. The concept of moral instruction was inherited by French dramatic theorists from the moralistic interpretation given to the works of Horace and Aristotle by those of their Italian Renaissance commentators who took Horace's liberal view of the useful in poetry as a dogmatic assertion, and endowed Aristotle's unexplained notion of catharsis with a moralistic aim which has since been much contested.[1] But the emphasis placed on the didactic function of drama in France during our period cannot be explained simply by the influence of scholars, for the interest shown in moral instruction appears at the same time that developments in theatrical technique gain the attention of theorists in France.

André Villiers has rightly pointed to the influence of the discovery of perspective, i.e. of a 'truer' spatial concept, on stage theory.[2] The importance of a stage decor using perspective, which gives a more realistic setting to the dramatic action, is that it relates the audience directly to the stage; the spectator is in the same space as the actor.[3] But the relation of the spectator to the 'real' space of the stage has obvious consequences for the presentation of the characters who appear in that space; they must be 'real' too. It is for this reason that dramatic theorists are so concerned with *mœurs*, or *bienséance*, since the characters' attributes must be recognizable to the audience.

[1] See Bray, R., *La Formation de la doctrine classique en France*, Paris, 1951, but also Kern, E. G., *The Influence of Heinsius and Vossius upon French Dramatic Theory*, Baltimore, 1949.
[2] See *Bibliography*. See also Védier, G., *Origine et évolution de la dramaturgie néo-classique*, Paris, 1955, for a study of developments in French painting in relation to the stage.
[3] Villiers (pp. 18–35) goes on to explain how this affects the theorists' arguments regarding the unities.

Dramatic theorists, however, are not advocating realism in the modern sense: their over-all conception of drama remains highly stylized. Indeed they are aware that only in a limited sense may reality be reproduced on the stage. Aristotle here becomes an ideal authority for the stage aesthetic in his definition of tragedy as the imitation of an action and in his insistence on verisimilitude. Indeed *vraisemblance* is a key element of drama for French dramatic theorists since it is important that things should appear to be real. Moreover, an action is *vraisemblable* if it upholds the audience's belief in the object of the dramatic illusion and secures their involvement in the action.

What, then, is the connection between moral instruction and the developments in theatrical technique? The content of any art which aims to teach must appear relevant to its audience. The dramatic illusion is now seen to provide this relevance, since the more the spectator can believe in the characters and what is happening on the stage, the more he is likely to accept the moral lesson offered. The immediacy of this lesson is enhanced by the spectator's feeling that he is a witness to the characters' actions. It is significant that the advocates of regular drama constantly attack those who remain faithful to the old techniques, unfavourable to the dramatic illusion, and who at the same time reject the concept of moral instruction. It is now necessary to examine in greater detail the relation of illusion to moral instruction.

Firstly, there is a clear preference for *vraisemblance* (a possible reality) over *vérité* (reality itself) as the essential feature of drama. Chapelain explains in his preface to Marino's *Adonis* that 'la vraisemblance . . . et non la vérité sert d'instrument au poète pour acheminer l'homme à la vertu';[4] the art of epic and dramatic poetry leads men to useful pleasure 'plus facilement . . . par le vray-semblable qui ne trouve point de resistance en eux, que par le vray, qui pourroit estre si estrange et si incroyable qu'ils refuseroient de s'en laisser persuader et de suivre leur guide sur sa seule foy'.[5] Truth, then, is sometimes stranger than fiction and becomes

---

[4] Chapelain, J., *Opuscules critiques*, ed. Alfred C. Hunter, Paris, 1936, p. 87.
[5] Gasté, A., *La Querelle du Cid: pièces et pamphlets publiés d'après les originaux*, Paris, 1898, pp. 364–5.

an obstacle to the spectator's involvement in the action. But the disposition of the spectator himself is important for his involvement: it is true that 'ce qui se représente soit feint', but the spectator must regard it as 'véritable'; if he fails to enter into the characters' feelings as 'réellement arrivants' he will lose the profit which poetry aims to give him.[6]

In this perspective the unities assume great importance. In his *Lettre sur la règle des vingt-quatre heures*, Chapelain remarks that were it not observed the spectator, noticing the 'fausseté' of the dramatic action, would not lend credence to it, 'sur quoi se fonde tout le fruit que la poésie pût produire en nous'.[7]

It is obvious from this statement that if what is portrayed on the stage were manifestly false the moral lesson would have no meaning for the audience. It is therefore important that the spectator should be able to relate what happens on the stage to his own experience, which is itself the criterion of what is true or false. D'Aubignac remarks that if the subject of drama is not 'conforme aux mœurs et aux sentimens des Spectateurs' the play will never succeed, however the poet may embellish it.[8] André Dacier, a classical scholar who was highly aware of developments in dramatic theory, and also critical of certain aspects of French seventeenth-century tragedy, concentrates rather on dramatic action, and those accidents productive of surprise which are legitimate in tragedy. He advises against the sudden collapse of a house or a stone thrown by chance because, there being no recognizable cause to which such events can be attributed, we impute them to pure chance and do not relate them to ourselves.[9] Thus *vraisemblance* must provide a more logical link in any sequence of events so that our involvement and belief in the action are not hindered.

This notion of what we may call *relatability* forms the basis for Dacier's reason why the truths of history cannot instruct of themselves:

---

[6] *Opuscules*, p. 121.
[7] Ibid., p. 117.
[8] Aubignac, Fr. H., Abbé d', *La Pratique du théâtre*, ed. P. Martino, Paris, 1927, p. 72.
[9] Dacier, A., *La Poétique d'Aristote*, Paris, 1692, Ch. ix, remarque 26, p.142.

L'Histoire ne peut instruire qu'autant que les faits qu'elle rapporte, luy en donnent l'occasion, et, comme ces faits sont particuliers, il arrive rarement qu'ils soient proportionnez à ceux qui les lisent, il n'y en a pas un entre mille à qui ils puissent convenir, et ceux mêmes à qui ils conviennent ne trouvent pas en toute leur vie deux occasions, où ils puissent tirer quelque avantage de ce qu'ils ont lû.[10]

Poetry, however, being concerned with things in general, 'est d'autant plus morale et plus instructive, que les choses generales surpassent les particulieres'; the latter 'ne conviennent qu'à un seul, et les autres conviennent à tout le monde'.[11] It is therefore not the facts of history which instruct, but the causes attributed to them; the latter are the concern of poetry.

Rapin is of a similar opinion to Dacier: the idea of virtue found in heroic poetry is more perfect than that found in history because the latter 'ne propose la vertu qu'imparfaite, comme elle est dans les particuliers', whereas poetry 'la propose sans aucune imperfection, et comme elle doit estre en general'.[12] Moreover: 'la vray-semblance sert à donner de la créance à ce que la Poësie a de plus fabuleux: elle sert aussi à donner . . . un plus grand air de perfection, que ne pourroit faire la verité même, quoy que la vray-semblance n'en soit que la copie. Car la verité ne fait les choses que comme elles sont; et la vray-semblance les fait comme elles doivent estre.'[13] Truth is nearly always defective 'par le mélange des conditions singulieres, qui la composent'; there is nothing in the world 'qui ne s'éloigne de la perfection de son ideé en y naissant' and we must seek 'des originaux et des modeles dans la vray-semblance, et dans les principes universels des choses' where 'il n'entre rien de material et de singulier, qui les corrompe'; this is where historical portraits are less perfect than those of poetry.[14] Thus drama must present an *already exemplary* reality to the spectator.

D'Aubignac offers the most complete argument on this aspect of *vraisemblance*. Drama, he says, does not portray

---

[10] Ibid., Ch. ix, rem. 5, p. 131.
[11] Ibid.
[12] Rapin, le Père R., *Les Réflexions sur l'éloquence, la poétique, l'histoire, et la philosophie*, Paris, 1684, iv, p. 127.
[13] Ibid., xxiv, p. 105.
[14] Ibid.

things 'comme elles ont esté' but 'comme elles devoient estre';
the poet must 'rétablir dans le sujet tout ce qui ne
s'accommodera pas aux regles de son Art, comme fait un
Peintre quand il travaille sur un modelle defectueux'.[15]
Professor Knight has pointed out that the Latin translation
of the Greek distorts Aristotle's thought; it should read
'possunt' rather than 'debent'.[16]

The further implications of d'Aubignac's attitude become
more apparent in his discussion of truth. He comments that
the *Vray* cannot be the subject of drama because 'il y a bien
des choses veritables qui n'y doivent pas estre veuës, et
beaucoup qui n'y peuvent pas estre representées'.[17] Thus
vraisemblance is a means of avoiding unacceptable subjects.
In the following statement d'Aubignac stresses the importance
of belief in our response to drama: it is true that Nero cut
open his mother's womb at her death but this barbarity,
although pleasing to its perpetrator, 'seroit non seulement
horrible à ceux qui la verroient, mais mesme incroyable, à
cause que cela ne devoit point arriver; et entre toutes les
Histoires dont le Poëte voudra tirer son sujet, il n'y en a pas
une, ... dont toutes les circonstances soient capables du
Theatre, quoy que veritables ...'[18] His conclusion is that
only 'le Vraysemblable' could 'raisonnablement fonder,
soustenir et terminer un Poëme Dramatique'.[19] Clearly
d'Aubignac's idea of belief is directly related to the moral
prejudice of the audience, for whom such acts as Nero's
should never have happened. *Vraisemblance* is, then, a
reordering of reality dictated by certain moral standards;
as well as being a means of keeping the play in contact
with reality, *vraisemblance* assumes the function of a moralistic control. As Professor Knight remarks, the phrase
'devaient arriver' implies that the poet 'doit corriger les faits
qu'il présente au nom de la bienséance et de la moralité'.[20]

[15] *Pratique*, p. 68.
[16] Knight, R. C., *Racine et la Grèce*, Paris, 1950, pp. 66-7.
[17] *Pratique*, p. 76.
[18] Ibid.
[19] Ibid., p. 77.
[20] *Racine*, p. 201. See also Genette, G., *Figures II*, Paris, 1969, pp. 71-3, and
Woshinsky, B., *La Princesse de Clèves: The Tension of Elegance*, The Hague,
1973, pp. 52-3.

A final reason for preferring *vraisemblance* to *vérité* is found in the concept of punishment of evil and reward of virtue. According to Chapelain the difference between history and a subject where the rules of *vraisemblance* have been observed is that in history events are not regulated and depend on fortune, the evil being enriched as well as the virtuous; poetry on the other hand: 'met le premier en considération l'universel et ne le traite particulièrement qu'en intention de faire tirer l'espèce, à l'instruction du monde et au bénéfice commun'. This is why in poetry 'la suite des actions, ou bonnes ou mauvaises, est toujours semblable, chacune en son genre; tout bon reconnu, tout méchant châtié, comme procédant da la vertu ou du vice dont la nature est de récompenser ou de perdre ceux qui les vont suivant'.[21]

La Mesnardière says simply that tragedy can only achieve its aim 'par l'utile exposition des Vertus recompensées, et des vices chastiez'.[22] For Scudéry in his *Observations sur 'Le Cid'* it is by means of punishment and reward that 'insensiblement, on nous imprime en l'ame l'horreur du vice, et l'amour de la vertu'.[23] Indeed there is a self-regarding instinct in the spectator since the thought of reward and punishment is largely what prompts us to act virtuously.[24]

However, this moral idealism on the part of dramatic theorists must not be taken for *naïveté*. They are aware that sometimes virtue goes unrewarded and vice unpunished. But in such cases how is the spectator to know what is good or bad? La Mesnardière's answer in the case of vice triumphant is that the poet must at least make sure that the virtuous are publicly praised by another character who admires their glorious acts.[25] He further recommends that if evil characters are not punished instantly they should be threatened with divine justice by a character 'qui exagere et qui deteste leur honteuse difformité'.[26] D'Aubignac agrees that the first rule

[21] *Opuscules*, p. 86.
[22] La Mesnardière, H.-J. Pilet de, *La Poétique*, Paris, 1640, p. 221.
[23] Gasté, p. 80.
[24] Scudéry, G. de, *L'Apologie du théâtre*, Paris, 1639, p. 16.
[25] *Poétique*, p. 223.
[26] Ibid., p. 224.

of drama is that virtue should always be rewarded or at least
praised, even in the midst of ill-fortune, and that vice should
always be punished, or in any case held in horror, even when
it is triumphant.[27] But for La Mesnardière total impunity
is wholly undesirable and he attacks Castelvetro for advocating
as the best form of tragedy a good man falling into misfortune; is it not better:

pour l'utilité de l'exemple, que les ames vertueuses voyent chastier
leurs contraires, et les vicieux leurs semblables, que si les gens de
probité avoient sujet de vaciller dans leurs saintes résolutions, voyans
mal-traitter la Vertu? et que les esprits mal nez receussent par la mesme
voye une espece d'exhortation qui les confirmast dans le vice, quand ils
verroient que les miseres feroient toute la recompense des meilleures
actions.[28]

The concept of punishment and reward therefore forms an
essential part of the moral reordering of reality represented
by *vraisemblance*.

Corneille is the only writer who voiced any strong
opposition to this rather simplistic moral attitude. He asserts
that we could never see an 'honnête homme' on stage 'sans
lui souhaiter de la prospérité, et nous fâcher de ses infortunes';
when such a man does experience misfortune we leave the
theatre aggrieved and angry with the author and actors; but
when our wishes are fulfilled and virtue is rewarded we go
home happy, wholly satisfied both with the play and those
who have performed it.[29] Although Corneille adds that:
'Le succès heureux de la vertu, en dépit des traverses et des
périls, nous excite à l'embrasser; et le succès funeste du crime
ou de l'injustice est capable de nous en augmenter l'horreur
naturelle, par l'appréhension d'un pareil malheur',[30] it seems
that for him the satisfaction of the spectator's basic sense of
justice (as opposed to a more objective view of right or wrong)
is more important than the fulfilment of any positive didactic
aim.

[27] *Pratique*, pp. 8-9.
[28] *Poétique*, pp. 170-1. Scudéry complains in his *Observations* that virtue is
excluded at the end of *Le Cid*, when Chimène's vice is rewarded with a husband
(Gasté, p. 80).
[29] Corneille, P., *Writings on the Theatre*, ed. H. T. Barnwell, Oxford, 1965,
pp. 6-7.
[30] Ibid., p. 7.

Indeed in the first *Discours* Corneille points out that the Ancients neither punished evil nor rewarded good, and that often criminals were punished out of all proportion to their crime.[31] Corneille explains the origin of punishment and reward in drama by our natural siding with virtuous people; it is not a precept of art but a usage we have adopted, 'dont chacun peut se départir à ses périls'.[32]

But Corneille also considers the case of his own plays. He comments in the letter which precedes *La Suite du menteur* that, if punishment and reward is a rule of drama, then he has disobeyed it: it is certain that Dorante's behaviour is not morally good, yet he obtains the real object of his desire.[33] It is interesting to contrast this statement with one made much later in the *Examen* of *La Place royale*: not only does Corneille make a concession to simplistic moral concepts but he argues for the necessity of punishment in comedy though not in tragedy:

Cet enlèvement lui[Angélique] réussit mal; et il a été bon de lui donner un mauvais succès, bien qu'il ne soit pas besoin que les grands crimes soient punis dans la tragédie, parce que leur peinture imprime assez d'horreur pour en détourner les spectateurs. Il n'en est pas de même des fautes de cette nature, et elles pourraient engager un esprit jeune et amoureux à les imiter, si l'on voyait que ceux qui les commettent vinssent à bout, par ce mauvais moyen, de ce qu'ils désirent.[34]

Can we really believe that Corneille intended to provide a moralistic end to this play? Or is the implication that the levity of comedy must be balanced by some obvious moralistic safeguard?

The most interesting point made in the above statement is, however, that great crimes do not require punishment because their portrayal in all their horror is sufficient to deter spectators from committing them. Indeed one means of moral instruction, Corneille considers, consists: 'en la naïve peinture des vices et des vertus, qui ne manque jamais à faire

---

[31] Ibid., pp. 5-6.
[32] Ibid., p. 6.
[33] Ibid., p. 185.
[34] Ibid., pp. 95-6. It is difficult to agree with Professor Barnwell that 'Corneille is protesting against a narrowly moralistic view of drama and against merely edifying dénouements' (*Writings*, p. 246, n. 8). Surely he justifies such an edifying denouement in certain cases.

son effet, quand elle est bein achevée, et que les traits en
sont si reconnaissables qu'on ne les peut confondre l'un
dans l'autre, ni prendre le vice pour vertu. Celle-ci se fait
toujours aimer, quoique malheureuse; et celui-là se fait
toujours haïr, bien que triomphant'.[35] We are then automatically edified by the realistic portrayal of good and evil
characters despite the consequences of their actions.

The most explicit justification for this concept comes in
the *Épître dédicatoire* to *Médée* (1639): in this play

> vous trouverez le crime en son char de triomphe, et peu de personnages
> sur la scène dont les mœurs ne soient plus mauvaises que bonnes; mais
> la peinture et la poésie ont cela de commun . . . que l'une fait souvent
> de beaux portraits d'une femme laide, et l'autre de belles imitations
> d'une action qu'il ne faut pas imiter. Dans la portraiture, il n'est pas
> question si un visage est beau, mais s'il ressemble; et dans la poésie, il
> ne faut pas considérer si les mœurs sont vertueuses, mais si elles sont
> pareilles à celles de la personne qu'elle introduit. Aussi nous décrit-elle
> indifféremment les bonnes et les mauvaises actions, sans nous proposer
> les dernières pour exemple; et si elle nous en veut faire quelque horreur,
> ce n'est point par leur punition, qu'elle n'affecte pas de nous faire voir,
> mais par leur laideur, qu'elle s'efforce de nous représenter au naturel.[36]

Art therefore reflects the moral neutrality of reality and
portrays good and bad indifferently. But we are also confronted with the problem of the relation of beauty to the
morally good, for the two are not equivalents; Corneille
believes that just as an artist can paint a beautiful portrait
of an ugly woman a dramatist can present a beautiful imitation
of an evil act. Since the criterion of beauty is the degree of
exactness of portrayal and since this exactness enables us to
recognize moral qualities more easily, beauty is not the
morally good in itself but that which leads us to it. In this
case the artist automatically fulfils a moral purpose by the
fact that his art is an imitation of nature.[37]

The Aristotelian principle of imitation is for d'Aubignac a
moral choice in itself because drama imitates human actions

[35] Ibid., p. 5.
[36] Ibid., p. 180. Racine in his preface to *Phèdre* comments that in his play 'le
vice y est peint partout avec des couleurs qui en font connoître et haïr la
difformité' (*Œuvres*, iii, p. 303).
[37] For a wider discussion of these issues, see Phillips, H., '*Vraisemblance* and
Moral Instruction in Seventeenth-Century Dramatic Theory', *Modern Language
Review*, vol. 73, 1978, pp. 267–77.

'pour les enseigner'.[38] Dramatic action shows us 'la force de
la Vertu brillante au milieu méme des persécutions: elle y est
souvent couronnée; et quand méme elle y succombe, elle
demeure toûjours glorieuse'; drama reveals all the deformities
of vice, which is often punished and, when not, always held
in abomination; consequently the spectators 'tirent
d'eux-mémes et naturellement cette conséquence', and drama
must principally instruct 'par la seule connoissance des
choses representées'.[39] Even the most common people learn
that the advantages given by fortune are false and that the
guilty are punished; the proof is in what they see on the stage
itself.[40] The force of the dramatic illusion is such that
'un homme supposé les rend capables de penetrer dans les
plus profonds sentimens de l'humanité, touchant au doigt
et à l'œil ... dans ces peintures vivantes des veritez qu'ils ne
pourroient concevoir autrement'.[41] Moreover, the people
never leave the theatre without taking with them 'l'idée
des personnes qu'on leur a representées, la connoissance des
vertus et des vices, dont ils ont veu les exemples'; their
memory 'leur en fait des leçons continuelles, qui s'impriment
d'autant plus avant dans leurs esprits qu'elles s'attachent à
des objets sensibles, et presque toûjours presens'.[42] Our
experience in the theatre becomes an integral part of our
experience in real life by means of an affective memory.
The significance of imitation for d'Aubignac is that it affords
impressions which are assimilated into our personal experience
and used to regulate our future conduct.

Dramatic theorists, however, strongly emphasize that
moral instruction in drama does not consist in preaching a
sermon since our experience in the theatre must be pleasurable. *Vraisemblance*, the criterion of illusion, is also a
necessary condition of the pleasure found in drama. Chapelain
in his letter to Godeau distinguishes false pleasure from the
true pleasure which 'se fait par l'ordre et par la vraisem-

---

[38] *Pratique,* p. 318.
[39] Ibid., pp. 318–19. Kern in this context points to the influence of Vossius
(pp. 124–7).
[40] Ibid., p. 9.
[41] Ibid.
[42] Ibid.

blance'.[43] It had been objected to d'Aubignac that the rigour
of the new rules would lead to the exclusion of some of the
finest aspects of stories which are true because the most
noteworthy events occur in different places. His reply again
establishes *vraisemblance* as a condition of pleasure: 'les
regles du Theatre ne rejettent pas les notables incidens
d'une Histoire; mais elles donnent les moyens de les ajuster
en telle sorte, que sans choquer la vray-semblance des Temps,
des Lieux, et des autres circonstances d'une Action, ils
puissent y paroistre, non pas, à la verité, telles qu'ils ont
esté dans l'effet, mais tels qu'ils doivent estre pour n'avoir
rien que d'agreable'.[44]

Although Chapelain regards instruction as the real aim of
poetry, he insists that this can only be achieved by pleasure
alone; moreover, without pleasure there is no poetry and
'plus le plaisir se rencontre en elle, plus est-elle poésie, et
mieux acquiert-elle son but qui est l'utilité'.[45] Rapin, much
later in the century, reaffirms that poetry is useful only
in so far as it is pleasurable and 'l'importance de cet Art est
de plaire'.[46] In his *Apologie* Scudéry sees utility as a direct
consequence of pleasure in that of all the forms of moral
instruction, drama is certainly the most 'agreable', and
consequently the most 'utile'.[47] Indeed the success of drama
has been such that *l'utile* and *le plaisant* are now inseparable.[48]

But here theorists encounter a problem of emphasis, or
of a balance to be maintained between the pleasurable and
the profitable. Dacier warns us that poets must seek more to
instruct than to please and that they must regard *l'agréable*
only as a means of conveying the useful.[49] Scudéry sees the
problem rather as one of maintaining moral awareness when
he remarks that one must avoid so concealing 'ce qui doit
instruire dans les Poëmes, par ce qui doit dellecter' that
'l'esprit n'en face point le discernement, et n'en recueille
pas, le fruict qu'il en doit attendre'.[50] Too great an emphasis
on pleasure is therefore likely to impair the effectiveness of
moral instruction, since the pleasurable is not necessarily to

[43] *Opuscules*, pp. 124–5.
[44] *Pratique*, p. 29.
[45] *Opuscules*, p. 97.
[46] *Réflexions* , xi, p. 94.

[47] *Apologie*, p. 3.
[48] Ibid., p. 26.
[49] *Poétique d'Aristote*, p. xvi.
[50] *Apologie*, p. 13.

be equated with the good.

In the early part of the century, however, at a time of reaction against previous theatrical traditions, many writers strongly attacked the notion of moral instruction and emphasized *plaire* exclusively. Mareschal, in the preface to *La Généreuse Allemande*, argues that the aim of drama is action, whose proper end is to please. Ogier stresses that different times and different nations (presumably a reference to the Ancients) do not share the same idea of beauty in poetry; although all men must agree on those things necessary for the sovereign good, each man may follow his own path in the case of objects simply 'plaisans et indifferens' such as poetry.[51] Since the theatre falls into such a cateogry this absolves it from any moral purpose. Religion and the sovereign good are entirely separate matters.

Ogier's historical perspective is also evident in d'Urfé's preface to his *Sylvanire*. D'Urfé recounts that when the poets of antiquity invented poetry it was meant to instruct people with greater authority by means of an agreeably told story; thus the principal aim was profit, pleasure being derived only 'par accident', in other words, as a by-product.[52] However, he continues, our century is so rich in preachers who save men from vice and inspire them to virtue that 'nostre Poësie infailliblement demeureroit inutile, si elle faisoit seulement profession d'instruire'.[53] So for d'Urfé drama in a Christian society would, if its object were didacticism, be a superfluous institution. The pulpit and the stage, profit and pleasure, must remain separate. It is then natural that d'Urfé should admit that, following the practice of his own age, his aim has been to please and only in passing to instruct.[54] Thus pleasure alone is of drama's essence whereas profit may or may not arise.

The most outspoken opponent of moral instruction in drama is undoubtedly Corneille. His statement of principle

[51] Lawton, H., *Handbook of French Renaissance Dramatic Theory*, Manchester, 1949, p. 123.
[52] *Par accident* (from *per accidens*) is a complement to the term *per se* which refers to something of the essence of an object: *par accident* thus means 'not inseparably connected with' and does not refer to chance.
[53] Urfé, H. d', Preface to *La Sylvanire ou La Morte vive*, Paris, 1627.
[54] Ibid.

begins in the boldest of manners when he considers the difference between Dorante in *Le Menteur* and its sequel: 'mais pour moi, qui tiens avec Aristote et Horace que notre art n'a pour but que le divertissement, j'avoue qu'il est ici bien moins à estimer qu'en la première comédie, puisque avec ses mauvaises habitudes, il a perdu presque toutes ses grâces, et qu'il semble avoir quitté la meilleure part de ses agréments lorsqu'il a voulu se corriger de ses défauts.'[55] Pleasure has clearly been sacrificed to a moralistic aim. Furthermore, those who endow drama with the lofty aim of instruction 'sont injurieux à l'artisan, dont ils ravalent d'autant plus le mérite, qu'ils pensent relever la dignité de sa profession, parce que, s'il est obligé de prendre soin de l'utile, il évite seulement une faute quand il s'en acquitte, et n'est digne d'aucune louange'.[56] Corneille expresses his admiration for those who achieve the fusion of the pleasurable and the profitable, especially when they are not obliged to do so. He denies, however, that in the opposite case artists are guilty of breaking any rule and adds that he would blame them only for not having set themselves a worthy enough objective, or for not possessing 'assez de charité pour prendre l'occasion de donner en passant quelque instruction à ceux qui les écoutent ou qui les lisent'.[57]

His position is clear in that provided poets have found the means to please 'ils sont quittes envers leur art; et s'ils pèchent, ce n'est pas contre lui, c'est contre les bonnes mœurs et contre leur auditoire'.[58] *Plaire* is thus entirely separate from *instruire* and is indeed the primary aim of the poet. The laws of art stand apart from the laws of morals. This does not give leave for the poet to be immoral; he must still take into account the sensibility of his audience, as Corneille indicates by the reference to 'bonnes mœurs'; but avoiding the immoral is not the same as proposing its opposite. It is also important to note that Corneille's defence and justification is found in the reference to his public. *Plaire* involves little more than the satisfaction of this public, with all the vagueness this implies. It would of course be wrong

---

[55] *Writings*, p. 183.
[56] *Writings*, p. 184.
[57] Ibid.
[58] Ibid.

to say that d'Urfé and Corneille think of art as something trivial. The *Discours* in themselves show drama as a serious art. But the first principle must be its autonomy and the poet's freedom from any outside obligation.

The most important debate on pleasure and utility formed part of the controversy over *Le Cid*. Corneille's defence of his play was based on the pleasure he had given his public; indeed the attitude of many of his supporters is illustrated by a statement in one of the *Querelle*'s anonymous tracts, in which the author affirms that, never having read Aristotle and being entirely ignorant of the rules, he judges the merits of plays simply according to the pleasure he receives.[59] Corneille's opponents in this dispute produced only one reasonable voice, ironically that of Chapelain, who had been delegated to conduct an enquiry into the matter. Far from engaging in outright condemnation, which was the dominant tone of Scudéry's *Observations*, Chapelain could not have been more conciliatory.

Indeed he is careful to present both sides of the question:

Les uns trop amis, ce semble, de la volupté, veulent que le Delectable soit le vray but de la Poësie Dramatique; les autres plus avares du temps des hommes, et l'estimant trop cher pour le donner à des divertissemens qui ne fissent que plaire sans profiter, soustiennent que l'Utile en est la veritable fin.[60]

In his opinion both views are correct because one must conceive that those who advocate pleasure are 'trop raisonnables pour en autoriser un qui ne fust pas conforme à la raison'; therefore, to do them justice we must assume that:

ils ont entendu parler du plaisir qui n'est point l'ennemy, mais l'instrument de la vertu, qui purge l'homme, sans dégoust et insensiblement, de ses habitudes vicieuses, qui est utile parce qu'il est honneste, et qui ne peut jamais laisser de regret ny en l'esprit pour l'avoir surpris, ny en l'ame pour l'avoir corrompuë.[61]

He even comes to the conclusion that both sides are in agreement; 'puisqu'il est vray que si ce Plaisir n'est l'Utilité mesme, au moins est-il la source d'où elle coule necessairement; que quelque part qu'il se trouve il ne va jamais sans elle, et que tous deux se produisent par les mesmes voyes'. In

---

[59] Gasté, p. 231.   [60] Ibid., p. 359.   [61] Ibid.

this sense we can all agree that a play is good 'quand elle produit un contentement raisonnable'.[62] It is obvious that Chapelain, unlike Scudéry, carefully distinguishes between pleasure and utility; the pleasurable is but the source of the profitable. It is therefore interesting to see in the former statement that, just as he has separated the false from the true pleasure according to aesthetic criteria, he separates a pleasure which may edify from one which may corrupt.

So far I have dealt with *pleasure* and utility. La Mesnardière envisages the problem from a slightly different angle, that of *divertissement*. He asserts that 'il faut . . . [que] la Tragedie soit attachée au profit du Spectateur, et qu'elle fasse pénétrer les bons sentimens dans son ame parmi le divertissement'.[63] Thus the spectator must be able to enjoy himself at the same time as he is being instructed, the phrase 'parmi le divertisse-ment' suggesting that instruction does not monopolize diversion. La Mesnardière defines exactly what he means by this term in a statement which at once reminds us of Chapelain and goes beyond him: 'Le Divertissement . . . est un puissant attrait qui se trouve dans les manieres par lesquelles elle instruit, et qui la rend agreable avant qu'elle soit utile, pour estre à la fin tous les deux.'[64] La Mesnardière's use of the term enables him to make the point that the pleasurable and the profitable are fused in a single experience, and that the spectator is unable to distinguish the one from the other.

We find, moreover, that, just as *vraisemblance* is a means of involving the spectator in the dramatic action, pleasure is a means of involving him in the instruction he receives and of obviating his natural reluctance to be taught. The need to palliate the austerity of moral precepts by means of pleasure is sometimes spoken of in terms of a medicine which needs to be administered to sick people in an acceptable form, rather like a sugared pill.[65] Rapin argues that we are more receptive to moral instruction and less resistant to the constraints of virtue when it is presented to us in a way

[62] Ibid., p. 360.
[63] *Poétique*, p. 141.
[64] Ibid., p. 166.
[65] See *Apologie*, pp. 3–4.

which gives us a pleasurable experience.[66]

For some writers moral instruction is even more effective when the spectator is completely unaware of it. Balzac asserts that 'la Comedie doit agir sur l'ame . . . finement et . . . imperceptiblement'; moreover, there must be 'de l'illusion et du charme, de la fraude et de la tromperie dans les moyens qu'elle employe, pour arriver à sa fin'.[67] This emphasis on deceit is further explained by Balzac when he says that the stratagem of virtue demands that vice should be fought by the same means as 'certaines armes couvertes de myrthe, et . . . certains hommes vestus de Femmes, qui ont autrefois tué des Tyrans': we must 'couvrir un dessein courageux sous une apparence effeminée'.[68] Scudéry uses a similar metaphor: drama, like 'ces Dames adroites', leads men to instruction 'feignant de ne les mener qu'au divertissement'; thus:

cette charmante et sage Mestresse, travaille à les rendre sages eux-mesmes, lorsqu'ils pensent qu'elle ne songe qu'à leur plaire . . . cette fidelle, mais adroite guide, les jette insensiblement, dans le chemin de la vertu, feignant de prendre celuy de la volupté: et leur cache un ameçon sous l'appas d'un si doux plaisir, qu'il les arreste sans qu'ils y pensent, qu'il leur fait suivre, ce qu'ils taschoient d'esviter.[69]

But here there is no degree of awareness on the part of the spectator, for he is led to virtue 'insensiblement'. He is undergoing this experience in spite of himself; once his attention is held by what is pleasurable, he becomes the essentially passive recipient of whatever moral instruction is forthcoming.

If the spectator is deceived to such an extent, how is he then to distinguish between the morally good and the merely pleasurable? If the illusion can be so successful cannot the spectator be easily corrupted too? It is doubtless for this reason that Boileau emphasizes that the author's personality must be beyond reproach.[70] Indeed Henri Peyre is only half correct when he observes that Boileau 'insiste non tant sur la

---

[66] *Réflexions*, ix, pp. 92–3.
[67] Balzac, J. L. Guez de, *Œuvres*, Paris, 1665, ii, 518.
[68] Ibid.
[69] *Apologie*, pp. 4–5.
[70] Boileau-Despréaux, N., *Œuvres complètes*. Introduction par A. Adam. Textes établis et annotés par Françoise Escal, Paris, 1966, *Art poétique*, Chant IV, 91–110.

moralité de l'art que sur celle de l'artiste',[71] for it is clear
that in Boileau's view only the morally upright person can be
relied upon to write morally sound verse.

One solution to the problem of the difficulty spectators
may have in distinguishing between good and bad in drama is
of course the open punishment of vice and reward of virtue.
But in real life vice is not always punished nor virtue infallibly
rewarded. One other solution is that the content of speeches
should contain moral advice in the nature of maxims or
sententiae. But how are we to accommodate man's reluctance
to be taught with this method of instruction, especially when
instruction is more effective if the spectator is unaware of it?
To what degree is drama permitted to teach in an undisguised
fashion?

The author of the *Discours à Cliton* is uncompromising
in his attitude towards direct moralizing: we do not go to the
theatre to be admonished or for moral lessons, and spectators
do not wish to be considered so unintelligent that they need
the action to be explained by a prologue, nor so debauched
'qu'on doive tousjours et par tout crier contre leurs vices,
et leurs mauvaises mœurs, nos chaises publiques estant
destinées à cette fonction'.[72] La Mesnardière comments that
in a play one may use 'quelques sentences graves' but 'il faut
qu'elles y viennent, sans y estre attirées de force'; one must
avoid preaching in drama and the most refined sententiae are
no more than 'un Résultat des Actions de grande consideration,
sur les événemens desquelles on a formé ces propos'.[73] Moral
maxims are thus born from the dramatic action itself.

Balzac discusses this problem in great detail and strongly
attacks the school of moralizers: although they may please,
he says, it is not how poets should please, particularly when
they appeal to intelligent people.[74] His major objection is
that dogmatizing detracts from the naturalness of drama
because the characters 'discourent seulement au lieu de

---

[71] Peyre, H., *Qu'est-ce que le classicisme?*, Paris, 1933, p. 128.
[72] Gasté, p. 261. Dacier considers that the chorus is useful as 'le moyen d'étaler
tous les sentiments qu'on doit inspirer aux peuples, et de leur faire connoître ce
qu'il y a de vicieux ou de louable dans les caractères qu'on introduit' (p. xvi).
[73] *Poétique*, p. 217.
[74] *Œuvres*, ii, 517.

parler; c'est-à-dire ils parlent en Beaux esprits, et ne parlent pas en Honnestes gens'.[75] One would say that they have learnt things by rote, with the consequence that they are wrongly called actors; 'Ce sont de veritables Recitateurs.'[76] Moreover this method of instruction sins against the necessity of imitation, for the characters wish to instruct 'directement et sans artifice, par la voye commune des Preceptes; au lieu qu'ils devroient instruire avec adresse, par le moyen de l'imitation'.[77] His conclusion is not unnaturally that 'Moralité' and 'Instruction': 'doivent s'y espandre invisiblement et doucement . . . ; Il faut sentir l'instruction; Mais il ne faut pas la voir'.[78] Balzac unmistakably emphasizes, therefore, the need to maintain the dramatic illusion, which would be seriously undermined by the unnaturalness of characters preaching directly to the audience.

Clearly Balzac argues the need to accept the rules of an art form. The anonymous author of the *Discours à Cliton* explains that if the poet wants to instruct 'il le doit faire subtilement, et comme en passant, par le jeu, et par le recit de ses Acteurs, et non par une leçon estudiée et par un chœur attaché à sa piece'.[79] Corneille too is conscious that the dramatic illusion would suffer since, for example, a character in the height of passion would be unable to formulate maxims: therefore one must use them sparingly and avoid speeches of this sort which are too general or too prolonged.[80] La Mesnardière criticizes maxims which are too speculative and which have no practical value.[81] Thinkers, he continues, are rare on the stage and even if they were not, they would feel passion like other men: thus the playwright must never give them 'ces belles abstractions de la condition humaine que nous n'avons jamais veües'.[82]

The question of emotion is emphasized by d'Aubignac when he says that all speeches which set out to instruct are a defect in any play because they are naturally 'froids et languissans', and being general maxims:

[75] Ibid. 515.
[76] Ibid. 517.
[77] Ibid. 517.
[78] Ibid. 513.

[79] Gasté, pp. 261–2.
[80] *Writings*, p. 4.
[81] *Poétique*, p. 218.
[82] Ibid., pp. 218–19.

qui, pour instruire, vont seulement à l'esprit et ne frappent point le cœur; ils éclairent et n'échauffent pas; et quoy qu'ils soient souvent assez beaux et bien exprimez, ils ne font que toucher l'oreille, sans émouvoir l'âme: de sorte que l'Action du Theatre, où nous cherchons quelque chose qui remuë nos affections, et qui fasse quelque impression sur nostre cœur, nous devient peu sensible, et consequemment peu capable de nous divertir.[83]

Corneille advises that sententiae should always be applicable to individual cases, to avoid them becoming just commonplaces which never fail to bore the spectator and slow up the action.[84]

In the *Pratique* d'Aubignac speaks at great length on the use and nature of moral sententiae which for him constitute one means of moral instruction. D'Aubignac objects not to the sententiae themselves but to the 'stile Didactique', the 'propositions universelles, faites sans art et avec des expressions languissantes'.[85] Furthermore those characters who appear with the demeanour of a pedagogue are not heeded because they make the most serious play look ridiculous.[86] Thus the usefulness of these maxims is restricted, all the more because in the Abbé's experience, spectators do not easily accept that a character who has strayed from the path of virtue should return to it because of '(les) beaux preceptes qu'on luy vient débiter'. It needs to be rather the influence of events 'qui l'oblige de reprendre des sentimens raisonnables'.[87] He stresses therefore the importance of example.

If such maxims are used it must be with the following restrictions. Firstly they must refer directly to the subject of the tragedy, 'en sorte qu'il semble que celuy qui parle, ait presents à l'esprit les interests du Theatre, ... car par ce moyen le Poëte ne se rend pas suspect de vouloir instruire le Spectateur par la bouche de ses Acteurs et ses Acteurs ne sortent point de l'Intrigue, qui les oblige d'agir et de parler'.[88] The actors must not break the illusion by speaking directly to the audience. The second piece of advice is that the playwright must 'parler avec figure', that is to say, using

---

[83] *Pratique*, pp. 314–15.
[84] *Writings*, p. 4.
[85] *Pratique*, p. 319.

[86] Ibid., p. 316.
[87] Ibid., p. 319.
[88] Ibid., p. 320.

questions and irony for '[la figure] y ajoûte quelque mouvement, et c'est ce qui la tire de la simplicité de l'Echole pour
la faire passer avec grâce sur le Theatre'.[89] Thirdly, these
maxims must be short 'afin de ne pas donner au Theatre le
temps de se refroidir'.[90]

Moral sententiae, then, clash with the dramatic illusion and
with drama as a pleasurable experience, whose criterion is
vraisemblance. But sententiae also hinder emotional involvement, itself essential for the experience of pleasure, as implied
in the coupling of plaire and toucher in the works of, for
example, Racine and Boileau.[91] The clearest connection
between pleasure and emotion is found in Rapin's Réflexions:

ce plaisir qui est proprement celuy de l'esprit, consiste dans l'agitation
de l'ame émeüe par les passions. La Tragedie ne devient agreable au
spectateur, que parce qu'il devient luy-mesme sensible à tout ce qu'on
luy represente, qu'il entre dans tous les differens sentimens des acteurs,
qu'il s'interesse dans leurs avantures, qu'il craint et qu'il espere, qu'il
s'afflige, et qu'il se rejoüit avec eux. Le theatre est froid et languissant,
dés qu'il cesse de produire ces mouvemens dans l'ame de ceux qui y
assistent.[92]

The need to make emotional involvement with characters
serve the ends of moral instruction greatly influenced the
discussion of catharsis, whose components of pity and fear
give rise, according to Aristotle, to 'the particular tragic
pleasure'.

[89] Ibid., pp. 320–1.
[90] Ibid., p. 321.
[91] See Racine, Œuvres, ii, 368, and Boileau, Art poétique, Chant III, 25–6.
[92] Réflexions, xviii, pp. 143–4.

II

CATHARSIS AND ITS FUNCTION

It has already been pointed out that French dramatic theorists inherited the moral orientation given to catharsis principally from Aristotle's Italian commentators. Their interpretation has since been contested by modern scholars who point to errors in the understanding of the Greek terms. To find the origin of a moralistic catharsis solely in the inadequacy of scholarly translations is, however, an over-simplification. First of all, catharsis easily fits into that tradition of Christian morals which emphasizes the place of passion in man's nature and his need to control it. Yet, tradition alone cannot account for the prominence of catharsis in seventeenth-century dramatic theory. Once again the reason for its importance must be sought in the aesthetic developments already alluded to.

An important condition of drama is the excitement of passion. For La Mesnardière this must be the prime object of the playwright.[1] He further advises that the spectator should be able to participate fully in every passion portrayed.[2] Chapelain too remarks that if this does not happen then the spectator could not assimilate the good that poetry aims to do him.[3]

Here the dramatic illusion is important since the spectator must be able to believe in the characters and their emotions. In his *Observations* Scudéry says that the poet who aims to arouse the spectator's passions by those of his characters, however strongly portrayed they may be, can never achieve this if what he wishes to convey is not 'vray-semblable'.[4] Later in the century, when the controversy over the moral function of drama was no longer in the same key, the basic notions of *vraisemblance* remain. Boileau remarks that

---

[1] *Poétique,* p. 73.
[2] Ibid., p. 74.
[3] *Opuscules,* p. 121.
[4] Gasté, p. 75.

'L'esprit n'est point ému de ce qu'il ne croit pas'[5] and similarly Racine asserts in his preface to *Bérénice* that 'Il n'y a que le vraisemblable qui touche dans la tragédie.'[6]

It is Chapelain, however, who unmistakably connects catharsis with illusion: 'A l'élection succède la *foi*, ou la créance que l'on peut donner au sujet; point important sur tous autres pour ce qu'ils disent qu'où la créance manque, l'attention ou l'affection manque aussi; mais où l'affection n'est point il n'y peut avoir d'émotion et par conséquent de purgation, ou d'amendement ès mœurs des hommes, qui est le but de la poésie.'[7] He too doubts that the force of passion could be reproduced on the stage if it does not have the support of *vraisemblance*.[8] It is worth noting that Chapelain sees *vraisemblance* in the subject as being a necessary condition for *vraisemblance* in the play. In order to involve us, the characters have not only to act credibly within the framework of the play, they must also be posed as credible by the subject. Catharsis, in which we must identify enough with a character to feel pity for him amid the unfortunate consequences of his 'criminal' act and to fear those consequences for ourselves, depends for its effect, therefore, on the dramatic illusion, which is underpinned by the notion of *vraisemblance*.

For the moment, however, our primary concern is with the function of catharsis, and Chapelain's use of the word *purgation* introduces us straightaway to the problem of definitions, which will determine whether catharsis is a moral or a purely aesthetic experience. Aristotle says simply that tragedy is 'the imitation of an action ... with incidents arousing pity and fear, wherewith to accomplish its catharsis of such emotions'.[9] Before discussing seventeenth-century theorists it will perhaps be helpful to look at the views of two twentieth-century commentators on the *Poetics* on the nature of catharsis.

---

[5] *Art poétique*, Chant III, 50.
[6] *Œuvres*, ii, 367.
[7] *Opuscules*, p. 85.
[8] Ibid., p. 119.
[9] *Aristotle on the Art of Poetry*, ed. I. Bywater, Oxford, 1909, Chapter 6, 1450a.

In his lectures on the *Poetics* Humphrey House considers that to speak of purgation is a fundamental error: he asks: 'What is it that can be evacuated? It cannot be the emotions of pity and fear themselves, because it is good that people should have them; it cannot be a morbid element in them because nothing is said about their having a morbid element.'[10] His own definition of catharsis is that:

A tragedy arouses the emotions from potentiality to activity by worthy and adequate stimuli; it controls them by directing them to the right objects in the right way; and exercises them, within the limits of the play, as the emotions of the good man would be exercised. When they subside to potentiality again after the play is over, it is a more trained potentiality than before . . . Our responses are brought nearer to those of the good and wise man.[11]

But another term involving difficulties of interpretation is *such emotions*. Are we to include in these, passions other than pity and fear, thus making it easier to attribute a moral function to catharsis? On this point there are conflicting views among modern commentators. While House considers that 'other passions are not excluded from the tragic experience', thus not limiting *such emotions* to pity and fear,[12] M. Hardy argues that it is a question of pity and fear exclusively, of a coupling which appears elsewhere in the *Poetics*, for the words *ton toiouton* have a simply demonstrative value: 'nous voilà déjà loin d'une purification des passions'.[13]

But what sort of experience is catharsis according to these two commentators? M. Hardy denies that it is moralistic in nature: we all more or less need, he says, to feel the emotions of pity and fear; tragedy, like song and unlike real life, allows us to experience them pleasurably and without any harm coming to us, catharsis thus being for the soul 'une sorte de médication, de traitement, d'hygiène'.[14] House, however, contrasts Aristotle's views on passion with those of Plato, for whom the excitement of emotion in poetry

---

[10] House, H., *Aristotle's Poetics: a Course of Eight Lectures*, London, 1956, p. 105.
[11] Ibid., pp. 109-10.
[12] Ibid., p. 103.
[13] Aristotle, *Poétique*, ed. J. Hardy, Paris, 1952, pp. 16-17.
[14] Ibid., p. 18.

leads to an excess of it in real life. The theory of catharsis is Aristotle's answer to these objections and enables him to give poetry a necessary place in human life and in the state; House concludes, 'The theory of catharsis cannot be taken out of this wider ethical context; and any attempt to isolate it and to speak of it as if it is in the modern sense of the term an independent "aesthetic" theory is a distortion of Aristotle's whole treatment of the matter.'[15]

Among seventeenth-century authors Racine and Boileau upheld the theory of an aesthetically orientated catharsis. One of the most important hints regarding Racine's views on catharsis is found in his translation of the Aristotelian formulation: '[Une action] ne se fait point par un récit, mais par une représentation vive qui, excitant la pitié et la terreur, purge *et tempère* ces sortes de passions. *C'est-à-dire qu'en émouvant ces passions, elle leur oste ce qu'elles ont d'excessif et de vitieux, et les rameine à un estat* modéré et conforme à la raison.'[16] Although Racine uses 'purger' he is clearly not advocating evacuation and considers only the tragic emotions. Professor Vinaver comments that Racine wishes not to rid us of these emotions but 'les réduire à un état d'équilibre parfait où, au lieu d'ébranler notre vision du vrai, elles l'intensifient et l'éclairent'.[17] Professor Knight remarks that Racine narrowly avoids giving tragedy a moralistic aim and that by writing *reason* instead of *virtue* he puts the idea on a plane 'où la morale se rencontre avec l'esthétique'.[18]

Boileau's view of catharsis in the *Art poétique* reflects the general tone of this work, where the emphasis is on the aesthetic rather than on the moral aspect of poetry: he writes:
Si d'un beau mouvement l'agréable fureur
Souvent ne nous remplit d'une douce 'terreur',
Ou n'excite en notre âme une 'pitié' charmante,
En vain vous étalez une scène savante.[19]
He does not therefore refer to the function of pity and fear,

[15] *Aristotle's Poetics*, p. 100.
[16] Racine, J., *Principes de la tragédie*, ed. E. Vinaver, Manchester, 1944, pp. 11-12. Racine's additions are italicized by Vinaver.
[17] *Principes*, p. 61.
[18] *Racine*, p. 202.
[19] *Art poétique*, Chant III, 17-20.

merely to the fact that they are excited. But he has perhaps underlined these two terms in order to distinguish the real from the theatrical emotions. The latter are in a sense artificial; moreover, we willingly submit ourselves to these feelings and we wish to enjoy them, hence 'douce' and 'charmante'. In any case they appear to have no moral content. The spectator experiences an emotional adventure without dire consequence to himself.[20]

One other writer deserves to be mentioned here, particularly because his remarks were made in firm opposition to those who advocated new directions in the early part of the century. For Mareschal, in his preface to *La Généreuse Allemande* (1631), it is not so much a choice between a moral or aesthetic catharsis as utter rejection of the notion itself. He considers it to be no less than an obstacle to an aesthetic experience in the theatre. He mentions that the aim of a play is to promote action, and the aim of action is pleasure; but Aristotle 'en donne deux contraires [aims], qui sont la compassion et la crainte'. Mareschal admits that these emotions should be present in tragedy, which always ends in disaster, but finds this 'si voisin de l'horreur' that even the authors of antiquity, seeing 'comme ils se contredisoient en leur fin propre, et que l'esprit pouvoit s'effaroucher plustost que de se rendre à la peur ou à la compassion', reduced the catastrophe to a *récit*, thus shielding our eyes from bloodshed. He concludes that the Ancients' taste is the opposite of '[les] delicatesses de nos Peuples', who, instead of pity and fear excited by 'objets funestes', desire consolation and joy 'par un agreable passage de la douleur au plaisir, et un changement de succez heureux, que le Ciel ou la seule patience fait treuver à la vertu tant de fois traversée'.

Many seventeenth-century authors, of course, ascribe a moral function to catharsis, not, however, without introducing a certain confusion and inconsistency into their use of terms. In his *Apologie* Scudéry states simply that the aim of catharsis is to 'appaiser les passions', but examples in the rest of the work suggest that he means much more than this. In the case

---

[20] See Sister Haley, *Racine and the Art Poétique*, pp. 160–82, for the aesthetic orientation of Racine's and Boileau's view of catharsis.

of Orestes pursued by the Eumenides, he asks: 'Est-il une ame assez sanguinaire, pour ne fremir point à l'aspect de ce chatiment? et qui pour s'exempter d'un semblable, ne quite sa cruelle inclination? Il en est ainsi de tous les crimes.'[21] Scudéry, then, envisages eradication rather than mere moderation.

In his straightforward definition of catharsis La Mesnardière reveals nothing unorthodox: catharsis is an imitation of suffering 'qui produit par elle-mesme la Terreur et la Pitié, et qui sert à modérer ces deux mouvemens de l'Ame'.[22] Thus at first sight he refers only to moderation and confines it to the tragic emotions alone. Later, he remarks that 'la vertu consiste à regler nos Passions, mais non pas à n'en avoir point', and throughout the *Poétique* he greatly emphasizes the importance of rectifying any passions which lead the hero into dire misfortune. Molière too in the preface to *Le Tartuffe* doubts the possibility of eradication, wondering 's'il n'est pas mieux de travailler à rectifier et adoucir les passions des hommes, que de vouloir les retrancher entièrement'.[23]

In the second *Discours* Corneille speaks at length of catharsis. His initial interpretation of Aristotle's phrase is little more than a translation; tragedy is useful in such a way that through pity and fear 'elle purge de semblables passions'.[24] Later, however, he is more explicit: he repeats Aristotle's remark that we pity those who suffer undeserved misfortune, fearing similar consequences for ourselves, and comments that pity refers to the sufferer and the fear which follows to ourselves; this passage in itself, he continues, explains the manner in which the *purgation* of passion works; the pity we feel for such a misfortune 'nous porte à la crainte d'un pareil pour nous; cette crainte, au désir de l'éviter: et ce désir, à purger, modérer, rectifier et même déraciner en nous la passion qui plonge à nos yeux dans ce malheur les personnes que nous plaignons, par cette raison commune, mais naturelle et indubitable, que pour éviter l'effet il faut

---

[21] *Apologie*, p. 19.
[22] *Poétique*, p. 8.
[23] Molière, *Œuvres*, ed. E. Despois and P. Mesnard, Paris, 1873–1900, iv, pp. 382–3.
[24] *Writings*, p. 28.

en retrancher la cause'.[25] He too, therefore, extends the range of passions subject to purgation.

But there is one definition of catharsis which, although centred on the tragic emotions themselves, has a distinct moral purpose. Le Père Menestrier, in his work on ancient spectacle, explains that by catharsis the Greeks intended to moderate passion and prepare men for 'tous les fâcheux événemens de la fortune en les apprivoisant . . . par les spectacles avec la compassion et la crainte'.[26] The same idea had been explained earlier in connection with the French stage by Sarrasin who wrote that pity and fear were passions to be moderated and reduced to 'une mediocrité raisonnable'; at a performance of tragedy the spectator 'acquiert une médiocrité des passions, lors qu'[il] s'accoûtume à voir souvent les objets qui les excitent dans nos esprits'.[27] Just as a doctor becomes accustomed to horrible wounds so it will be with the spectator 'qui voit tous les jours des miseres'; he will be moved by them but only to the same extent as the wise man.[28] For Sarrasin the moderation of pity and fear makes us in some way receptive to virtue and trains us to experience the correct reactions to misfortune in real life.[29]

The fullest explanation of this particular notion of catharsis is found in Rapin's *Réflexions*. He begins with the orthodox statement that tragedy 'rectifie l'usage des passions en modérant la crainte et la pitié' but adds that these two emotions are 'des obstacles à la vertu'.[30] This last phrase is clarified later when he refers to Aristotle's consideration that tragedy is more useful than philosophy since it is a public lesson whereby 'elle instruit l'esprit par les sens, et . . . rectifie les passions par les passions mesmes, en calmant par leur émotion le trouble qu'elles excitent dans le cœur';

---

[25] Ibid., pp. 28–9.

[26] Menestrier, le Père C.-F., *Des représentations en musique anciennes et modernes*, Paris, 1681, p. 78.

[27] Sarrasin, J.-F., *Discours de la tragédie ou remarques sur l'Amour tyrannique de M. de Scudéry*, n.p., 1683, pp. 70–1.

[28] Ibid., p. 71.

[29] M. Hardy says wrongly of this sort of catharsis that 'Une version aussi peu chrétienne, puisqu'elle fait de la pitié une faiblesse, ne pouvait convenir aux théoriciens français du XVIIe siècle' (pp. 19–20).

[30] *Réflexions*, x, p. 93.

Aristotle, he continues, had found two great faults to correct in man, namely pride and insensitivity, to which tragedy provides a remedy: 'elle rend l'homme modeste, en luy representant des Grands humiliez; et elle le rend sensible et pitoyable, en lui faisant voir sur le theatre les étranges accidens de la vie, et les disgraces imprévûës, ausquelles sont sujettes les personnes les plus importantes'.[31] But because man is naturally timid and compassionate he may go to extremes of pity and fear, and 'la trop grande crainte peut diminuer la fermeté de l'ame'; tragedy corrects these weaknesses in such a way that we become less overawed by the frequent misfortunes of those in higher positions than ourselves; we thus cease to fear ordinary mishaps since those of the *Grands* are so much more terrible; 'Et comme la fin de la Tragedie est d'apprendre aux hommes à ne pas craindre trop foiblement des disgraces communes, et à ménager leur crainte: elle fait estat aussi de leur apprendre à ménager leur compassion pour des sujets qui la meritent. Car il y a de l'injustice d'estre touché des malheurs de ceux, qui meritent d'estre miserables.'[32] In this view, therefore, pity and fear constitute faults in themselves, and are not the means of eradicating other passions; moreover, Rapin introduces an element of comparison with others into the experience, for we learn not to fear ordinary misfortunes after having witnessed the disasters which befall kings. The main concern is therefore with the worthiness of the object to which we apply our pity and fear. Thanks to catharsis a sense of balance is restored to our reactions to our own misfortunes and to those of others.

But there is evidence to suggest that Rapin does not exclude a more purely pleasurable experience of the tragic emotions. Following the previous passage he writes that it is not enough for tragedy to use terrible and moving events in order to rid people 'de ces vaines frayeurs, qui peuvent les troubler, et de ces sottes compassions qui peuvent les amollir'; Aristotle says that poets must use 'ces grands objets de terreur et de pitié comme les deux plus puissans ressorts qu'ait l'art, pour produire le plaisir, que peut donner la Tragedie'.[33]

---

[31] *Réflexions*, xvii, p. 142.   [32] Ibid., p. 143.   [33] *Réflexions*, xviii, p. 143.

André Dacier's remarks on the *Poetics* are interesting for, while many of the previous points appear together in his work, he develops the notion of catharsis which has just been discussed. Although at first sight there is still some terminological confusion, Dacier is more aware than most of the problems involved. His general definition of catharsis is that a tragedy is 'l'imitation d'une action allegorique et universelle, qui convient à tout le monde et qui par le moyen de la compassion et de la terreur modere et corrige nos passions'; Dacier goes on to criticize the rules of his own time where tragedy merely excites passions 'au lieu de les calmer ou de les éteindre'.[34] Thus he conceives of moderation *and* correction, whereas the mention of 'calmer . . . ou éteindre' suggests moderation as an alternative to eradication. What of the passions involved in catharsis? His translation of Aristotle's phrase is '[Une imitation] . . . qui par le moyen de la compassion et de la terreur, acheve de purger en nous ces sortes de passions, et toutes les autres semblables.'[35] Thus there is not only purgation, but this is extended to passions other than pity and fear.

Dacier, aware of the need to explain how pity and fear can be purged, and simultaneously purge other passions, is led to define the term *purgation* itself. The Academicians and the Stoics, he comments, applied it to passion with the meaning of 'chasser' or 'déraciner', an interpretation unsuitable for us because it is beyond the power of tragedy to achieve this; the Peripatetics, however, were persuaded that only excess in passion was harmful and that, when regulated, the passions were useful, even necessary; the term 'purgation' thus meant to remove their sinful excess and to reduce them to a 'juste modération'.[36] This is the aim assigned to tragedy. Catharsis does not purge us of passions but indeed *moderates* them for our moral good.

But how do pity and fear fit into this perspective? Here the most commonly accepted notion of catharsis is fused with that of Sarrasin and Rapin: Dacier says of pity and fear that: '[La tragédie] les excite en nous mettant devant les yeux

---

[34] *Poétique d'Aristote*, pp. viii–ix.
[35] Ibid., Ch. vi, rem. 7, p. 78.
[36] Ibid., p. 78.

les malheurs, que nos semblables se sont attirez par des fautes involontaires, et elle les purge, en nous rendant ces mêmes malheurs familiers, car elle nous apprend par là de ne les pas trop craindre, et à n'en être pas trop touchez quand ils arrivent veritablement.'[37] As in the case of Rapin accustoming ourselves to misfortune is an essential feature of the moderation of pity and fear. But the two concepts are more directly linked in the following statement, where catharsis is:

un assez grand bien qu'elle fait aux hommes, puisqu'elle les [spectators] prépare à supporter courageusement tous les accidens les plus fâcheux, et qu'elle dispose les plus miserables à se trouver heureux, en comparant leurs malheurs avec ceux que la tragedie leur represente . . . En purgeant la terreur et la compassion, elle purge en même temps toutes les autres passions qui pourroient nous précipiter dans la même misere, car en étalant les fautes qui ont attiré sur ces malheureux les peines qu'ils souffrent, elle nous apprend à nous tenir sur nos gardes pour n'y pas tomber, et à purger et à modérer la passion qui a été la seule cause de leur perte.[38]

Not only is tragedy the medicine which purges passion, since it teaches the ambitious man to moderate his ambition and so on,[39] but at the same time we derive consolation in comparing our own misfortunes with those which have a truly tragic dimension.

Thus catharsis is for most dramatic theorists an essential part of moral instruction in the theatre. Although there is some confusion whether harmful passions are eradicated from within us or merely modified by catharsis, no doubt exists regarding its place in the tragic experience, be it an aesthetic or a moral one. But if catharsis does have a moral function, how is it to be brought about?

[37] Ibid., pp. 78-9.   [38] Ibid., p. 79.   [39] Ibid., rem. 8, p. 81.

III

THE AESTHETIC CONDITIONS
OF CATHARSIS

In the eyes of dramatic theorists catharsis is not just an abstract phenomenon; its effectiveness is seen to depend on several practical considerations, such as the choice of an appropriate hero and the nature of the fault he commits, which determine whether or not the tragic emotions are aroused in the spectator.

It will again be helpful to begin by referring to the *Poetics*, where Aristotle advises against three sorts of plot which exclude the possibility of feeling pity and fear: a good man must not pass from happiness to misery nor a bad man from misery to happiness; and an extremely bad man must not pass from happiness to misery since 'pity is occasioned by undeserved misfortune, and fear by that of one like ourselves'.[1] The ideal tragic hero is therefore 'a man not pre-eminently virtuous and just, whose misfortune, however, is brought upon him not by vice and depravity but by some error of judgement'.[2] The important elements here, then, are fault, personality, and situation.

The nature of the character and the fault he commits are closely connected in La Mesnardière's *Poétique* although his approach is slightly different from Aristotle's. His first consideration is that the hero who suffers must appear 'bon et vertueux presqu'en toutes ses actions' and he emphasizes *almost* because 'il suffit qu'il commette une faute médiocre qui lui attire un grand malheur, sans qu'il se noircisse encore par un crime détestable, dont mesme l'exemple est mauvais'.[3] Our reaction to the tragic hero is therefore in some way determined by the nature of the *faute médiocre* which is here opposed to a *crime détestable*. The former term is defined more exactly when La Mesnardière remarks that 'Les fautes

---

[1] *Poetics*, Ch. 13, 1453a.
[2] Ibid.
[3] *Poétique*, p. 18.

seront mediocres, si elles ne sont point du nombre de ces détestables crimes qui partent d'une ame noire; mais de ces fragilitez que nous appelons des erreurs.'[4] Aristotle's 'error' remains but is equated with the human weaknesses which cause men's misfortunes. However, La Mesnardière explains that the hero experiences unhappiness not just because he is subject to 'quelques imperfections' but 'pour avoir fait une faute qui merite d'estre punie',[5] in other words for allowing his weakness to overcome his better judgement.

Dacier reproduces Aristotle's formula in its general outline but significant changes occur in his translation of 'error', which directly inserts catharsis into the perspective of Christian morals: since characters may be neither very virtuous nor very bad 'il faut necessairement qu'ils tiennent le milieu'; this is found only in those 'qui péchent par foiblesse et qui tombent dans des fautes involontaires'; they are 'méchans, parce qu'ils péchent', and 'bons, parce qu'ils péchent malgré eux, par infirmité'.[6] 'Error' here becomes 'sin'. The transformation is easy to understand for *hamartia* has the meaning of sin in the Greek New Testament. But Dacier is more explicit about the tragic flaw when he describes it as 'une faute involontaire qu'on a commise, ou par ignorance, ou par imprudence, et malgré soy, vaincu par une violente passion dont on n'a pu être le maître, ou enfin par une force majeure et extérieure, pour executer des ordres ausquels on n'a pû ny dû desobeïr'.[7] Like La Mesnardière Dacier emphasizes a weakness closely associated with passion and man's inability to control it, and indeed attempts to reduce the moral responsibility of the hero.

One other element already noted as important was personality and this too is related to the nature of the flaw. Weakness does not include outright vice and La Mesnardière makes a clear distinction between a *faute médiocre* and a *crime détestable*; furthermore the act must not result from an 'âme noire' and Dacier has described the fault as 'involontaire'. Indeed most theorists agree with Aristotle

---

[4] Ibid., p. 20.
[5] Ibid.
[6] *Poétique d'Aristote*, Ch. xiii, rem. 8, p. 182.
[7] Ibid., rem. 10, pp. 182–3.

that the ideal hero is neither good nor bad; for La Mesnardière he must be good in almost all his actions. A *faute médiocre* is thus a single wayward act committed at the height of passion, resulting not from an evil personality but from a weakness inherent in all men, which has great and terrible consequences for those in high places.

One significant conclusion that can be reached here is that action is of prime importance. La Mesnardière emphasizes that the act and not habit is the subject of tragedy, and the poet must apply his art not 'aux méchantes inclinations qui font cét homme vicieux, mais à la mauvaise action qui produit ses infortunes'.[8] Theorists, therefore, pay much attention to the cirumstances which lead to this. Dacier's definition of the *faute involontaire* points to situations where characters are under some form of external obligation.

This leads us to a further example of a pitiable character, whose justification is the very irony of circumstance. La Mesnardière speaks of 'l'Ignorance des personnes qui deviennent mal-heureuses pour des fautes qu'elles ont faites sans les avoir premeditées'; moreover, there is no subject which better excites passion than 'les peines de ces Heros, qu'on ne peut nommer innocens, pource qu'ils ont fait de grans crimes, mais qui meritent d'étre plaints, à cause qu'ils les ont commis sans en avoir aucun dessein'.[9] (We remember that *ignorance* was part of Dacier's definition of the fault.) An obvious example of this is Oedipus who, having committed incest and parricide, is none the less possessed of 'une innocence si claire, au moins pour la volonté . . . qu'encore qu'il nous semble horrible par les forfaits abominables qui se rencontrent en lui, il nous fait beaucoup de Pitié, pource qu'ils lui sont arrivez, plustost qu'il ne les a commis'.[10] There is thus a desire to recuperate the tragic hero as far as circumstances allow: the crime is separated from the person by his unawareness.

Some authors offer us specific examples of characters who commit a *faute médiocre* in order to illustrate their theories.

---

[8] *Poétique*, p. 20. Habit, according to some theorists, is the domain of the epic. See Dacier, p. v and Ch. xxviii, rem. 37, pp. 496–7.
[9] *Poétique*, pp. 83–4.
[10] Ibid., p. 84.

As shown above, La Mesnardière, is interested in a hero who, although technically guilty of crime, is himself morally blameless. But he also makes a case for *excusing* one who is morally guilty. His discussion of Orestes and Meleager was prompted by his desire to refute Castelvetro's views on Aristotle, where the Italian commentator maintained that neither character mentioned sinned in ignorance or while blinded by passion, and that both were 'parricides de volonté deliberée'.[11] Replying to this opinion La Mesnardière agrees that these crimes are horrid, but not so much that they cannot be excused in some way, especially when they are considered 'sans préoccupation d'esprit'.[12]

Orestes' case is clear; La Mesnardière does not exalt this 'mauvais fils' for killing his mother but forgives him for protecting oppressed innocence and returning to his state to kill his enemies. While not approving the reversal of justice in order to gain a crown, 'je l'excuse d'estre severe envers ces cruels parricides, de soumettre ces adulteres à toutes les rigueurs des loix qu'ils ont laschement violées en la mort d'un si grand Roy, et de leur faire souffrir les peines qu'ils ont meritées par l'insolence de leur vie'.[13]

The case of Meleager and Althaea is more complex. Meleager had killed Althaea's brothers because they had insulted Atalanta, and in revenge for this killing Althaea caused the death of Meleager. Castelvetro had seen no passion in this act, seeking it rather in Meleager's death. But La Mesnardière stresses the act because it is in the murder that we must seek 'l'Ignorance, les Passions, et l'Aveuglement, pour voir s'il sera possible d'y treuver quelques motifs qui excusans sa promptitude, laissent naistre la Compassion sur les malheurs de ce Heros'. Meleager is 'criminel' for the violence used against members of his family, but he deserves pity because he is no longer himself when he commits this act; 'sa passion fait son crime'.[14] Compassion is thus directly related to an excuse. The case of Althaea is slightly more interesting: certainly the mother is inhuman

[11] Ibid., p. 178.
[12] Ibid., p. 180.
[13] Ibid., pp. 181-2.
[14] Ibid., p. 187.

in the murder of her son but he himself showed cruelty in his own murders; her impiety has at least the advantage of approaching a religious duty in that she acts to appease the soul of the princes killed for rather trivial reasons; 'Enfin si la passion l'aveugle, on voit que son aveuglement a un extréme rapport à celui de la Justice: et que si elle n'a plus d'yeux pour connoître son propre Fils, c'est pource qu'il est trop coupable, et qu'il lui paroist tout sanglant du parricide de ses Freres.'[15] There is an essential irony in this attitude for we are invited both to excuse and to condemn a character for his act, which in turn provides an excuse for the revenge of another character.[16]

Interesting comments on the relation of catharsis to specific tragic characters are found in Racine's prefaces to his own plays. In the first preface to *Andromaque*, where he defines tragic characters as having 'une bonté médiocre, c'est-à-dire une vertu capable de foiblesse', he sees the cause of their misfortune as 'quelque faute qui les fasse plaindre sans les faire détester',[17] or, as we read in *Britannicus*, 'quelque imperfection'.[18] Characters are, therefore, basically virtuous but subject to weakness. Professor Knight remarks that the flaw in Racine is neither, as in La Mesnardière, 'une tare morale qui mérite d'estre punie' nor 'un geste ou une parole irréfléchie' but 'un égarement inhérent au personnage et qui vient d'une passion irradicable et meurtrière'.[19]

Racine further considers the problem in his preface to *Phèdre* where he tells us that Phèdre has all the qualities required by Aristotle:

En effet, Phèdre n'est ni tout à fait coupable, ni tout à fait innocente. Elle est engagée par sa destinée, et par la colère des Dieux, dans une passion illégitime, dont elle a horreur toute la première. Elle fait tous ses efforts pour la surmonter. Elle aime mieux se laisser mourir que de la déclarer à personne. Et lorsqu'elle est forcée de la découvrir, elle en parle avec une confusion qui fait bien voir que son crime est plutôt une punition des Dieux qu'un mouvement de sa volonté.[20]

---

[15] Ibid., pp. 195–6.
[16] Cf. Corneille, *Writings*, p. 100, where Corneille says of Médée that 'on excuse sa vengeance après l'indigne traitement qu'elle a reçu de Créon et de son mari . . .'.
[17] *Œuvres*, ii, 36–7.
[18] Ibid., 243.
[19] *Racine*, p. 203.
[20] *Œuvres*, iii, 299.

Here, then, is another example of separating crime from will. What is important in *Phèdre* is not 'goodness' or 'badness' but degrees of guilt or innocence.

If, as Racine holds, the tragic protagonists have 'quelque faute qui les fasse plaindre sans les faire détester' it is apparent that they must have qualities which do not alienate our sympathy. Corneille likewise speaks of '[le] premier acteur, pour qui nous devons toujours ménager la faveur de l'auditoire'.[21] The presentation of the hero who must arouse our pity if catharsis is to be effective is, therefore, of prime importance.

One element which dramatic theorists discussed at length was that of *mœurs*:[22] according to La Mesnardière they are 'les vrais Principes du bonheur ou de l'infortune'[23] and 'par nos Mœurs nous sommes bons ou mauvais'.[24] But a major discussion arose over the interpretation of Aristotle's goodness of *mœurs*. Aristotle writes:

> In the characters there are four points to aim at. First and foremost, that they shall be good. There will be an element of character in the play, if ... what a personage says or does reveals a certain moral purpose; and a good element of character, if the purpose is revealed good. Such goodness is possible in every type of personage, even in a woman or a slave ...[25]

Bywater's translation thus emphasizes both the moral aspect and excellence of its kind. Hardy, however, omits any reference to the former: 'Il y aura caractère si ... les paroles ou les actes décèlent une conduite; le caractère sera bon si elle est bonne.'[26] The problem is whether *goodness* is moral or aesthetic.

In the preface to his *Apologie* Scudéry says rather vaguely that *mœurs* must be 'absolument bonnes'; but in his *Observations* he remarks that Aristotle requires that *mœurs* should be for the most part good and that 's'il y faut introduire des personnes pleines de vices, le nombre en soit

21 *Writings*, p. 47.
22 We have retained the French term to avoid repetition of *character* and also possible ambiguity.
23 *Poétique*, p. 107.
24 Ibid., p. 113.
25 *Poetics*, Ch. 15, 1454a.
26 *Poétique*, ed .Hardy, p. 50.

moindre que des vertueuses'.[27] This mention of vice clearly marks *bonnes* as moral. Similarly La Mesnardière comments that Aristotle prescribed more virtue than vice for the stage[28] and later introduces the notion of *mœurs exemplaires*,[29] an original gloss on Aristotle. La Mesnardière also tells us that poets must try to introduce characters 'qui ayent de nobles attitudes, et des sentimens éxemplaires, bien qu'ils commettent quelques fautes'.[30] Thus, although goodness has moral associations, it does not exclude the possibility of a flaw.

Some writers, however, see *mœurs* as purely aesthetic. This is principally because the second quality of *mœurs*, that they should be *convenables*, is merged with *bonté*. Corneille is firm in his declaration that 'goodness' is 'le caractère brillant et élevé d'une habitude vertueuse ou criminelle, selon qu'elle est propre et convenable à la personne qu'on introduit'.[31] This confusion of *bonté* and *convenance* is also found in Chapelain's *Discours de la poésie représentative*: poets call *bienséance* not 'ce qui est honnête' but 'ce qui convient aux personnes, soit bonnes, soit mauvaises, et telles qu'on les introduit dans la pièce'.[32]

But for those theorists who see in goodness of *mœurs* a moral component, what is the concrete expression of that goodness most likely to retain our sympathy and compassion? One of La Mesnardière's requirements is 'beaucoup de douceur, de constance et de modestie dans la personne qui souffre',[33] for it is natural to pity 'ceux que l'on voit endurer avec beaucoup de patience, et mesme de résignation à la volonté de Dieu'.[34] It is interesting to note the mention made here of divine responsibility for the hero's misfortune. Appropriately La Mesnardière adds that in the case of a hero fulminating against heaven we shall most likely be unmoved, feeling that blasphemy itself is deserving of misfortune.[35] He advises that the hero should speak respectfully of heavenly power even when it is responsible for his misfortune;[36] the poet must never allow that 'la plus juste colere emporte si

[27] Gasté, p. 81.
[28] *Poétique*, pp. 146–7.
[29] Ibid., p. 140.
[30] Ibid., p. 141.
[31] *Writings*, p. 14.

[32] *Opuscules*, p. 130.
[33] *Poétique*, p. 75.
[34] Ibid., pp. 75–6.
[35] Ibid., p. 76.
[36] Ibid., p. 102.

fort son Héros, qu'il en perde et le jugement, et le respect qui est deu aux Potentats de la Terre'.[37]

But it is equally important that the hero's utterances should be commensurate with his social position; he must never 'débonder en injures, indignes d'un honneste homme, et moins encore en blasphémes, odieux aux âmes bien faites'.[38] Moreover, 'aprés avoir fait les plaintes sortables à sa condition, et proportionnées à ses maux, le Poëte doit le remettre dans un état raisonnable, plus tranquille et plus moderé; et penser que les crieries, les transports et la fureur sont de fort mauvais moyens pour exciter la Compassion'.[39] An audience of 'honnestes hommes' must not be shocked by anything they find unacceptable. The hero's language must consist of 'parolles ... lugubres' and 'accens pitoyables' which must be 'pour des sujets légitimes',[40] for it is true that 'les honnestes soumissions et les souplesses d'esprit sont des moyens infaillibles pour attendrir toutes les ames'.[41] Humility is clearly more effective because nothing is more ridiculous or intolerable than 'les arrogans mal-heureux'.[42]

We must, then, never have reason to despise the tragic hero and hence to impair our involvement in his misfortune. In a comment which is remarkable for its similarity with Corneille's theory of *admiration*, first expressed twelve years later, La Mesnardière asks that: 'sans témoigner un courage lasche et rampant, indigne de sa condition, [la personne mal-heureuse] plaigne son infortune par des accens si pitoyables, que l'Auditeur ait autant d'admiration pour sa vertu, que de douleur pour sa disgrace'.[43]

There are, therefore, certain attitudes of characters to their crime which may also constitute a means of preventing the alienation of our sympathy: one consists of: 'le Repentir de ceux qui ont commis des crimes, et ... la longue Incertitude de ceux qui en vont commettre; qui, aprés avoir balancé entre les bons sentimens et les meschantes actions, ne prennent

[37] Ibid., p. 104.
[38] Ibid., p. 101.
[39] Ibid., p. 76.
[40] Ibid., p. 97.
[41] Ibid., p. 79.
[42] Ibid.
[43] Ibid., p. 77.

le mauvais parti que pource qu'ils sont aveuglez de la passion qui les transporte'.[44] The poet must never expose the atrocious acts of evil that are repellent to nature itself without ensuring that the characters about to commit them experience some feelings of virtue which seem for a moment to hold them back.[45] Thus a 'crime détestable' is possible in tragedy provided that one of these two features is present. La Mesnardière's justification of this reminds us of his definition of the *faute médiocre*: the poet must not presume that 'les horribles desseins de l'inceste et du parricide soient un sentiment naturel qui naisse dans l'esprit humain comme une pensée ordinaire'; he must show that 'ces tentations furieuses n'attaquent jamais une ame, qu'elle ne reçoive à l'instant des conseils de la Raison, qui seroient assez puissans pour l'empescher de succomber, si elle les vouloit entendre, et ne pas suivre ses passions, et les mouvemens déréglez d'une nature corrompuë'.[46]

But as much as hesitation before the act the poet may portray 'un aigre et cuisant Repentir dans la Personne coupable; qui venant à considerer l'atrocité de son forfait dans cette froideur honteuse qui suit l'exécution des crimes, connoist l'énormité du sien'.[47] The aim of this 'incertitude exemplaire' is to show that nature is never so blind in the planning of great crimes that reason does not make itself heard, 'et ne lui donne des conseils capables de l'en retirer, si elle ne se plaisoit point dans les perils qui l'environnent: Et partant que les passions, pour violentes qu'elles soient, ne forcent jamais une ame, si elle n'est assez lasche pour vouloir estre forcée'.[48] It is as if La Mesnardière were afraid that, were evil to be shown as absolute in all circumstances, the idea of moral instruction in the theatre would be seriously undermined.

But how are these attitudes to be expressed in dramatic terms? One means La Mesnardière considers legitimate is suicide, which gives us a fine example of *Rescipiscence* or

---

[44] Ibid., p. 225. Cf. Racine's justification of *Phèdre, Œuvres*, iii, 299.
[45] Ibid.
[46] *Poétique*, p. 226.
[47] Ibid., p. 230.
[48] Ibid., pp. 232-3.

'un genereux Desespoir, . . . les deux Sentimens heroïques de la Morale des Payens'; he cites Phaedra as an example.[49] But how can one who has just recommended respect for the Christian God uphold the example of suicide and stoic morality? La Mesnardière is well aware of the problem, writing that such suicides should be imitated at least in the feelings which prompt them, but 'on n'en doit pas imiter les genereuses actions'; although Christianity condemns suicide it allows 'les grandes âmes' to be deeply affected by their country's misfortunes or their *gloire*; those forbidden to imitate Lucretia's suicide after the loss of her honour may draw from her example 'une instruction salutaire pour faire mourir les vices qui possible leur ont causé ce que fist à cette Heroïne la vanité de Collatin'.[50] We learn from the characters' feelings rather than from their acts. La Mesnardière is convinced that the result of this hesitation and remorse is that 'le Poëme . . . peut tirer les bonnes Mœurs des plus pernicieux exemples, et les sentimens vertueux des plus meschantes actions'.[51]

It is evident that the tragic flaw must not be excessive and that the hero's qualities should attract and not alienate our pity. Moreover, fear is aroused by the punishment of an evil act. But if there is to be pity in the first place some similarity must exist between the spectator and the tragic protagonist; equally, if punishment is to be effective, the spectator must be able to relate these consequences to himself. The exact nature of the relation of spectator to hero, and the interpretation of Aristotle's remark that 'pity is occasioned by undeserved misfortune, and fear by that of *one like ourselves*'[52] were indeed matters to which theorists gave much attention.

La Mesnardière is strict in his definition; he contests Castelvetro's idea that only the people can enjoy tragedy and emphasizes the characters' rank, for their actions must be those of kings, princes, imperial governors who enjoy good fortune before their fall.[53] He instead limits the effect of

[49] Ibid., pp. 205-6.
[50] Ibid., p. 207.
[51] Ibid., p. 232.
[52] *Poetics*, Ch. 13, 1453a.
[53] *Poétique*, p. 17.

catharsis to those of the same order because only princes can be 'effrayez des disgraces de leurs semblables'.[54] La Mesnardière cannot understand how Castelvetro's man of low condition could be greatly affected by the fall of the House of Troy.[55] But he slightly relaxes his stricture when he says that the profitable in tragedy is reserved 'aux grandes Ames; soit que l'illustre naissance, les éminentes dignitez, ou la bonne nourriture leur donnent cette condition'.[56] It is the lower orders, then, who are excluded from enjoying tragedy.

Dacier considers tragedy as 'une action allegorique et universelle, qui convient à tout le monde';[57] but while he stresses that tragedy portrays the misfortunes which befall 'those like ourselves',[58] he does not abandon the notion of rank, for tragedy is 'une imitation des actions des plus grands personnages, qu'elle represente encore plus grands qu'ils n'étoient, en les faisant pourtant semblables'.[59] How can these two ideas be reconciled? Dacier's views become clearer from an examination of his reply to Corneille who attacked Paolo Beni, the originator of La Mesnardière's restriction, for interpreting *semblables* too literally, especially since there were no kings in Athens.[60] Corneille points out that although the audience carry no sceptre by which they may resemble kings on the stage the latter are men and as such susceptible to misfortune; they experience the same passions as the spectators who 'prêtent ... un raisonnement aisé à faire du plus grand au moindre' and who believe that, 'si un roi, pour trop s'abandonner à l'ambition ... tombe dans un malheur si grand qu'il lui fait pitié, à plus forte raison lui qui n'est qu'un homme du commun doit tenir la bride à de telles passions, de peur qu'elles ne l'abîment dans un pareil malheur'.[61] There is thus an affective similarity between stage king and spectator which includes the possibility of committing similar errors and suffering similar misfortune.

On this point Dacier gives us a more detailed explanation: 'mais dira-t-on, s'il n'y a que les malheurs de nos semblables,

[54] Ibid., p. N.
[55] Ibid.
[56] Ibid. p. P.
[57] *Poétique d'Aristote*, p. viii.
[58] Ibid., p. xiii.
[59] Ibid., Ch. ii, rem. 17, p. 22.
[60] *Writings*, p. 29.
[61] Ibid., pp. 29-30.

qui nous donnent de la crainte, la Tragedie n'en donne point, puisqu'elle n'expose que les malheurs des Princes et des Rois, et des personnages les plus illustres: ou si elle en donne, c'est aux personnages de ce rang-là'.[62] He severely criticizes Corneille's solution because it would prove Aristotle wrong: if misfortune caused by passion produced fear in everybody, the misfortune of kings would frighten the *peuple* like that of any other man: Aristotle would therefore err in saying that fear arises from 'la misere de nos semblables'. But, he continues, Aristotle has shown that tragedy is 'une fable universelle, qui regarde tous les hommes in general';

ce n'est ny Edipe, ny Atrée, ny Thyeste, c'est un homme ordinaire à qui on donne le nom qu'on veut; mais pour rendre son action plus grande et plus croyable, le Poëte luy donne un nom illustre qui soit connu; cependant quoyque cette fable soit renduë singuliere par l'imposition des noms, elle ne change pourtant pas de nature au fond, et demeure toûjours generale; c'est toûjours un homme ordinaire qui agit sous le nom d'un Prince ou d'un Roy.[63]

Thus Aristotle rightly called these kings and princes *nos semblables*, for the poet imitates not the actions of kings but those of men; 'c'est nous qu'il represente'.[64] The aristocratic ethos of tragedy, very marked in the works of d'Aubignac and La Mesnardière, is thus lost. Kings in tragedy are not real kings because the latter, contrary to Corneille's suggestion, cannot be ordinary men.

Dacier justifies his interpretation of tragic character and action, itself inspired by Aristotle's notion of poetry as universal, by defining a pity which:

présuppose toûjours que les gens qu'elle regarde, sont gens de bien; car on n'en auroit pas pitié si on croyoit qu'ils meritassent le mal qu'ils ont; mais ce sont des gens d'une probité ordinaire et commune, comme tout ce qu'on appelle les honnêtes gens; s'ils étoient vertueux et justes dans un souverain degré, on n'auroit que de l'horreur pour leur misére. En un mot la pitié, comme la crainte, demande quelque espece d'égalité entre celuy qui souffre et celuy qui compatit.[65]

But if it is ourselves that we pity in tragedy, why is it

[62] *Poétique d'Aristote*, Ch. iii, rem. 6, p. 179.
[63] Ibid., pp. 180-1.
[64] Ibid., p. 181.
[65] *Poétique*, Ch. xiii, rem. 7, p. 181.

necessary to make the situation more credible by the provision
of celebrated names? Can we not believe in this portrait of
ourselves? Clearly Dacier is missing an essential point in the
relation of hero to spectator in that princes and kings are in
more special positions, and their passions are in service to
courses of conduct not within the ordinary man's experience.
Moreover, the audience's response may be prompted by this
very factor, something well understood by Corneille. Dacier's
opinions, however, do not prevent him from writing of
le merveilleux that tragedy and epic poetry imitate 'ce qu'il
y a de plus excellent, elles doivent donc étaler les Incidens
extraordinaires et merveilleux'.[66]

Both Corneille and Dacier devote some time to the
question whether or not men of low rank can be the principal
characters of a tragedy. In the Épître to the 1650 edition of
Don Sanche Corneille asks the following question: if it is true
that fear of a similar fate is aroused in us by the suffering of
those like ourselves could it not be better aroused by the
misfortune of those 'de nôtre condition', whom we resemble
more, than 'par l'image de ceux qui font trébucher de leurs
trônes les plus grands monarques, avec qui nous n'avons
aucun rapport qu'en tant que nous sommes susceptibles des
passions qui les ont jetés dans ce précipice: ce qui ne se
rencontre pas toujours'?[67] It would be unwise to over-
interpret this statement, as does Bray despite his final
reservations.[68] Even here Corneille does not abandon the
notion of hero: although, he says in the second Discours,
there is no need to portray only the misfortunes of kings on
the stage, those of other men could find a place only 's'il
leur en arrivait d'assez illustres et d'assez extraordinaires pour
la mériter et que l'histoire prît assez de soin d'eux pour nous
les apprendre'.[69] The hierarchy in mankind is preserved and
we are far from the drame bourgeois of the eighteenth
century. Ordinary men must still commit extraordinary acts.

Dacier's approach is almost the opposite of Corneille's, for
he admits that things sufficiently extraordinary and tragic
may happen to people of middle and low social status; but

[66] Ibid., Ch. xxv, rem. 23, p. 400.
[67] Writings, p. 196.
[68] Formation, p. 332.
[69] Writings, p. 30.

they cannot succeed, not because of the action itself, but because of the lowness of the characters; tragedy 'n'exige pas que l'action qu'elle represente soit importante et grande par elle-même, il suffit qu'elle soit tragique, elle la rend grande par les noms qu'elle donne à ses personnages, qu'elle va prendre . . . parmy ceux qui ont le plus de fortune et de réputation. La grandeur de ces hommes illustres, rend l'action grande, et leur reputation la rend vray-semblable et croyable'.[70] This is surely an admission that kings must be the subject of tragedy, for it is their special position which makes the action *grande*. Dacier is nearer Corneille than he wishes to think.

So far pity and fear have been treated as a single entity. It is also necessary to consider the separation of the two tragic emotions, which is determined by attitudes held towards the hero's misfortune, itself often seen in terms of punishment for a criminal act. La Mesnardière remarks that the spectator will be moved by 'la force de l'Exemple . . . qui oblige le Poëte de finir la Tragédie par la punition des vices, qui donne de la terreur'.[71] But we must be careful that those who suffer this punishment are those who possess the qualities of 'coupables malheureux',[72] we must also avoid portraying the misfortune of innocent and virtuous people, or the success of very evil characters.[73]

This leaves us for the moment with the ideal tragic hero. But an important problem arises here in that he too is punished and, according to La Mesnardière, to excess: he asserts that, 'Les Mœurs sont fort exemplaires dans les Sujets pitoyables, puisqu'ils exposent toujours les severes punitions de quelques fautes legeres; soit pour donner de la pitié des Personnes affligées; soit pour avertir l'Auditeur de se tenir net de tout crime, afin de ne pas tomber entre les mains d'une Justice qui punit rigoureusement mesme les fautes mediocres'.[74] This excess of punishment is, in La Mesnardière's opinion, like the hyperbole which uses untruth to persuade

---

[70] *Poétique*, Ch. xiii, rem. 9, p. 182.
[71] *Poétique*, pp. 216–17.
[72] *Poétique*, p. O.
[73] Ibid., pp. 107–8. For Dacier punishment of evil and reward for virtue produces only 'le plaisir qu'on trouve à la Comédie' (Ch. xiii, rem. 32, p. 199).
[74] Ibid., pp. 144–5.

of the truth, for 'les Chastimens de Theatre passent jusqu'à la cruauté pour faire craindre la Justice'.[75] Surely if these faults, especially those committed in ignorance, are punished out of all proportion to their gravity (and the tragic hero is good apart from one single error) do we not risk arousing indignation rather than pity?

Later it is almost as if La Mesnardière is aware of this: in the case of *grands personnages*, 'Si leurs peines étoient moindres, si elles étoient supportables, et un peu plus proportionnées à la patience humaine, leur puissante Exagération ne produiroit dans nos Esprits que la Terreur et la Pitié.' But 'depuis qu'elles dégénérent en cruautez execrables, et en souffrances horribles, elles ne peuvent engendrer que des effets qui leur ressemblent'.[76] In this context it is therefore interesting to read in the *Poétique* that 'le mouvement de la Crainte étant un effet légitime de nôtre Poëme tragique, [le Poëte] peut exposer des Héros qui soient capables de grans crimes'[77] and that perhaps Aristotle would even allow the central character of tragedy to be 'absolument mauvais dans les Sujets odieux qui doivent produire la Crainte'.[78] Fear is thus accorded an autonomous function and catharsis is no longer seen as embodying both tragic emotions at the same time.

One objection to the use of a very evil character as the subject for tragedy is that the spectator does not identify with him because, as Corneille says, we are not as evil, his crimes being thus beyond our capability.[79] But perhaps this is La Mesnardière's point in that all the horror of extreme justice is heaped upon somebody who is in any case morally beyond the pale and with whom we would not wish to associate ourselves. By isolating terror in a subject of this kind we lessen the load on the sympathetic tragic hero and we take less account of his moral responsibility. But it is also clear that the usefulness of catharsis in moral instruction is thus seriously undermined.

[75] Ibid., pp. 145.
[76] Ibid., pp. 323-4.
[77] Ibid., p. 19.
[78] Ibid., p. 145.
[79] *Writings*, p. 31. See also Dacier, Ch. xiii, rem. 5, p. 179.

This of course leads us to a point where pity must be preferred to fear: La Mesnardière comments that if we are allowed to 'introduire sur le Théatre les excellentes Personnes qui ont souffert de grans outrages, et celles qui les ont commis' it is preferable to 'choisir les premieres, qui excitent nôtre Pitié par leurs malheurs déplorables, que de prendre les dernieres, qui nous font transsir d'horreur à l'aspect de leurs cruautez'.[80] Thus the possibility of portraying a good man suffering at the hands of a tyrant is reintroduced and La Mesnardière prefigures Corneille's justification of martyrs on the stage. La Mesnardière's reason for his preference is that 'la Commiseration est infiniment plus douce, plus humaine et plus agréable que la terreur et l'effroy'.[81] He agrees that fear is useful but, since it is a disagreeable emotion, 'elle ne doit regner que dans les Sujets horribles qui exposent le chastiment des parricides'.[82] Within the subject itself the poet must try to ensure that 'la Terreur soit beaucoup moindre que les sentimens de Pitié'.[83] Moreover, he advises poets 'd'introduire rarement de ces criminels detestables, et de ne se point servir d'une dommageable licence, dont l'usage est plus nuisible qu'il ne peut estre avantageux'.[84] This means that the poet's attention is almost wholly concentrated on the emotion of pity. D'Aubignac too agrees in his *Dissertation* on Corneille's *Oedipe* that 'la compassion est le plus parfait sentiment qui regne au Théatre'.[85] But if we eliminate fear how are we encouraged to eradicate within ourselves the fault which leads to the tragic hero's misfortune?

Indeed what of the hero and his flaw? La Mesnardière remarks that pity can be aroused only 'par la triste ressemblance d'une Action peu criminelle, qui attire un grand malheur'.[86] Furthermore 'il vaut mieux que la Compassion, qui est un sentiment plus doux, et qui naist des calamitez

[80] *Poétique*, p. 19.
[81] Ibid.
[82] Ibid., p. 22.
[83] Ibid., p. 21.
[84] Ibid., p. 19.
[85] Granet, l'Abbé Fr., *Recueil de dissertations sur plusieurs tragédies de Corneille et de Racine*, 2 vols., Paris, 1739, ii, 34.
[86] *Poétique*, p. 143.

des personnes imparfaites, *moins coupables que malheureuses*, fasse impression sur les esprits'.[87] In the *Poétique* La Mesnardière constantly dilutes the nature of the act committed by Aristotle's tragic hero. From the possibility of portraying an *execrable faute* we come to *une Action peu criminelle*. The recuperation of the tragic hero is complete.

This emphasis on pity has not been overlooked by previous commentators. Louis Herland, in his analysis of d'Aubignac's *Dissertations* on three of Corneille's tragedies, sees a growing tendency towards a preference for the unhappy lover, thus suggesting a certain influence from the salons.[88] Professor Barnwell reflects that perhaps Beni's restriction upon fear had influenced French theorists in this respect.[89] While not wishing to exclude these factors, it would seem that one important reason for this emphasis lies in the rank attributed to tragedy and the relation of characters to the audience.

It has already been observed that tragedy befell people in high places. While much of d'Aubignac's *Dissertations* is concerned with appropriate portrayal of kings in tragedy, at the same time he doubts the usefulness of showing the populace that kings are not shielded from misfortune and that they are ·equally subject to divine retribution, which may in turn entail the misfortune of their people. For this reason he criticizes Corneille for choosing the Oedipus myth as a fitting subject for tragedy: 'C'est leur [the populace] donner sujet, quand il arrive quelque infortune publique, d'examiner toutes les actions de leur Prince, de vouloir pénétrer dans les sécrets de leur cabinet, de se rendre juges de tous leurs sentimens, et de leur imputer tous les maux qu'ils souffrent, et qui ne doivent être que la punition de leurs propres iniquités.'[90] The people must be maintained in their belief that kings are always favoured by heaven and that they are 'par tout innocens, et que personne n'a droit de les estimer coupables'.[91] Thus, when portraying sovereigns

---

[87] Ibid., p. 22. Our italics.
[88] 'Les Qualités du personnage de tragédie', *Mélanges de la Société toulousaine d'Études classiques*, Toulouse, 1946, vol. ii, 205–22, pp. 208–9.
[89] *Writings*, p. 223, n. 6.
[90] Granet, ii, 31–2.
[91] Ibid., 32.

on the stage, 'il n'y faut rien mêler qui sente le déreglement des mœurs, il en faut retrancher toutes les circonstances qui peuvent faire mal penser de leur conduite, il faut empêcher que les peuples s'imaginent d'être châtiés pour des crimes d'autrui sans être les premiers coupables'.[92] In the *Pratique* d'Aubignac asserts that because of the love and respect we have for our princes we cannot believe that they can be evil, nor tolerate that 'leurs Sujets, quoy qu'en apparence mal-traittez, touchent leurs Personnes sacrées, ny se rebellent contre leur Puissance, non pas mesme en peinture'; he does not believe that 'l'on puisse faire assassiner un Tyran sur nostre Theatre avec applaudissement, sans de tres-signalées précautions'.[93] Here the restrictions imposed on the tragic hero are dictated by the need to safeguard the state from rebellion.

La Mesnardière is more explicit regarding the virtues of a monarch: he must be so courageous that he fears no danger nor finds anything impossible in the course of a just war; he must be so wise that he never retracts his decisions and so liberal that he proves himself the giver and not the usurper of his kingdom's wealth; finally, he must be so good that he treats his subjects as he himself would wish to be treated, were he a private citizen.[94] La Mesnardière concludes that we must revere in princes 'cette puissance indépendante dont ils ne sont que la figure: Et bien qu'ils soient imparfaits aussi bien que les autres hommes, on doit cacher leurs défauts, pource qu'ils président aux hommes comme Lieutenans de Dieu: ou si l'on en dit quelque chose, il faut en parler pour les plaindre, et non pas pour les condamner'.[95] Thus kings, as representatives of God, are beyond criticism. How could we revere as our sovereign one who is subject to our own imperfections? It is significant that d'Aubignac rarely speaks of a moralistic catharsis and that La Mesnardière holds to the notion that the appreciation of tragedy is reserved strictly for a social élite.

This change of emphasis regarding the tragic emotions provides an appropriate introduction to the discussion of Corneille's theories of catharsis. Corneille merits special

[92] Ibid., 33.
[93] *Pratique*, pp. 72-3.
[94] *Poétique*, p. 120.
[95] Ibid., p. 102.

consideration because much of the second *Discours* and parts of the *Examens* are devoted to catharsis or at least to explaining the various discrepancies between Aristotle's ideas and his own dramatic practice. His analysis of the problem leads him to an entirely different conception of tragic emotion.

Corneille uses as the basis for his argument Aristotle's categories of character and plot. His view of the evil man falling into misfortune is orthodox in that we experience no pity or fear because of our lack of identity with him.[96] A problem however arises with the prescription of a virtuous man falling into misfortune (which should arouse our indignation) because martyrs would in this case be banished from the stage; but *Polyeucte* has succeeded in spite of this prescription along with Héraclius and Nicomède, 'bien qu'ils n'impriment que de la pitié et ne nous donnent rien à craindre, ni aucune passion à purger, puisque nous les y voyons opprimés et près de périr, sans aucune faute de leur part dont nous puissions nous corriger sur leur exemple'.[97] Our attention is immediately drawn to the prominence given to pity and to the absence of any tragic flaw. Corneille's definition of Aristotle's ideal tragic hero is however more or less orthodox: he is a man 'ni tout à fait bon, ni tout à fait méchant, et qui, par une faute, ou faiblesse humaine, tombe dans un malheur qu'il ne mérite pas'.[98]

As his attitude towards Polyeucte suggests, Corneille too is interested in separating the tragic emotions. According to him Aristotle did not intend that they should always go together and one is sufficient to effect purgation, with the condition that 'la pitié n'y peut arriver sans la crainte', whereas 'la crainte peut y parvenir sans la pitié'; the Count's death in *Le Cid* arouses no pity but can better purge in us the pride which produces envy of another's glory 'que toute la compassion que nous avons de Rodrigue et de Chimène ne

---

[96] *Writings,* pp. 33–4.
[97] Ibid., p. 33. Cf. Dacier on Polyeucte: 'De quelque maniere qu'on regarde le martyre, ou comme un mal ou comme un bien, il ne peut exciter ny la pitié ny la crainte, et par consequent il ne purgera pas les passions, ce qui est l'unique but de la Tragedie . . .' (Ch. xiii, rem. I, p. 177).
[98] Ibid., p. 31.

purge les attachements de ce violent amour qui les rend à plaindre l'un et l'autre'.[99] Thus whereas La Mesnardière required different subjects to be used Corneille uses different characters to arouse each emotion within the same play. Indeed Corneille establishes the principle that a perfect tragedy consists in arousing pity and fear by means of principal characters like Rodrigue and Placide but that it is not an absolute necessity, since one may use different characters to arouse each emotion in turn, as in *Rodogune*, 'et même ne porter l'auditeur qu'à l'un des deux, comme dans *Polyeucte*, dont la représentation n'imprime que de la pitié sans aucune crainte'.[100] There can, then, despite a previous statement, be pity without fear. But the importance of using different characters in this way is that it allows him to establish the possibility of the very good or the very bad character: he repeats Aristotle's opinions regarding these two types but adds:

quand ces deux raisons cessent, en sorte qu'un homme de bien qui souffre excite plus de pitié pour lui que d'indignation contre celui qui le fait souffrir, ou que la punition d'un grand crime peut corriger en nous quelque imperfection qui a du rapport avec lui, j'estime qu'il ne faut point faire de difficulté d'exposer sur la scène des hommes très vertueux ou très méchants dans le malheur.[101]

The possible portrayal of extremely virtuous or evil characters is actually opposed by Corneille to Aristotle's ideal tragic hero, whose *bonté médiocre* is often scorned in the *Examens*. Corneille has little time for the weakness which leads to the *faute médiocre*, as is evident from the following statement regarding *Polyeucte*: 'Ceux qui veulent arrêter nos héros dans une médiocre bonté, où quelques interprètes d'Aristote bornent leur vertu, ne trouveront pas ici leur compte, puisque celle de Polyeucte va jusqu'à la sainteté, et n'a aucun mélange de faiblesse.'[102] A more forthright statement comes in the *Examen* of *Le Cid* where Corneille asserts

---

[99] *Writings*, p. 34.
[100] Ibid., p. 36. Professor Barnwell points out that 'It is apparent that for Corneille fear was secondary to pity and only introduced because of his need to come to terms with the idea of catharsis interpreted as moral purification' (*Writings*, n. 25, p. 224).
[101] Ibid.
[102] Ibid., p. 117.

that a woman who is in duty bound to obtain her lover's death 'a les passions plus vives et plus allumées que tout ce qui peut se passer entre un mari et sa femme'; moreover:

la haute vertu dans un naturel sensible à ces passions, qu'elle dompte sans les affaiblir, et à qui elle laisse toute leur force pour en triompher plus glorieusement, a quelque chose de plus touchant, de plus élevé et de plus aimable que cette médiocre bonté, capable d'une faiblesse, et même d'un crime, où nos anciens étaient contraints d'arrêter le caractère le plus parfait des rois et des princes dont ils faisaient leurs héros.[103]

Thus Corneille once again rejects the notion of fault altogether.

The feeling of elevation aroused by Chimène's conduct leads us to the notion of *admiration*, which Corneille considers the most appropriate tragic emotion. The fullest explanation is perhaps found in the *Examen* of Nicomède,[104] where Corneille explains that in his play 'la grandeur de courage y règne seule, et regarde son malheur d'un œil si dédaigneux qu'il n'en saurait arracher une plainte'.[105] This hero of mine, he continues, is somewhat unorthodox in that he does not seek pity for his excessive misfortune; moreover it has been shown that 'la fermeté des grands cœurs, qui n'excite que de l'admiration dans l'âme du spectateur, est quelquefois aussi agréable que la compassion que notre art nous ordonne d'y produire par la représentation de leurs malheurs'.[106] Indeed in the *Au Lecteur* he writes of 'la compassion que notre art nous commande de *mendier* pour leurs misères'.[107] There is still compassion, Corneille remarks, but it does not draw tears; its effect is limited to putting the spectators 'dans les intérêts de ce prince, et à leur faire former des souhaits pour ses prospérités'.[108] Pity is now reduced to little more than a desire to witness the hero's success.

Corneille even endows our admiration for Nicomède's

[103] Ibid., p. 102.
[104] Although the term *admiration* appears in the *Au Lecteur* of the 1651 edition (*Œuvres*, v, 504) this formula is reproduced almost word for word in the *Examen*.
[105] *Writings*, p. 151.
[106] Ibid., p. 152.
[107] *Œuvres*, v, 504. My italicization.
[108] *Writings*, p. 152.

virtue with a moral function, asserting that it is a means of purgation surer than that effected by pity and fear, for 'L'amour qu'elle nous donne pour cette vertu que nous admirons nous imprime de la haine pour le vice contraire.'[109] But whether the moral orientation of *admiration* applies in all cases is seriously open to doubt. In his second *Discours* Corneille agrees that Cléopâtre is very evil and is prepared to commit parricide to retain her crown; yet all her crimes 'sont accompagnés d'une grandeur d'âme qui a quelque chose de si haut, qu'en même temps qu'on déteste ses actions, on admire la source dont elles partent'.[110] Surely there is no positive moral quality implied here. What are we to understand by *admiration*?

It is clear that the meaning of *admirer* given by Furetière and reproduced by Professor Barnwell, i.e. 'regarder avec étonnement quelque chose de surprenant ou dont on ignore les causes', is inadequate.[111] Corneille himself provides us with an answer in his definition of *bonté de mœurs* as 'le caractère brillant et élevé d'une habitude vertueuse ou criminelle, selon qu'elle est propre et convenable à la personne qu'on introduit'.[112] Significantly this statement immediately precedes the description of Cléopâtre quoted earlier. *Admiration* is therefore a form of appreciation of the style in which an evil or virtuous act is committed, as long as the style is commensurate with the character's rank. In a sense, therefore, it is irrelevant that Nicomède himself is virtuous, and the moral function Corneille gives to *admiration* is his way of covering his tracks in his departure from strict Aristotelian principles.

Corneille's attitude towards a moralistic catharsis is no less than one of total scepticism. Excepting his own method he doubts whether any purgation ever takes place[113] and remarks that Aristotle's notion is merely 'une belle idée', never really translated into practice; he asks those who have seen his plays to ask themselves if it is by way of the things

---

[109] Ibid.
[110] Ibid., p. 14.
[111] Ibid., n. 7, p. 261.
[112] Ibid., p. 14.
[113] Ibid., p. 32.

that have moved them in plays that 'ils en sont venus par
là jusqu'à cette crainte réfléchie', and whether 'elle a rectifié
en eux la passion qui a causé la disgrâce qu'ils ont plainte'.[114]
Corneille, the dramatist, is alone in referrring the matter to
the spectator himself.

In his stand on catharsis Corneille has a partisan of no
mean stature in Saint-Évremond, who criticizes Aristotle's
notion as making things worse rather than better, seeing a
danger in the idea of an excess of pity 'qui fait passer les
maux d'autruy en nous mémes'.[115] He explains that there
was less virtue than misfortune presented on the Greek stage
'de peur qu'une ame élevée à l'admiration des Héros, ne fût
moins propre à s'abandonner à la pitié pour un misérable'.[116]
Aristotle, realizing the possible harm in this, believed he had
found a remedy in a purgation which nobody has yet understood; is there anything more ridiculous 'que de mettre la
perturbation dans une ame, pour tâcher après de la calmer
par les réflexions qu'on lui fait faire sur le honteux état où
elle s'est trouvée'.[117] He doubts whether 'une ame accoûtumée
à s'effrayer sur ce qui regarde les maux d'autrui, puisse être
dans une bonne assiette sur les maux qui la regardent elle-
même'.[118] Our becoming accustomed to the misfortunes of
others adds to our weakness rather than to our moral
resistance.

This is not to say that Saint-Évremond excludes affliction
altogether, but it must be of a particular type. He explains
that afflication must have 'quelque chose de touchant' and
end with 'quelque chose d'animé, qui puisse faire sur nous
une impression nouvelle', 'par une bonne fortune, qui finit
les malheurs avec la joye', or 'par une grande vertu qui attire
nôtre admiration'; sometimes it may end in death and arouse
in us 'une nouvelle commiseration propre et naturelle à la
tragédie', but this must never be after long lamentations
'qui donnent plus de mépris pour la foiblesse que de compassion pour le malheur'.[119] Pity is not absent, but clearly
admiration is the more important of the two and, as in the
case of Corneille, totally alien to an atmosphere of weakness

---

[114] Ibid.
[115] *Œuvres*, iii, 328.
[116] Ibid., iv, 178.
[117] Ibid.
[118] Ibid., 177.
[119] Ibid., iii, 342.

and grief.

The most important statement on the individual components of catharsis comes in Saint-Évremond's definition of pity and fear in *De la tragedie ancienne et moderne*: fear is frequently no more than 'une agréable inquiétude qui subsiste dans la suspension des esprits; c'est un cher interêt que prend notre âme aux sujets qui attirent son affection';[120] we can, he continues, say the same about pity for 'Nous la dépoüillons de toute sa foiblesse, et nous lui laissons tout ce qu'elle peut avoir de charitable et d'humain'; I like, Saint-Évremond goes on, to see a great man lament his misfortune even to the extent of arousing compassion and provoking tears, but 'je veux que ces larmes tendres et généreuses regardent ensemble ses malheurs et ses vertus, et qu'avec le triste sentiment de la pitié nous ayons celui d'une admiration animée, qui fasse naître en nôtre âme comme un amoureux desir de l'imiter'.[121] Pity and fear are almost void of any corrective value, fear being reduced to an emotion of an aesthetic nature, remarkably similar to the pity which Corneille postulates for Nicomède; although Saint-Évremond admits a form of pity involving only the central character, the emphasis is unmistakably on our emulation of the tragic hero. There is, moreover, no mention of the tragic flaw to be avoided by the spectator, but this is because there is no suggestion of a similarity of experience between audience and hero. The moral quality of *admiration*, more positive than in Corneille, is a desire to imitate the hero's virtue, while the actual nature of his downfall is not discussed.

What, then, is the function of catharsis? For the most part it has a moralistic orientation in that by pitying the misfortunes of others and fearing such consequences for ourselves we come to eradicate, or at least moderate, the harmful passions and inclinations which lead to error. There does, however, arise a problem in the way our experience of pity and fear stands in relation to our experience of these harmful passions. If the desired result of the dramatic art is achieved, and we are involved to the extent of actually feeling jealousy and its like, are we at the same time sufficiently removed from the characters to pity them and fear the consequences of their acts for ourselves? If so, then the tragic experience is one of both participation *and* judgement.

But judgement does not mean rejection of the tragic hero. Indeed, the success of catharsis, as it is described by most of the dramatic theorists discussed above, depends on an acceptance of human frailty. Moreover, while this frailty manifests itself in a disastrous error of moral judgement, we are asked to sympathize more with the hero's suffering amidst the consequences of his act than to condemn the act itself. The greater emphasis of La Mesnardière and d'Aubignac on pity rather than on fear is proof of this. La Mesnardière even attempts to excuse the hero for his error when he asserts that the act may be committed in ignorance or at a moment when the hero is not himself (for he is good apart from this act) and may thus be considered as separate from the person. Such an attitude is strangely at odds with the simplistic code of punishment of vice and reward of virtue, also a part of drama, and perhaps exemplifies the eternal dilemma of non-rigorist moral thinking, where an understanding of the act must ultimately be accommodated with the need to punish it. There is, in the light of the views discussed in this chapter, a grain of truth in Senault's remark that: 'La Misericorde naturelle est presque toujours injuste, elle considere la peine, et ne regarde pas l'offense, elle voudroit rompre les prisons pour en tirer les parricides, et les criminels ne luy sont plus odieux quand ils deviennent miserables.'[122]

[122] Senault, le Père J.-F., *L'Homme criminel ou la corruption de la nature par le péché selon les sentiments de saint Augustin*, Paris, 1644, p. 451.

IV

HISTORICAL ARGUMENTS AND DOCTRINAL AUTHORITIES

Those writers and religious moralists who alleged that drama can only be a corrupting influence in society can no longer be left out of the picture. But before turning our attention to drama, its content and effect, there is one important aspect of the *querelle* to consider first. It may be seen in one sense as a conflict of authorities, that is to say, a conflict between the ardent opponents of drama who uphold the works of the Church Fathers as the only reliable doctrine on the matter and those who undertake the defence of drama and use for this purpose the works of St. Thomas Aquinas and St. Francis of Sales, where we find less categorical statements regarding attendance at theatrical performances.[1] For those anxious to defend drama and at the same time salve their religious conscience the two authorities mentioned are obvious choices. Dubu finds it no coincidence that Richelieu was a Thomist and sees his standpoint as partly political;[2] nor is it an accident that d'Aubignac, an erstwhile admirer of Richelieu, should include quotations from the *Summa* in his *Dissertation sur la condemnation des théâtres*.[3] Thus, in a sense, attitudes towards doctrinal authorities are often an indication of those adopted towards drama.

The most resounding clash of authorities in our period came in 1694 when le Père Thomas Caffaro not only used St. Thomas and St. Francis in his defence of drama but even attempted to deduce arguments in his favour from Tertullian, St. Cyprian, and many others who are the very sources which, according to some, allow no ambiguity. Furthermore Caffaro

---

[1] St. Thomas will be a source of reference in many of the following chapters where we discuss the particular issues of the *querelle*. Here we are interested only in general considerations arising from his use as a source for the justification of drama.

[2] 'De quelques rituels . . .', *Année canonique*, Part I, p. 100.

[3] Aubignac Abbé d', *Dissertation sur la condamnation des théâtres*, Paris, 1666, pp. 246-9.

was highly critical of those theologians who tended to confuse ancient drama with that of the seventeenth century and indeed cast doubts on the relevance of the Fathers' doctrine to the seventeenth century. This situation was not allowed to stand: thundering replies proclaimed the doctrinal validity of the Fathers, while Bossuet undertook the reconciliation of St. Thomas's declarations with those of the Church. The importance of the question of authorities is revealed in Bossuet's assertion that: 'L'autorité ecclésiastique s'est fait reconnaître: par ses soins la vérité a été vengée; la saine doctrine est en sûreté, et le public n'a besoin que d'instruction sur une matière qu'on avait tâché d'embrouiller par des raisons frivoles.'[4]

Firstly, however, it is necessary to consider briefly the rejection of the relevance of the Fathers' doctrine to the seventeenth century as formulated in d'Aubignac's *Dissertation* and Caffaro's *Lettre*. D'Aubignac's basic aim is to put the problem in its proper historical context, the main point being that the Fathers' condemnation of drama as a pagan act of religion is no longer valid, since the charge of idolatry cannot now be levelled against the seventeenth-century theatre;[5] he concludes that one cannot condemn 'un divertissement que les Papes et les Princes Chrêtiens ont aprouvé depuis qu'il a perdu les caracteres de l'impieté qui le rendoient abominable'.[6] This subject was of course discussed by d'Aubignac at an earlier date in his ambitious *Projet pour le rétablissement du theatre françois*, where he considers that the progress of the French theatre is arrested by the common religious prejudice against drama,[7] and declares the need for a royal edict proclaiming that this

---

[4] Bossuet, J.-B., *Maximes et réflexions sur la comédie*, 9 May 1694, in Urbain and Levesque, *L'Église et le théâtre*, pp. 169–70. On Bossuet's intervention see Dubu, 'De quelques rituels . . .', part I, pp. 120–1 and Dubu, ibid., part II, pp. 97–8. This 'contamination' of St. Thomas forced religious moralists to find another more suitable 'modern' authority, which came in the form of a work against drama allegedly written by St. Charles Borromeo. This matter is discussed in Dubu, 'De quelques rituels . . .', parts I and II, and 'Pour une étude canonique des rituels', *Année canonique*, vol. vii, 1960, pp. 27–32.

[5] *Dissertation*, p. 90.

[6] Ibid., pp. 101–2.

[7] *Pratique*, p. 387.

prejudice is now unfounded.[8]

While the works of d'Aubignac and Caffaro mentioned above are the most important in the question of defending drama by a historical approach, before discussing the ideas of Caffaro, it would perhaps be helpful to examine statements by others who were more directly concerned with drama as an art form. Scudéry was not unaware of the way in which those who blindly accepted the Fathers' doctrine as eternal precepts understood the history of drama: he mentions in his *Apologie* that some Fathers even wrote approvingly of drama but that the latter's present-day opponents show their ignorance in being unable to distinguish between the drama of antiquity and that of their own time.[9] Chappuzeau too contends that the Fathers and the Church in general decried only indecent or bloody spectacles.[10] Corneille himself did not allow the condemnation of drama to go unmentioned: significantly it is in the *Épître* to *Théodore* (1646) that he writes that St. Augustine was not declaiming against plays similar to our own and that those whose scruples or zeal make them stubborn opponents of drama have little or no grounds for basing their arguments on his authority; although it was with some justification that the saint condemned the theatre of his own day, it is unfair to extend this condemnation to that of our own which, for the most part, offers only 'des exemples d'innocence, de vertu et de piété'.[11]

The tone of Caffaro's critical approach to the problem is set when he boldly remarks that until now he believed that things were forbidden because they were bad, not bad

---

[8] Ibid., p. 394.
[9] *Apologie*, pp. 1-2.
[10] Chappuzeau, S., *Le Théâtre françois*, Lyon, 1674, p. 24.
[11] *Œuvres*, v, 9-10. For Corneille's evolution in this matter see Couton, G., *La Vieillesse de Corneille (1658-84)*, Paris, 1949, pp. 151-8. M. Couton notes that Nicole in the text of 1667 (I have used the definitive text of 1675) sees Corneille as the one playwright who attempted to purify the theatre of its most reprehensible vices (p. 154). But the reasoning behind Nicole's compliment is exposed when Nicole adds that since one can prove that Corneille's plays are still 'très contraires à l'Evangile' with how much more authority can we condemn the rest.

because they were forbidden.[12] He begins by going to the most controversial source of all, the Bible, and declares that, however much one reads the Scriptures, they contain no specific or formal condemnation of drama.[13] But his major problem is the difference he finds between the pronouncements on drama of the Fathers and the Scholastics. He will therefore use a rule of St. Cyprian whereby reason must be used in the case of those things upon which the Bible is silent. In this way will he be able to reconcile the theologians' conclusions with those of the Fathers.[14]

Caffaro also undertook to find justifications of drama in the works of the Fathers themselves. He quotes sources too numerous to mention here, but one example in particular is indicative of his earnestness: Caffaro notes that St. Cyprian, when speaking of David dancing before the Ark, admits that it is not evil to sing or dance, although there is no excuse for Christians who witness the lascivious dances etc. performed in the praise of idols; it is easy to conclude, Caffaro continues, that St. Cyprian 'ne condamne pas absolument les Danses, les Chants, les Opéras et les Comédies, mais seulement les Spectacles qui représentoient les fables en la maniere lascive des Grecs et des Romains, et qui se celebroient en l'honneur des Idoles'.[15] This is in fact a gratuitous gloss on St. Cyprian's words which contain no reference to drama. In any case, from the same example Pégurier is able to draw the opposite conclusion to Caffaro, explaining that, since St. Cyprian condemns lascivious dances, he automatically condemns opera and other dramatic forms.[16]

Caffaro, like d'Aubignac, is anxious that the religious problem should be put in its proper historical perspective and claims that only the excesses of ancient drama provoked

---

[12] Caffaro, le Père Thomas, *Lettre d'un théologien illustre par sa qualité et par son mérite, consulté par l'auteur pour savoir si la comédie peut être permise, ou doit être absolument défendue*, in Urbain and Levesque, *L'Église et le théâtre*, pp. 67-119, p. 90 (henceforward this work will be referred to as U/L).

[13] Ibid., U/L, p. 70.

[14] Ibid., p. 70.

[15] Ibid., p. 85. See St. Cyprian, *De Spectaculis*, Ch. 3 in Migne, *Patrologiae*, iv, col. 782.

[16] Pégurier, l'Abbé L., *Réfutation des sentiments relâchés d'un nouveau théologien*, Paris, 1694, pp. 50-1.

the Fathers' anathema.[17] But here too his optimism leads
him astray for he adds that if the Fathers had themselves
witnessed the contemporary theatre 'conforme aux bonnes
mœurs et à la droite raison', they would not have decried it
so and would have subscribed to the views of St. Thomas.[18]
He justifies his argument by the observation that the nearer
the Fathers came to the seventeenth century, the more their
attacks diminished in anger; this is, according to him, because
drama was being reformed as opposed to earlier times when
they declaimed more fervently against the abominable
circumstances with which it was often accompanied; he adds
that 'Ce n'est pas pour cela que les derniers le cedent en
science et en sainteté aux premiers, c'est que la Comédie
se change.'[19] It is unfortunate that *naïveté* is Caffaro's
greatest fault; he writes at a time when the plays of Regnard
and Dancourt could hardly be considered shining examples of
'bonnes mœurs'.

The arguments against the applicability of the Fathers'
doctrine to seventeenth-century drama provoked a number of
strongly worded replies. Among them is a work by Voisin
which is an explicit attack on d'Aubignac's *Dissertation*;
because much of it is devoted to the actor we shall deal with
it later. More generally the replies to Caffaro are often
encumbered with numerous counter-quotations which
provide 'corrected' interpretations of the Fathers' works.[20]

The first of Caffaro's arguments, as already stated, was
that the Bible contained no formal precept against drama.
Many years before Rivet had dealt with the same issue: his
answer was that the general rules we find in the word of God
provide certain principles 'par lesquels avec la ratiocination,
nous tirons des conclusions contre toutes sortes de vices et
excés'; therefore 'de la condamnation des choses moindres
sous mesme genre, nous inferons celles des plus grandes'.[21]

[17] *Lettre d'un théologien*, U/L, p. 77.
[18] Ibid.
[19] Ibid., p. 86.
[20] See, however, Ériau, J.-B., *Pourquoi les Pères de l'Église ont condamné le théâtre de leur temps*, Paris, 1914.
[21] Rivet, A., *L'Instruction chrétienne touchant les spectacles publics*, The Hague, 1639, p. 39.

Coustel uses the same argument in his reply to Caffaro.[22]

Caffaro had also suggested that the Fathers condemned only the excesses of drama. Coustel argues that at the time of the Emperors spectacles were less infamous yet were still condemned by the Fathers.[23] Pégurier points out that the Church Councils of the past condemned not only ancient drama but also that of their own time.[24] Salvian is mentioned as an example of one who declaimed against spectacles organized by Christians.[25] Indeed Lebrun is, as had been Vincent in 1647,[26] at pains to emphasize that not all tragedies or comedies of antiquity were as horrible or as infamous as some have suggested,[27] thereby implicitly invalidating Caffaro's argument regarding the condemned excesses of ancient drama.

The religious moralists reply equally to the view that now drama has become dissociated from its origins in the pagan religion it no longer has idolatrous connotations. Lamy utterly rejects this line of defence; in his opinion 'Les Spectacles sont criminels par leur origine', the latter being found in 'le vin, l'insolence, la violence et le désir de médire'.[28] Drama is thus tainted by some sort of original sin. This is precisely the charge rejected by both Scudéry and Chappuzeau who attempt to establish the status of drama by references to its noble origins. But La Grange, in his reply to Caffaro, agrees that all spectacles had their origins in superstition, that they have been refined for the needs of pleasure and retained for political considerations only.[29] Drama, he adds later, became separated from its religious origins because authors sought to satisfy their own

---

[22] Coustel, P., *Sentiments de l'Église*, Paris, 1694, p. 7.

[23] Ibid., pp. 54–5.

[24] *Réfutation des sentiments relâchés*, p. 139.

[25] There is a translation into French of Chapter IV of Salvian's *Le Gouvernement, ou providence de Dieu* in Rivet's work beginning at p. 97. There was an edition of this work published in 1580 and several in the seventeenth century, including a translation by du Ryer in 1634.

[26] Vincent, Ph., *Traité des théâtres*, La Rochelle, 1647, pp. 12–13.

[27] Lebrun, le Père P., *2ième Discours*, pp. 78 seq.

[28] Lamy, B., *Nouvelles réflexions sur l'art poétique*, Paris, 1678, p. 194.

[29] La Grange, Ch. de, *Réfutation d'un écrit favorisant la comédie*, Paris, 1694, pp. 10–11.

advantage rather than that of the gods.[30]

If drama as a whole is condemned for its origins, it is logical to continue to attribute pagan qualities to seventeenth-century drama, and a priest's letter, included in Voisin's treatise, proclaims just this in unequivocal terms when he says that 'Enfin ces pieces infames . . . rétablissent l'idolatrie, qui est l'origine du Theatre.'[31] Voisin holds somewhat contradictory views: in his preface he admits that contemporary drama is no longer consecrated to idols although plays still contain vestiges of the paganism from which they derive;[32] later, however, he asks, 'la Comedie en elle-mesme n'est-elle pas un reste de l'Idolatrie, ayant esté inventée par les demons, et consacrée à de fausses divinitez?'.[33] Vincent extends this reasoning to attendance at theatrical performances for going to the theatre, 'c'est se rendre aux lieux que l'idole s'étoit affectés, et en quelque façon renouveller les anciens hommages qu'on y rendoit à Sathan, . . .'[34] Thus theatre-going which, according to Vincent, bears the marks of idolatry as long as it exists[35] is an act of idolatry in itself.

Frain du Tremblay, in his *Nouveaux Essais de morale*, focuses attention on the content of plays and asks whether they can be wholly purged of idolatry when the gods of antiquity are always present.[36] This was indeed a subject of fierce controversy in the seventeenth century, particularly regarding the epic.[37] La Grange, however, adds to Frain's contribution when he describes opera as beginning 'par l'invocation d'une Divinité, comme de Venus, de Cupidon, ou de quelque autre. On introduit une Actrice, qui d'un air de respect pour la Divinité qu'elle invoque, chante au milieu d'une symphonie parfaite en ses accords, des Vers à sa

---

[30] Ibid., pp. 16–17.
[31] Voisin, J. de., *La Défense du traitté de Monseigneur le prince de Conti touchant la comédie et les spectacles, ou la réfutation d'un livre intitulé: Dissertation sur la condamnation des théâtres*, Paris, 1671, *Lettre I*, p. 475. Since there are two letters in Voisin's work the present one will be known as *Lettre I*, and the other as *Lettre II*.
[32] Ibid., p. xlviii.
[33] Ibid., p. 69.
[34] *Traité des théâtres*, p. 61.
[35] Ibid.
[36] Frain du Tremblay, J., *Nouveaux Essais de morale*, Paris, 1691, p. 188.
[37] Where this specifically concerns drama, see Chapter XI.

loüange: Cette fausse Divinité ne les entend pas, mais le vrai Dieu les entend.'[38] This is a theme one can expect to re-encounter when discussing the particular aspects of a play's content.

A more subtle attitude towards the charge that idolatry is still found to be a part of drama is held by the authors of the *Décision*.[39] They acknowledge that it is with serious foundation that the Fathers' authority is challenged, for it appears that once idolatry, impurity, and dissolution are no longer associated with drama the early Fathers of the Church regard it as no more than 'une vaine curiosité'.[40] Furthermore, the Church Councils have been moderate in condemning drama only when performed on feast days, as in the Councils of Milan at the time of St. Charles; even modern authors like St. Thomas and St. Francis are not much opposed to attendance at the theatre.[41] Their answer to these problems, however, is that the Fathers condemned drama either because of idolatry and impiety, *or* 'par la raison generale, que [les Comedies] portent ordinairement à la corruption des bonnes mœurs; comme à exciter ou à enflammer notablement les passions, quelque soin que l'on ait apporté d'en reformer de temps en temps les abus'.[42] This fact, they continue, points to the truth of the proposition that drama is evil morally speaking and in its 'usage ordinaire'; this is why it has always been condemned by the Church.[43] Hence the Fathers provide not only circumstantial condemnation (i.e. idolatry) but general principles concerning corruption which constitute permanent rules. The *Décision*'s case is strengthened by the fact that St. Cyprian himself writes that, even when drama ceases to be idolatrous, Christians should never attend spectacles 'qui pour estre exempts de crime ne sont pas exempts de vanité, et dont le pompeux appareil a trop de la

---

[38] *Réfutation d'un écrit*, p. 70.
[39] For *Bibliography* see under Pégurier.
[40] *Décision faite en Sorbonne touchant la comédie, du 20 mai 1694, avec la Réfutation des sentiments relâchés d'un nouveau théologien*, Paris, 1694, pp. 2-3. It is interesting to note in the introduction to this work that the *Décision* was in fact prepared during the year 1693, thus *before* the *affaire Caffaro*.
[41] Ibid., pp. 3-5.
[42] Ibid., pp. 15-16.
[43] Ibid., p. 16.

liberté du siècle'.[44] Pégurier reminds us that Tertullian too
bases his arguments on concupiscence and considers spectacles
as a form of *volupté*.[45]

Those who defend drama sometimes, however, point for
their self-justification to the more conciliatory views of St.
Thomas and St. Francis. The religious moralists were thereby
confronted with an embarrassing problem, since these two
writers were no heretics but respected doctrinal authorities.
In the *Summa* St. Thomas does not specifically refer to
drama; he analyses rather the nature of games (*ludi*) which
may be considered legitimate for recreation.[46] His first point
is that 'just as weariness of the body is dispelled by resting
the body, so weariness of the soul must needs be remedied
by resting the soul: and the soul's rest is pleasure . . .'[47] St.
Thomas continues by suggesting that this rest may be
effected by 'words or deeds wherein nothing further is sought
than the soul's delight', and these are called 'playful or
humorous'.[48] Caffaro is in no doubt that this includes some
form of drama. Indeed in view of the later discussion of the
actor it may be inferred that drama, (and more particularly
comedy) is included in 'such words or deeds'. Aquinas is,
however, careful to add a number of conditions which would
prevent any excesses being committed.[49]

The embarrassment felt by religious moralists before the
leniency of such an exposition is well illustrated by Bossuet's
comment that it must be admitted with the respect due to
such a great man that 'il semble s'être un peu éloigné, je ne
dirai pas des sentiments dans le fond, mais plutôt des

---

[44] *Des spectacles*, trans. Deschaussé, Paris, 1640, p. 181. Surprisingly this is
dedicated to Richelieu.

[45] *Réfutation des sentiments relâchés*, p. 26.

[46] The term *games* is of course ambiguous. In the context of our discussion of
St. Thomas it refers to 'words and deeds' destined to provide pleasure and therefore has intellectual connotations. The French term *jeux* is more ambiguous for
Caffaro uses it also in the sense of gambling. This distinction must be borne in
mind in later discussions, especially Chapter VIII.

[47] Thomas Aquinas, Saint, *Summa Theologica*. Literally translated by the Fathers
of the English Dominican Province, 22 vols., London, 1937, IIa. IIae, 168, a. 2,
vol. 13, p. 296.

[48] *Summa*, IIa. IIae, 168, a. 2, ad. 2, vol. 13, p. 297.

[49] These will be discussed at greater length in the chapter devoted to the question
of *divertissement*.

expressions des anciens Pères sur le sujet des divertisse-ments'.[50] But Bossuet doubts whether St. Thomas refers to any form of drama at all, explaining that in the article in question the saint is attempting to discover whether there are things 'plaisantes, joyeuses', which can be permitted in life, in other words, whether there are innocent recreations; and in this article of the *Summa*, he adds, there is not one single word about drama but a general discussion of those activities 'nécessaires à la recréation de l'esprit'.[51]

The arguments of Bossuet that have briefly been examined here concern the substance of St. Thomas's reasoning. In the works of other religious moralists who reply to Caffaro's letter, one means of eluding the essential problem is found in the explanation of St. Thomas's method. The reasoning of the *Décision* is that: 'Cette idée de la Comedie separée de toutes circonstances, dont S. Thomas a parlé, est une idée *generale et speculative* de la Comédie que l'on peut regarder comme une chose de soy indifferente, qui n'est ny bonne ny mauvaise. Mais elle n'a pas cette indifference dans son usage, et lorsqu'on la considere avec les circonstances qui l'accompagnent ordinairement.'[52] Furthermore the authors point to another passage in the *Summa* where St. Thomas regards attendance at spectacles as bad since it helps incline men to vice and cruelty.[53]

The second means of invalidating St. Thomas's arguments comes in an attempt to discredit him as a reliable source of doctrine. Gerbais, another opponent of Caffaro, tries to distinguish between the theologian and the philosopher in Aquinas, who has dealt with the matter of drama not as the former, since he makes not a single reference to revealed truth, but as the latter, 'en raisonnant sur les principes d'une morale toute naturelle, et sur le témoignage de quelques Philosophes anciens qu'il allegue, et qui ont reconnu dans les Jeux une espece de vertu, peu recommandée neanmoins dans les Conciles et chez les Peres'.[54] Such conclusions, Gerbais

---

[50] *Maximes et réflexions*, U/L, pp. 252-3.
[51] Ibid., pp. 226-7.
[52] *Décision faite en Sorbonne*, pp. 10-11. Our italics.
[53] See *Summa*, IIa. IIae, 167, a. 2, ad. 2, vol. 13, pp. 288-91.
[54] *Lettre d'un docteur de Sorbonne*, pp. 23-4.

adds, based on purely human principles, are not always the safest rules for Christians to follow, particularly when they favour pleasures against which they must be on their guard.[55] It is interesting to note that this is precisely Coustel's criticism of Caffaro, who used not tradition but 'les vaines subtilitez d'un raisonnement humain et philosophique'.[56] Finally, Bossuet sees St. Thomas as unreliable for having used ancient philosophers and concludes that, for reasons which do not detract from St. Thomas' profound erudition, we must not always expect from him an altogether exact interpretation of the Fathers, especially when he undertakes to accommodate them with Aristotle, who was certainly not the source of their ideas.[57]

St. Francis of Sales is, of course, much closer to our period, the first edition of *L'Introduction à la vie dévote* appearing in 1608. There are two sections of the work which interest us, the twenty-third chapter of the first part which specifically mentions drama, and chapters XXXI–XXXIV of the third part which refer to dancing in particular and recreation in general.

The explicit reference to drama is in the twenty-third chapter of the first part entitled *Qu'il faut purger de l'affection aux choses inutiles ou dangereuses*, where he says that 'Les jeux, les bals, les festins, les pompes, les comédies, en leur substance, ne sont nullement choses mauvaises ains indifférentes, pouvant être bien et mal exercées.'[58] The important notion in this statement is that drama may be considered indifferent in nature; the essential thing for St. Francis is the attitude of the spectator for he goes on to say that, 'encore qu'il soit loisible de jouer, danser, se parer, ouïr d'honnêtes comédies, banqueter; si est-ce que d'avoir de l'affection à cela, c'est chose contraire à la dévotion, et extrêmement nuisible et périlleuse. Ce n'est pas mal de le faire, mais oui bien de s'y affectionner'.[59] Two points are worthy of attention; there is, firstly, a permissible degree of

---

[55] Ibid., p. 28.
[56] *Sentiments de l'Église*, p. 3.
[57] *Maximes et réflexions*, U/L, p. 259.
[58] *Introduction à la vie dévote*, ed. F. Henrion, Tours, 1939, p. 75.
[59] Ibid., pp. 75–6.

such diversions, and, secondly, 'd'honnêtes comédies' are not inconceivable. It is true, however, that St. Francis's attitude is a little more strict later in the chapter when he says: 'Mais n'est-ce pas une chose ridicule, ains plutôt lamentable, de voir des hommes faits s'empresser et s'affectionner après des bagatelles si indignes, comme sont les choses que j'ai nommées, lesquelles outre leur inutilité, nous mettent en péril de nous dérégler et désordonner à leur poursuite?'[60] This is why, he continues, we must purge ourselves of these affections, and although such activities are not always in opposition to devotion 'les affections néanmoins lui sont toujours dommageables'.[61] But it is the degree to which men become obsessed with diversion rather than the nature of the diversion itself that concerns St. Francis.

As in the case of St. Thomas, replies to the use of St. Francis in defence of drama emphasize the speculative nature of his considerations. The general tendency of religious moralists was to dismiss this use in a few lines and pass on to something else. The more detailed discussions of St. Thomas are perhaps explained by the fact that he spoke of the actor finding his justification in the recreation of society.

However, Voisin does deal with St. Francis at some length in his treatise in defence of the Prince de Conti. Voisin's interpretation of the passages examined in this chapter is that in the opinion of St. Francis diversion tends in common practice towards evil and one can think it indifferent only 'en considerant les Bals, et les Comedies dans une speculation metaphysique, et par une abstraction d'esprit, les separant de toutes leurs circonstances'. One must conclude from this that 'on ne peut pas dire, en parlant des Bals, et des Comedies selon la pratique commune, et ordinaire, que ce soient des choses indifferentes'.[62] He also emphasizes that one must put into practice the advice given by St. Francis.[63] Here he clearly provides his own gloss on the text because the conditions given by St. Francis come in his discussion of dancing. The *Décision* too remarks that the saint attaches so

---

[60] *Introduction à la vie dévote*, pp. 76–7.
[61] Ibid., p. 77.
[62] *Défense*, p. 468.
[63] Ibid., pp. 468–9.

many conditions to diversion that it is easier to desist than to observe them.[64] Although the inclusion of balls in the first statement of St. Francis we have quoted above points in some way to the validity of this view it none the less remains true that the saint's attitude by no means constitutes a categorical interdict. He leaves much to the individual conscience, something other theologians are not prepared to do.

But the principal point in the first passage of St. Francis we have quoted is that the nature of drama is indifferent and that the important consideration is rather the way it is used. This is very much an argument favoured by those who defend drama. Scudéry comments in his *Apologie* that it is unjust to condemn drama, which is in itself good, because 'des mains peu sçavantes, luy auront laissé des fautes qui certainement ne sont pas en l'Art'.[65] Dacier, in his commentary on Aristotle's *Poetics*, emphasizes that no fault can be imputed to the arts 'car les arts ne pechent point';[66] moreover, 'les accuser de quelque faute, c'est soûtenir que l'art de tirer fait manquer le but où l'on vise. Cela étant, quand on dit qu'une telle chose est une faute de l'art; on veut dire que c'est la faute de l'ouvrier qui a peché contre les regles de son Art'.[67] In his preface he remarks that 'Puis que la Tragedie n'a aucun defaut qui ne vienne du dehors, il s'ensuit de là qu'elle est bonne par elle-mesme, et par consequent utile.'[68]

There is a hint of the notion of indifference even among those who oppose drama. Conti writes of drama that: 'Dans cette idée generale, il n'est ny bon ny mauvais; il est susceptible de toutes sortes de sujets, et de toutes sortes de circonstances; et tant qu'il demeure dans cette indetermination, qui n'a d'estre que dans l'esprit des hommes, et dans les livres de la Poëtique, il n'est digne ny d'approbation, ny

[64] *Décision faite en Sorbonne*, p. 118.
[65] *Apologie*, p. 11.
[66] *Poétique d'Aristote*, Ch. xxvi, rem. 6, p. 428.
[67] Ibid.
[68] *Poétique d'Aristote*, p. xiv. The notion of indifference was used to calm the conscience of Anne of Austria, the Sorbonne doctors telling her that the practice of the Church had much changed since the days of 'cette severité Apostolique' (see Mlle de Motteville, *Mémoires pour servir à l'histoire d'Anne d'Autriche*, 5 vols., Amsterdam, 1723, i, 343-4).

de blâme.'[69] He thus makes the important distinction between the idea of a play and a play perceived, between style as a concept and the effect of style; but he adds that it is not his intention to deal with drama in such a way because his study is concerned with morals and not with metaphysics: 'je veux parler de la Comedie comme on la joüe, et point du tout comme on ne la joüe pas'.[70]

Nicole has no time for such distinctions in the first place: to 'former une certaine idée metaphysique de la Comedie, et de purifier cette idée de toute sorte de peché' is a way of accommodating one's conscience with the illicit pleasure drama affords; he adds that a way of guarding oneself against such an illusion is to consider drama 'non dans une speculation chimerique, mais dans la pratique commune et ordinaire dont nous sommes témoins'.[71] How interesting, then, to note that Caffaro, in excusing his conduct to Bossuet, says that he had formed a metaphysical idea of a good comedy without reflecting that things in theory are not always the same in practice.[72]

Coustel too considers that drama is more than 'une chimere' or 'une idée purement métaphysique', and that one must always consider the accompanying circumstances, since drama is 'une espece d'action moralle' which includes actors, the aims of drama, the spectator, its effects, and the time and occasion of performances.[73] Lelevel is concerned with the effect of drama; although he concedes that decor, music, verse or prose are indifferent in themselves, 'si chacune de ces choses est accommodée à la corruption de la nature; si toutes unies ensemble elles conspirent à faire oublier Dieu, à jetter l'homme du côté des sens, à remplir son cœur de l'amour des créatures, la Comédie sera-t'elle bonne, sera-t'elle indifferente?'.[74] One cannot even claim the benefit of the doubt for, as Lamy writes, even when plays are good in themselves, 'c'est-à-dire que sur le papier et dans la bouche

[69] *Traité de la comédie et des spectacles*, pp. 10-11.
[70] Ibid., p. 11.
[71] Nicole, P., *Traité de la comédie*, ed. G. Couton, Paris, 1961, p. 40.
[72] Caffaro, le Père Th., *Lettre à Bossuet*, U/L, p. 146.
[73] *Sentiments de l'Église*, pp. 28-9.
[74] Lelevel, H., *Réponse à la lettre du théologien défenseur de la comédie*, Paris, 1694, p. 7.

des Acteurs, elles n'auroient aucun venin', one could never say that their performance, with all the accompanying circumstances, is entirely innocent.[75]

These, then, are the principal arguments concerning the problem of authorities and historical interpretation. Above all, the religious moralists uphold the legitimacy of applying the Fathers' anathema to the drama of the seventeenth century. When a philosophical loophole appears they reject it because the theoretical possibility of good drama is considered irrelevant. It is equally irrelevant that St. Francis of Sales, much nearer our period than St. Thomas, should envisage the possibility of 'honnêtes comédies' for, as Gerbais remarks:

Quand j'accorderois toutes ces consequences, il ne s'en suivroit pas que saint François de Sales ait approuvé les Comedies d'aujourd'hui, dont il s'agit entre le Docteur [i.e. Caffaro] et moi. Car qu'il y ait des Comedies qui de leur nature soient indifferentes ou qu'il n'y en ait pas, il est sûr . . . que celles d'aujourd'hui ne sont point indifferentes.[76]

---

[75] *Nouvelles réflexions*, p. 194.
[76] *Lettre d'un docteur de Sorbonne*, p. 59.

V

THE MORAL RESPONSE
TO DRAMA

An examination of the views advancing a didactic function
for drama in the theorists' works led to the conclusion that,
if man was to be brought nearer to moral perfection, there
had to be a compromise with his imperfect nature. This
meant that the austerity of moral precepts should be tempered
by their presentation in a pleasurable form. Indeed both
Scudéry and Balzac advocate some measure of deceit; art will
present profit in the guise of a woman who at first sight
offers only pleasure. But this deceit has noble qualities since
it is in the service of man's improvement.

The religious moralists reject any such compromise with
man's corrupt nature and see drama as encouraging rather
than eradicating corruption. In this respect the religious
moralists' attitudes to the excitement and portrayal of
passion in plays assume great importance. Pégurier considers
that the spectator seeks in the dramatic experience only
pleasure; the poet must therefore arouse the spectator's
passions because, as Tertullian says, 'il n'y a point de plaisir
où il n'y a point d'émotion et d'affection'.[1] Lelevel doubts
whether we would attend the theatre at all 'si l'on n'y recevoit
pas les émotions agréables que des passions toûjours injustes,
mais naïvement respresentées, produisent en nous'.[2] The
excitement of passion is placed firmly in the perspective of
corruption when Lebrun remarks that 'la corruption du
cœur humain ne fait trouver du plaisir à la Comedie, qu'autant
qu'elle flatte ses passions et plaît à sa concupiscence'.[3]

Conti illustrates the difference of outlook between those
who attack and those who defend drama; while dramatic
theorists agree that drama's aim is to excite passions the aim
of the Christian religion 'est de les calmer, de les abattre, et

---

[1] *Réfutation des sentiments relâchés*, p. 106.
[2] *Réponse à la lettre*, p. 8.
[3] *2ième Discours*, p. 197.

de les detruire autant qu'on le peut en cette vie'.[4] Implicit in this view is the assumption that catharsis is inadequate in eradicating harmful passions. In any case the pleasure derived from the very experience of passion is illicit in itself.

But sometimes moralists single out specific passions in their attacks. The most common among these are love, ambition, jealousy, anger, and vengeance.[5] Such passions are, according to du Bois, contrary to the Christian religion which condemns 'ces vastes projets d'ambition, ces grands desseins de vengeance, et toutes ces avantures d'amour, qui forment les plus belles idées des poètes'.[6] Coustel comments that on the stage we never find Christian virtues like 'la douceur et l'humilité, le mépris des richesses, l'amour de la pauvreté et du silence', especially when they would hardly be to the taste of 'ces Dames mondaines qui s'y plaisent tant'.[7] The reason why Christian virtues have no place in drama is explained by Nicole; drama, he writes, requires 'quelque chose de grand et d'élevé selon les hommes ou du moins quelque chose de vif et d'animé'; this is not to be found in 'la gravité et dans la sagesse chrétienne'.[8]

The manner in which the dangerous passions are portrayed is often a cause of anxiety for the religious moralists. Voisin finds that in drama the passions are accompanied 'd'une image de grandeur, et de generosité'[9] while Pégurier complains that incest, adultery, and perjury are often portrayed as virtues 'pour rendre plus agreables les passions et les mouvemens dereglez du cœur'.[10] The *Décision* comments that ambition and vengeance become 'grandeur d'âme', and despair and stubbornness 'constance invincible'.[11] Drama, then, by exciting illicit passions, also propagates false values.

One dangerous passion which came under particularly close scrutiny from the religious moralists was profane love.

[4] *Traité de la comédie et des spectacles*, pp. 45-6.
[5] See Coustel, *Sentiments de l'Église*, pp. 40-1.
[6] In Racine, *Œuvres*, iv, 293.
[7] *Sentiments de l'Église*, p. 65. This is but one example of the virulent anti-feminism which pervades all the replies to Caffaro in 1694.
[8] *Traité de la comédie*, p. 53.
[9] *Défense*, p. 337.
[10] *Réfutation des sentiments relâchés*, p. 70.
[11] *Décision faite en Sorbonne*, p. 76.

It merits special attention here because dramatic theorists too believed that playwrights lowered the tone of their works by the excessive space given to it, and their views act as an effective contrast to the more categorical conclusions of drama's detractors.

There was no universal agreement regarding the extent to which love should be portrayed in drama. Chappuzeau in 1674 complains that contemporary taste demands too much.[12] Perrault explains the vogue as the result of the subservience of playwrights to the manners of the century, since the ladies who constitute the majority of the audience cannot suffer a hero if he does not resemble their lovers in manner and expression.[13] Rapin is concerned lest the tone of tragedy be lowered: 'C'est dégrader la Tragedie de cet air de majesté qui luy est propre, que d'y mêler de l'amour, qui est d'un caractère toûjours badin et peu conforme à cette gravité, dont elle fait profession.'[14]

Corneille is characteristically explicit in his ideas on the status of love in tragedy: in his first *Discours* he says that: 'Sa dignité demande quelque grand intérêt d'État, ou quelque passion plus noble et plus mâle que l'amour, telles que sont l'ambition ou la vengeance, et veut donner à craindre des malheurs plus grands que la perte d'une maîtresse.'[15] Love is not of course excluded but it must be content with a lesser role. Moreover, his proposal that ambition and vengeance are more suitable passions for tragedy is significant in the light of the views of the religious moralists on the same passions. Saint-Évremond too is concerned with priorities: in *Sur les caractères des tragédies* he explains that other passions 'servent à former le caractère au lieu de le ruiner'; to be much in love is to be possessed of 'une passion qui ne ruine pas seulement les qualités d'un caractère, mais assujetit les mouvemens des autres passions'.[16] Saint-Évremond does not wholly dissociate love from a moral context since it is an affective link between the spectator and the model hero;

---

[12] *Le Théâtre françois*, p. 41.
[13] Perrault, Ch., *Épistre à Bossuet* in *Saint Paulin, évesque de Nole*, Paris, 1686.
[14] *Réflexions*, xx, p. 147.
[15] *Writings*, p. 8.
[16] *Œuvres*, iii, 326–7.

rather he expresses the wish that we shall one day rediscover that form of love which acts as a spur to virtue.[17]

Boileau's views are not dissimilar to those of Saint-Évremond; he writes:

N'allez pas d'un Cyrus nous faire un Artamène.

Et que l'amour souvent de remords combattu,

Paroisse une foiblesse et non une vertu.[18]

Boileau is, however, unconcerned with moral scruples; his emphasis is on maintaining the status of the hero who must not become 'un berger doucereux'. Racine, too, having similarly stressed the heroic aspects of his characters in the first prefaces to *Alexandre* and *Andromaque*[19] (the heroic is often defined in opposition to the sentimental characters found in the novels of the period), asserts in his preface to *Phèdre* that 'les foiblesses de l'amour y passent pour de vraies foiblesses'.[20]

One of the most original statements on the subject of love comes in the Abbé de Villiers's *Entretiens sur les tragédies de ce temps* where he advocates a tragedy without any form of love, a passion which Timante, one of the characters in the dialogue, considers the only corrupting element in tragedy; as he explains, 'les autres passions ne sont point si engageantes'.[21] Moreover, we may see hatred, ambition, vengeance, and jealousy without fear because we have a natural horror for them, and characters who indulge in them earn only our reproach.[22] The absence of love will thus ensure that there is no danger to our moral constitution when we attend the theatre.[23]

Villiers is, however, the only commentator among those who defend drama to speak of love's evil effect. Boileau goes as far as to dissociate himself from the 'tristes esprits' who deprive the stage of one of its richest adornments, and who describe Chimène and Rodrigue as poisoners:

[17] Ibid., iv, 182.
[18] *Art poétique*, Chant III, 100-2.
[19] *Œuvres*, i, 518-19 and ii, 34-5.
[20] Ibid., iii, 302.
[21] *Granet*, i, 19.
[22] Ibid.
[23] Ibid., p. 28.

L'amour le moins honnête, exprimé chastement,
N'excite point en nous de honteux mouvement.
Didon a beau gémir, et m'étaler ses charmes;
Je condamne sa faute en partageant ses larmes.[24]

Boileau emphasizes that one is not necessarily blinded by
love to the moral issues involved, although he is careful to
speak only of love expressed 'chastement'. Paradoxically
Corneille sees a positive moral value in drama's portrayal
of love when, in his preface to *Attila*, he is compelled to
defend his art against the attacks of religious moralists.
He even points to the usefulness of catharsis; although love
is often the soul of drama, 'l'amour dans le malheur n'excite
que la pitié, et est plus capable de purger en nous cette
passion que de nous en faire envie'.[25]

Thus, for most of our commentators love is acceptable
if used correctly. The position of the religious moralists
allows of no such compromise. The rigorist theological view
of love is found in Senault's *Homme criminel*: 'Il n'est
permis à personne dans nostre Religion de se faire aymer;
c'est un attentat que de vouloir acquérir les libertez qui
n'appartiennent qu'à Dieu, c'est diviser son Empire que
de luy desbaucher ses sujets; Il veut que tous ses esclaves
soient ses Amans, et selon les maximes de Saint Augustin
nous devons à Dieu tout nostre amour.'[26] In the specific
case of drama Nicole writes that, since love is the strongest
impression that sin has made on our souls, something apparent
from the disorder it causes in society, there is nothing more
dangerous 'que de l'exciter, de la nourrir, et de détruire ce
qui la tient en bride et qui en arrête le cours'.[27] The love
referred to here is of course a concupiscent love which
excludes all but one person.

We are, however, also deceived by drama as to the true
nature of love. According to Nicole the fact that it appears
on the stage 'sans honte et sans infamie' encourages us to
view it in a favourable light.[28] One particular means of

---

[24] *Art poétique*, Chant IV, 97-8 and 100-3.
[25] *Writings*, p. 171.
[26] *L'Homme criminel*, p. 73.
[27] *Traité de la comédie*, pp. 42-3.
[28] Ibid., p. 43.

persuading us that love is legitimate is described by Coustel: 'un des plus malicieux artifices du demon, est de faire representer ce qui se passe dans le commerce d'une passion illegitime, sous le pretexte d'un mariage esperé, afin que les complimens étudiez qui se font, les messages, les lettres pleines de douceurs et de tendresses qui s'écrivent, soient moins suspectes à des ames simples et sans experience'.[29] Nicole himself argues that, although marriage makes good use of concupiscence, profane love is in itself always bad and dissipated; for this reason it is forbidden to excite it in oneself or in others.[30] One must, he continues, constantly regard love as a shameful effect of sin, always capable of poisoning one's soul, were it not for God's intervention: 'Ainsi de quelque honnêteté apparente dont les Comedies et les Romans tâchent de la revêtir, on ne peut nier qu'en cela même ils ne soient contraires aux bonnes mœurs, puisqu'ils impriment une idée agreable d'une passion vicieuse, et qu'ils en font même une qualité heroïque . . .'[31] This, Nicole adds, is because drama arouses concupiscence without at the same time giving rise to what constrains it; consequently the spectator feels only passion.[32] There is one more trap in the dramatists' portrayal of love which arises from the fact that a passion portrayed as honourable is even more dangerous 'parce que l'esprit la regarde avec moins d'horreur, et que le cœur s'y laisse aller avec moins de resistance'.[33] Making illicit love more respectable leads us to accept it.

Finally, Bossuet too agrees on the futility of attempting to legitimize love by marriage, remarking that 'encore que vous ôtiez en apparence à l'amour profane ce grossier et cet illicite dont on aurait honte, il en est inséparable sur le théâtre'.[34] The question of deceit also forms part of his argument for 'Le grossier que vous en ôtez ferait horreur, si on le montrait; et l'adresse de le cacher ne fait qu'y attirer les volontés d'une manière plus délicate, et qui n'en est que

[29] *Sentiments de l'Église*, p. 60.
[30] *Traité de la comédie*, p. 43.
[31] Ibid.
[32] *Traité de la comédie*, p. 44.
[33] Ibid.
[34] *Maximes et réflexions*, U/L, p. 185.

plus périlleuse lorsqu'elle paraît plus épurée.'[35] Thus the means of recognizing evil is removed from us. In any case Bossuet sees marriage as coming too late in a play to be an effective restraining force because our senses are already aroused; moreover, he concludes that marriage is too serious a subject for a spectator who seeks only pleasure and 'n'est que par façon et pour la forme dans la comédie'.[36]

But religious moralists consider love illicit not only because it is an effect of concupiscence but also because of its allegedly pagan qualities. Gerbais, while conceding that drama is no longer idolatrous and that sacrifices have ceased to be offered to Venus in a religious sense, remarks that 'les intrigues d'amour qui en sont presque inseparables, ne laissent pas d'honorer cette Déesse; et quoiqu'on ne les accompagne pas d'encens, il est au moins sûr que ces intrigues ne sont pas des offrandes qui puissent être presentées au veritable Dieu'.[37] The *idea* of love is worshipped no less than a personified goddess. Even the characters themselves may become objects of worship. Lamy writes that 'La Heroïne est le Dieu du Heros, et le Heros est celuy de la Heroïne.'[38] His conclusion is that even if a passionate love between two people is decent in the eyes of men it is certainly not Christian: 'Nôtre cœur est un autel où Dieu ne souffre point qu'on sacrifie impunément à d'autres qu'à luy, et qu'on y allume un feu étranger.'[39] The language of love too is supposed to exhibit idolatrous features. Coustel accuses Sévère in *Polyeucte* of speaking 'en vray idolâtre'; should words like 'sacrifier' and 'immoler', which are God's due alone, be used 'pour des Creatures, qui se regardent aprés cela comme de petites Divinitez, à qui l'on doit offrir de l'encens de toutes sortes de loüanges'?[40]

The moralists, then, attack the passions aroused in drama, on the one hand because their excitement is injurious to our spiritual welfare, and on the other hand because they are

---

[35] Ibid., p. 186.
[36] Ibid., p. 187.
[37] *Lettre d'un docteur de Sorbonne*, pp. 31-2.
[38] *Nouvelles réflexions*, p. 102.
[39] Ibid., p. 53.
[40] *Sentiments de l'Église*, p. 64.

often portrayed as virtues. The religious moralists further
contend that a major contribution to this deception regarding
the passions' true value is made by the presentation of the
hero or heroine. Conti explains that in *La Mort de Pompée*
Cornélie is commended because she makes vengeance a duty,
'qui attire le respect, et qui la fasse passer pour une personne
heroïque'.[41] Bossuet, replying to the argument that passion
in drama is portrayed as a weakness, exclaims 'Je le veux;
mais il paraît comme une belle, comme une noble faiblesse,
comme la faiblesse des héros et des heroïnes.'[42] He comments
that a young woman will learn how to love by seeing this
passion not in men but in a girl depicted as modest, chaste
and virtuous, 'en un mot dans une héroïne'.[43] Thus the poet
endows his principal characters with the kind of personality
which acts as a sanction to vice.

The writer who examined the phenomenon of the hero
in most detail was Bernard Lamy in his *Nouvelles réflexions
sur l'art poétique*. Lamy identifies in all of us a natural
movement towards God which manifests itself in a strong
inclination for *grandeur*; poets exploit this inclination by
offering us everything that is great and eminent in the world,
sometimes having recourse to exaggeration.[44] Lamy considers
such an offering as something very much short of the real
thing. Moreover, 'toutes les choses que rapportent les Poëtes,
sont capables d'arréter l'esprit, et de le tourner vers elles
par leur nouveauté, par leur rareté, par leur grandeur'.[45] In
other words our inclination for *grandeur* stops at the level of
the poet's creation and fails to reach its ultimate aim in God.

The heroes in poetry are therefore representative of
grandeur, since they are 'tous genereux et grans Capitaines',
being moreover courageous when faced with danger and
fearless in combat.[46] Such qualities, Lamy comments, are
no doubt virtues in a Christian but 'elles sont criminelles et
plûtôt des vices que des vertus, par le côté par lequel les

---

[41] *Traité de la comédie et des spectacles*, p. 41.
[42] *Maximes et réflexions*, U/L, p. 181.
[43] Ibid., p. 182.
[44] *Nouvelles réflexions*, pp. 15-16.
[45] Ibid., p. 25.
[46] Ibid., p. 39.

hommes corrompus les regardent et les admirent'.[47] Poetic
grandeur is no longer a copy of its higher form but a travesty
of it. As Lamy indicates, however, our opinion of the poet's
heroes does not change; even though they embody the
very passions whose portrayal as virtues we saw condemned
earlier, 'ils ne paroissent pas moins considerables parmy les
hommes, et moins cheris des Dieux; ainsi en consacrant leurs
personnes, ils consacrent leurs vices et rendent par ce moyen
la vengeance, l'ambition, l'orgueil et l'adultere honorables'.[48]

Lamy suggests that it is rather the poet's express purpose
to encourage us to find the justification of our own vices in
those of the heroes themselves. The poet achieves his aim by
depicting the hero as pious and as protected by God himself:
'[les poètes] font ces fictions pour plaire aux hommes qui
sont troublez dans leurs desordres par la crainte d'un Dieu
vangeur des pechez qu'ils commettent: de laquelle crainte
ils les délivrent en leur representant que de grands hommes
aimez des Dieux, ont fait ce qu'ils font, . . .'[49] Our fear of
a judging god is thus assuaged if this same god is seen to
approve of the sinful acts committed by a character who
has all the appearance of virtue. Another of the poet's
methods is to infer that the gods themselves are subject
to similar faults to our own. The justification of our sinful
acts is also to be found in the inference that the gods are
capable of the same acts. They are portrayed as quarrelsome
and adulterous and just as the poet endeavours to make men
appear as gods, he also tries to make the gods appear as men,
'leur attribuant des actions humaines et criminelles, afin
qu'elles ne passent plus pour telles . . .'.[50] Lamy explains our
acceptance of such procedures as a desire on our part to
enjoy both '[les] douceurs de la volupté, et [le] repos de la
bonne conscience'.[51]

The poet, in establishing our identification with the hero,
must also pay special attention to the nature of his hero's
virtues, something, as demonstrated earlier, dear to the hearts

[47] Ibid.
[48] Ibid., pp. 58-9.
[49] Ibid., p. 125.
[50] Ibid., p. 59.
[51] Ibid.

of those who write in favour of drama. Lamy informs us that the criteria for such virtues are to be found in those values we ourselves hold dear; in other words, poets must ·conceive of their heroes 'sur cette idée que les hommes à qui ils veulent plaire, ont de la vertu'.[52] In this way the most dissolute people are glad to see their own passions justified, 'c'est-à-dire de voir d'honnêtes gens, qui sont faits comme eux, et qui vivent comme eux'.[53] The spectator in drama is thereby more deeply convinced of the worth of his own values. But the quality of worldly virtue is swiftly dispatched by Lamy as consisting only 'dans l'observation de certaines bienséances, ausquelles on a attaché une idée d'honnêteté'.[54] Thus poets satisfy the vanity of society by confirming it in its false values, embodied by a hero rare and extraordinary.

One of the most important conclusions Lamy draws is that a sympathetic portrayal of the hero obscures the moral issues involved in a character's acts and he cites Dido as one example. This same character is used by Boileau to illustrate how we can preserve a moral sense even though we may pity the queen in her distressing love (described by Boileau as an example of 'l'amour le moins honnête, exprimé chastement'):[55]

Didon a beau gémir et m'étaler ses charmes,
Je condamne sa faute en partageant ses larmes.[56]

Lamy contends, however, that we are blind to the sin of Dido's passion precisely because she has all the excellent qualities of a virtuous character, 'qui font qu'on est affligé de voir une grande princesse reduite au desespoir par une passion qui semble innocente, puisque sa fin étoit un mariage honnête'.[57] We are deceived into thinking of Dido as virtuous because marriage is her ultimate aim.

The poet, then, encourages us to identify with the hero by modelling the latter's qualities on our own ideals. But this identification has serious consquences for our personality. Lamy explains that we become so involved in our interest for the hero that 'on entre dans toutes leurs passions'; moreover, 'on aime ce qu'ils aiment; on hait ce qu'ils

---

[52] Ibid., p. 62.
[53] Ibid., pp. 62-3.
[54] Ibid., p. 62.

[55] *Art poétique*, Chant IV, 101.
[56] Ibid., 103-4.
[57] *Nouvelles réflexions*, pp. 120-1.

haïssent; on se réjoüit, et l'on s'afflige avec eux'.[58] Our
pleasure is increased by the fact that these passions have the
appearance of innocence and are unaccompanied by any
painful circumstances.[59] Moreover, our involvement is so
intense that it is impossible 'qu'en même temps que nous
sommes liéz [à ceux dont il peint les mouvemens] par le
plaisir, nous ne soyons aussi brûlez des mêmes flammes'.[60]
This leads to a situation where: '[Le lecteur] est dans son
imagination ce qu'est ce Heros, et ce qu'il voudroit être luy-
même; ainsi il n'y a aucun mouvement de son cœur qui ne
soit rendu agissant, . . . Il n'y a point de passion dont il ne
ressente les agréables émotions . . .'[61] We therefore substitute
the hero's personality for our own. In Bossuet's words we
become 'un acteur secret dans la tragédie, on y joue sa propre
passion'.[62] For Yves de Paris too 'chacun est tout ensemble
spectateur et personnage'.[63]

According to Lamy man's need to substitute his own
personality for one he mistakenly considers more desirable
is based on a false evaluation of the terrestrial world.
Although creatures are made in the image of God, man
contemplates only the beauty of the former, represented in
poetry by 'une peinture tres-imparfaite'. Borrowing a
platonist image he says that just as the men in the cave
contemplate shadows, earth-bound minds consider only 'les
corps', since they fail to realize that 'les beautez passageres
d'icy bas ne sont que les ombres d'une beauté éternelle'.[64]
Thus man is convinced that creatures are the principle and
end of beauty, and not a mere expression of eternal beauty.[65]
Sin has once again corrupted our natural movement towards
God and has arrested our attention at the level of objects.[66]
In this way the hero's portrayal in all forms of poetry

[58] Ibid., p. 93.
[59] Ibid.
[60] Ibid., p. 132.
[61] Ibid., p. 98.
[62] *Maximes et réflexions*, U/L, p. 178.
[63] Yves de Paris, *Les Vaines Excuses du pécheur en ses passions*, 2 vols., Paris,
1662–4, ii, 315.
[64] *Nouvelles réflexions*, pp. 5–6.
[65] Ibid., pp. 6–7.
[66] Ibid., pp. 8–10.

deceives us into imagining the world more worthwhile than it is in reality. Lamy believes that we should instead cast earthly creatures from our mind and 'n'y penser jamais si ce n'est pour en connoître le neant: il faut rentrer dans soy-même, et considerer qu'elles ne nous peuvent donner cette beatitude que nous desirons'; it is from this duty, demanded both by our reason and our religion, that poets endeavour to deter us.[67] Not content with ourselves we yield to the poet's charms, seeking fulfilment in a fictional being and not as we should in God.

But the mere fact of substitution is not the sole cause of anxiety; it also takes place without our knowledge. Lamy informs us that the soul becomes united in some way 'avec l'objet de sa connoissance' and 'lorsqu'elle n'est occupée que des corps qui luy sont étrangers, elle sort d'elle-même, et ne peut par consequent connoître ce qui s'y passe'.[68] The aim of poets is therefore to 'remplir l'imagination de leurs Lecteurs d'une peinture vive des choses sensibles, qui les tienne toûjours hors d'eux-mêmes, et qui les empêche d'y rentrer'.[69] The result, of course, is that we lose complete control of the artistic experience.

This loss of control is further stressed in the moralists' examination of drama's aural and visual qualities, which are seen as contributing factors in the nature of drama as deceit. These discussions show too how much the religious moralists are aware of the attraction of a performance and of the way in which a text is given life by the actor.

For Lamy drama is the most dangerous form of poetry because 'Ce que l'on voit faire touche bien davantage que ce que l'on ne fait qu'entendre.'[70] Senault argues that the splendour of theatrical performances and the actors' costumes all contribute to make drama 'le plus charmant de tous les Divertissemens', he continues: '[la comedie] enchante tout à la fois les yeux et les oreilles; et pour enlever l'homme tout entier, Elle essaye de seduire son esprit, aprés qu'elle a charmé tous les sens. Il faut être de bronze et de marbre pour

---

[67] Ibid., p. 24.
[68] Ibid., pp. 27–8.
[69] Ibid., p. 28.
[70] Ibid., p. 191.

resister à tant d'appas.'[71] The significance of words like *charmer* and *enchantement*, encountered frequently in the moralists' works, must not be underestimated for their meaning is still very much that of *casting a spell*, as indeed the proximity of 'seduire son esprit' suggests. The visual sumptuosity of drama thus transforms the theatre into a temple of magic. Courtin even refers to the tales of antiquity and novels as 'cette espece de magie'.[72]

La Grange views the richness of presentation in the context of love's portrayal. One sees a girl in a magnificent room or pleasure garden, dressed in her most attractive finery, where she laments her suffering for love 'sans oublier les soûpirs, les larmes, et toutes les marques de transport'; then, in a desert strewn with rocks towering up to the skies, a young man appears 'qui croyant n'être point aimé, s'abandonne au desespoir'.[73] What young person, he asks, can resist such an experience? Coustel argues that all these rich elements of decor persuade men that life on earth has 'quelque chose d'aimable', whereas 'en comparaison des biens ineffables du Ciel, tout cela ne doive effectivement passer que pour des réveries et des songes'.[74] This manifestation of earthly riches helps yet again to turn man away from God and deceive him regarding their true value in everyday life.

Moralists also emphasize the damage done to the soul by hearing corrupting maxims in the theatre. Senault, in *L'Homme criminel*, comments that the soul is corrupted more easily by what it hears than by what it sees,[75] and support for this view comes from an unexpected quarter. In his *Apologie* Scudéry recommends that no dangerous maxims should be uttered by the characters in a play because: 'L'ouye est sans doute celuy de tous les sens qui approche le plus, du propre siege de l'entendement et de la raison, qui est le cerveau; si bien qu'il corrompt aussi plus facilement

---

[71] Senault, le Père J.-F., *Le Monarque, ou les devoirs du souverain*, Paris, 1661, pp. 231-2.
[72] Courtin, A. de, *Traité de la paresse ou l'art de bien employer le temps, en formes d'entretiens*, Paris, 1673, pp. 103-4.
[73] *Réfutation d'un écrit*, p. 67.
[74] *Sentiments de l'Église*, p. 55.
[75] *L'Homme criminel*, p. 443.

l'ame, si ce qu'on reçoit par luy n'est pas bon.'[76]

But in their examination of corruption through our sense of hearing the religious moralists give us more detailed considerations on those forms of writing most likely to endanger us. Lamy writes that whereas 'les Peintures ordinaires', which are expressed in only 'couleurs grossieres et materielles', make only a feeble impression upon us, poetry on the other hand, 'par l'harmonie et la cadence de ses Vers, en fait dans l'Ame de si vives et de si agreables, que l'on ne se doit pas étonner si un des Maîtres de l'Art a pû dire que les Poëtes renfermant leurs pensées dans les bornes d'un Vers, et donnant une prison étroite à leurs mots, sçavent par là enchaîner la raison avec la rime'.[77] Verse is thus a means of enslaving our minds so that, once again, we lose control of the artistic experience.

Verse is also highly effective in the excitement of passion, which leads to the abdication of our own personality. Lamy comments that poets 'donnent un tour à ce qu'ils disent qui n'est point ordinaire, et qui nous enchante de telle manière, que ne nous sentant plus nous-mêmes, nous entrons avec plaisir dans tous les sentimens et dans toutes les Passions qu'ils veulent exciter dans nôtre Ame'.[78] This is, of course, precisely what dramatic theorists wish us to do. Senault too, even in the conciliatory passage on drama in De l'usage des passions, notes that if the 'personnes vulgaires' look carefully at themselves they would freely admit that 'les vers du Theatre leur donnent de l'esmotion, et qu'ils impriment dans leurs ames tous les sentimens des personnages qu'ils font parler'.[79]

Corroboration of the view that a passion well expressed results in the undermining of the spectator's sound judgement comes, surprisingly, from Chapelain. In his Sentimens de l'Académie he remarks that Chimène's love for Rodrigue could be accepted as the most pleasurable aspect of the play, not because it is good but because it is well expressed.[80] Like

---

[76] *Apologie*, pp. 5-6.
[77] *Nouvelles réflexions*, pp. 1-2.
[78] Ibid., p. 3.
[79] Senault, Le Père J.-F., *De l'usage des passions*, Paris, 1641, p. 181.
[80] Gasté, p. 375.

the religious moralists he find that 'les passions violentes
bien exprimées, font souvent en ceux qui les voyent une
partie de l'effect, qu'elles font en ceux qui les ressentent
veritablement'.[81] Furthermore: 'Elles ostent à tous la liberté
de l'esprit, et font que les uns se plaisent à voir representer
les fautes, que les autres se plaisent à commettre. Ce sont
ces puissans mouvemens, qui ont tiré des Spectateurs du Cid
cette grande approbation, et qui doivent aussi la faire excuser.
L'Autheur s'est facilement rendu maistre de leur ame, apres
y avoir excité le trouble et l'esmotion.'[82] Clearly little
separates the religious moralists from some dramatic theorists
in terms of a psychology of the passions. It is rather the
secular optimism of the latter regarding the effects of drama
which is wholly unacceptable to the former, for whom the
mere possibility of danger makes of all drama a forbidden fruit.

But for the moralists verse is also an agent of deceit. In his
Poésies chrétiennes Godeau argues that in reading or hearing
poetry we are less free to use our reason 'pour reconnoistre
la verité des objets'; moreover, when poetry lays a trap 'elle
le couvre de fleurs si agreables et si éclatantes, qu'on ne le voit
pas, ou qu'on est bien aise d'y estre pris . . .'[83] Nicole
considers that a passion for which we should normally
experience horror becomes more attractive by the ingenious
way in which it is expressed.[84]

Another area where poets are accused of deceiving us by
their use of language is that of obscenity. In the first place
the very content of plays is often considered sufficiently
dangerous to be ruled out altogether. Vincent deplores those
plays which include magicians casting spells and characters
like Phèdre 'qui est éprise d'une flamme maudite, et brusle
d'un amour incestueux'.[85] Pégurier too attacks subjects
which involve incest and adultery, complaining that they are
often endowed with the quality of virtue.[86]

As far as Voisin is concerned, however decent the content

[81] Ibid., p. 414.
[82] Ibid.
[83] Godeau, A., *Poésies chrétiennes*, Paris, 1654, p. 12.
[84] *Traité de la comédie*, p. 57.
[85] *Traité des théâtres*, p. 9.
[86] *Réfutation des sentiments relâchés*, p. 70.

of a play may be, the form given to it by the poet 'n'a jamais l'honnesteté toute pure'; Voisin says of content that the poet 'la revest toujours de galanteries, et de ce qu'il estime pouvoir agréer davantage aux spectateurs'.[87] He further remarks that in most cases 'la forme détruit ce qu'il y a d'honneste dans la matiere, par des discours prophanes, pleins de dogmes et de maximes Payennes'.[88]

Vincent, however, discerns a superficial and unsuccessful attempt on the poet's part to lessen the obscenity by removing the linguistic excesses: it none the less remains that the content is still as dangerous as before; 'encores qu'il n'y ait pas de mots sales, ni des expressions qui facent rougir, la matiere en soy a le mesme reproche que celles du passé, qu'on confesse dissoluës'.[89] Replying to Caffaro's point that drama has undergone reform Pégurier agrees that plays are 'aussi épurées qu'elles l'ayent été dans un autre temps'; however, the reason for this is not the poet's concern for moral rectitude but rather his desire to comply with the taste of a century which prefers more *délicatesse* in its pleasures.[90]

Lebrun believes that the poet's attempt to conceal the horror of evil beneath acceptable expressions in fact undermines our ability to recognize it as such:[91] 'pour plaire au sexe, [les poètes] mettent par tout des envelopes; et comme on s'exerce à deviner, on va toûjours au-delà de ce qu'on avoit voulu dire. Qu'on ne s'excuse donc pas sur ce qu'on est reservé dans les termes.'[92] Couching obscenity in more delicate turns of phrase thus encourages us to seek it. Moreover, good taste is nothing more than deception.

Opera, while attacked on much the same grounds as other forms of drama, was specifically criticized for the affectivity of its music, which is seen to assist in the excitement of passion. The authors of the *Décision* declare that 'à la faveur de la Musique dont les tons sont recherchez et disposez

---

[87] *Défense*, p. 268.
[88] Ibid.
[89] *Traité des théâtres*, p. 15.
[90] *Réfutation des sentiments relâchés*, p. 86.
[91] *2ième Discours*, p. 93.
[92] Ibid.

exprés pour toucher, l'ame est bien plus susceptible des passions qu'on y veut exciter, et particulierement celle de l'amour, qui est le sujet le plus ordinaire de cette sorte de Comédie'.[93]

The last major element of dramatic presentation left for discussion is *vraisemblance*, a notion fundamental to the dramatic theorists' defence of moral instruction. Consider first of all the question of poetry and history. For most dramatic theorists poetry was seen in opposition to history and the subject of the former was not what had actually happened (*vérité*) but what might happen or might have happened (*vraisemblance*). Poetry is regarded as more instructive than history, which fails both to reveal the causes of evil-doing and to punish evil-doers. Chapelain suggested that all art which observed the rules of *vraisemblance* was able to remedy this, and we concluded that *vraisemblance* was in fact a reordering of reality according to a moral ideal.

Baillet, however, comments that poets deliberately contradict the truth 'pour faire voir que leur Art consiste dans la fiction' and 'de peur de se rencontrer avec les Historiens'.[94] The poets' rivalry with the historian induces them to portray characters quite differently from what they were in reality; Baillet would accept alterations to history (which for him includes the legends of antiquity) if poets were content to 'nous changer de mal en bien' and to portray men 'comme ils ont dû être en nous ôtant l'idée de ce qu'ils ont été effectivement . . .'[95] Unfortunately poets do precisely the opposite and depict historical figures 'tels qu'ils n'ont jamais dû être, et qu'ils n'ont point été'.[96] He cites as an example Racine's portrayal of Hippolyte who has been deprived of the innocence and chastity attributed to him for centuries past.[97]

Fiction itself is what Voisin disapproves of most in poetry. Plays in his opinion are bad because 'selon leur genre elles

[93] *Décision faite en Sorbonne*, p. 128.
[94] Baillet, A., *Jugements des sçavans sur les principaux ouvrages des auteurs*, 7 vols. Paris, 1722, iii, 267.
[95] Ibid.
[96] Ibid.
[97] Ibid., 268.

sont des representations fausses et imaginaires, ne representant
pas les choses telles qu'elles sont comme font les Histoires;
mais telles qu'elles les feignent ou les déguisent'.[98] But
Voisin also attacks the selection of incidents in plays: the
poet's aim is to show only what may occupy 'agreablement'
the spectators' minds, 'flatter plus doucement leurs sens, et
émouvoir plus fortement leurs passions, . . . preferant mesme
le mensonge à la verité'.[99] The poet chooses his material not
according to its historical value but according to its ability
to arouse our passions. For Rivet poetry sanctions evil even
when it accurately records certain historical facts, for poetry
tends to keep evil feelings alive by resuscitating past crimes;
quoting St. Cyprian he writes that 'L'horreur antique est
repetée par une action exprimée à l'image de la verité, afin
que ce qui a jadis esté commis, ne s'abolisse avec le siecle.'[100]
Bossuet's views on history and art are clear: what an error, he
declares, not to realise the distinction between history, 'l'art
de représenter les mauvaises actions pour en inspirer de
l'horreur' and poetry, 'celui de peindre les passions agréables
d'une manière qui en fasse goûter le plaisir'.[101] Bossuet
refers here to a form of historical writing which in itself
reveals a meaning whereas poetry can only corrupt.

Mensonge, then, in no way possesses the noble qualities
dramatic theorists attribute to it; it is no more than falsehood.
Moreover, among the theorists the term *vérité* refers for the
most part to historical fact and has little or nothing of a
moral concept. For certain religious moralists, however, *truth*
is nearer to that which is or has been ordained by God; there
is no reason for the poet's imagination to add to it.

Vraisemblance is not only relevant to the opposition of
poetry to history. Chapelain and Scudéry note that the
spectator's experience of emotion very much depends on the
degree of *vraisemblance* achieved in the presentation of a
play. Frain du Tremblay writes that it is rather the degree of
emotion displayed in the play which produces our belief in
the play as a real event; the poet's aim in composing his

[98] *Défense*, pp. 267–8.
[99] Ibid., p. 268.
[100] *L'Instruction chrétienne*, pp. 67–8.
[101] *Maximes et réflexions*, U/L, pp. 177–8.

works is 'de les rendre si vives et si touchantes, que l'imagination soit trompée et qu'elle croye assister à une action véritable, non pas à une representation'.[102] Bossuet too emphasizes the reality of the emotions communicated by the characters and the action of the stage: if, he says, we condemn indecent painting because we can appreciate it properly only by entering into the spirit of the artist, how much greater will be the effect of drama where 'tout paraît effectif', where these are not 'des traits morts et des couleurs sèches qui agissent', but living characters, 'de vrais yeux, ou ardents, ou tendres et plongés dans la passion, de vraies larmes dans les acteurs, qui en attirent d'aussi véritables dans ceux qui les regardent'.[103] The consequence of drama's ability to present the fictional as a living reality is that real reactions are elicited from the spectator. No difference is supposed between real and theatrical emotion. The religious moralists' complaint is that the dramatic illusion succeeds all too well.

Indeed Godeau is concerned at our reacting in the same way to fictional as to real people. In his *Églogues sacrées*, referring to the *Aeneid*, he remarks:

Combien de fois blamant l'inconstance d'Enée,
Ay-je plaint de Didon la triste destinée;
Combien souvent mes yeux pour ses fausses douleurs
Ont-ils laissé couler de veritables pleurs?[104]

The reference here is to the epic: Bardou, however, issues a warning when he says of drama,

Gardons-nous d'écouter d'amoureuses chimeres;
D'honorer de nos pleurs des maux imaginaires.[105]

Lamy develops this point when he asks: 'Est-ce pour des phantômes que Dieu a imprimé dans nôtre cœur toutes ces différentes affections d'estime et d'amour; ou pour nous attirer à luy, qui est notre centre . . . et nous separer des creatures, ausquelles nous ne pouvons nous attacher sans nous priver de nôtre felicité?'[106] The theme is familiar:

---

[102] *Nouveaux essais*, p. 155.
[103] *Maximes et réflexions*, U/L, p. 179.
[104] *Poésies chrétiennes*, no. xi, p. 223.
[105] Bardou, P., *Épistre sur la condamnation du théâtre.* A. M. Racine, Paris, 1694, p. 7.
[106] *Nouvelles réflexions*, p. 107.

we are ill-using emotions which God has created especially to bring us nearer to him; our tears are precious and if we are not to betray God's creation they must be directed to worthier objects. Fictional beings cannot be worthy.

The relation of emotion to *vraisemblance* was further examined by the religious moralists when they considered how dramatists succeed so well in exciting the spectator's passions. One point made in many of the theorists' discussions was that the audience should be able to relate directly to what was happening on the stage, that nothing should be unfamiliar to them, to the extent that d'Aubignac saw a play's success in terms of the subject's conformity to the customary beliefs and feelings of the spectators. It is interesting, then, that the authors of the *Décision* note themselves that if a playwright's subjects are to please they must conform to the disposition of the majority of the spectators 'qui sont des personnes du monde qui en ont les maximes et l'esprit'.[107]

Lamy echoes Rapin's remark that the passions portrayed become 'fades et de mal goust, si elles ne sont fondées sur des sentimens conformes à ceux du spectateur' when he comments that reading modern poetry is more dangerous than reading that of antiquity because modern poets are more aware of the *ressort* of the passions of their contemporaries; they know what coincides with their corrupt inclinations and what precisely is capable of moving them; thus, 'reglant leurs Ouvrages sur ces connoissances, ils attaquent les hommes par où ils sont le plus sensible: de sorte qu'ils peuvent beaucoup nuire'.[108] Drama is not a moral reordering of reality but an exploitation of it.

As usual, Lamy's views on the subject of *vraisemblance* are supported by more general considerations. He explains that just as 'l'esprit aussi ne peut se porter à connoître que ce qui luy paroît veritable' the will can love only those things which are good, or which at least have the appearance of good.[109] This is why 'toutes les fables dont la fausseté est évidente, loin de plaire paroissent ridicules: elles ne

---

[107] *Décision faite en Sorbonne*, p. 75.
[108] *Nouvelles réflexions*, p. 220.
[109] Ibid., p. 73.

plaisent que lorsque l'artifice du Poëte est tel qu'il enchante en quelque façon, et que l'on s'imagine quasi qu'elles sont veritables'.[110] That poets, in order to please, take so much care to hide their lies behind 'l'apparence de la verité', is further proof that our mind is made for the truth.[111] Man's joy in reading fiction is, however, an obvious sign of his corruption because he prefers the appearance of truth to truth itself, just as we have seen that 'il quittoit la veritable grandeur pour courir aprés son ombre'.[112] Man is all too ready to exchange the real for the substitute world and in so doing place earthly considerations above those of eternal good.

Lamy also approaches the question of *vraisemblance* and pleasure. The poet, he tells us, must beware not to 'proposer des choses comme veritables, dont l'erreur peut être apperçeüe par les sens', since an untruth cannot be pleasing if it does not have the appearance of truth.[113] Pleasure is thus directly related to the degree of success of the illusion. He says later that if for example the unity of time is violated, whatever the pleasure the reader experiences in allowing himself to be deceived, 'il est impossible qu'il ne s'apperçoive trop sensible-ment que ce qu'on luy dit est une fable, et par consequent il ne s'en degoûte'.[114] The pleasure of the spectator in allowing himself to be deceived is important for it indicates that he enjoys being deceived.

But here we encounter a difficulty in Lamy's argument. He gives as an example of our love of images a father scolding his son. This *enchants* us so much that we think we are witnessing the actions of a *real* father. He goes on to say, however, that this image is not pleasant in itself because we should not enjoy being in the company of the father while he is admonishing his son; 'mais cependant la peinture qu'en font les Poëtes n'a rien que de charmant'.[115] Lamy then discusses Aristotle's idea that we derive our pleasure from the exactness of the imitation rather than from the

[110] Ibid.
[111] Ibid., p. 76.
[112] Ibid., pp. 76-7.
[113] Ibid., p. 118.
[114] Ibid., pp. 152-3.
[115] Ibid., pp. 79-80.

subject itself.[116] His own view of this pleasure is that it comes:

de ce que les hommes, quoy que tres-attachez à leurs sens ont un certain sentiment naturel qui leur fait preferer ce qui est spirituel aux choses materielles, et qui les oblige par exemple d'estimer davantage que les corps mêmes, l'art avec lequel une personne ingenieuse les represente: d'où vient que toutes ces imitations et ces peintures des Poëtes leur sont plus agreables que les choses mêmes.[117]

But if we are in a state of mind sufficient to appreciate the hand which paints we are not then experiencing the total involvement with the hero Lamy has alleged earlier. We are aware of beholding something fictional and, according to Lamy, the realization of this should displease us.

This was indeed an issue taken up during the *affaire Caffaro*. The authors of the *Décision* mention that it could be argued that in the theatre our sight and imagination are satisfied by the vivid and natural performance of the actor 'sans y interesser le cœur'; we praise the actor and his art without necessarily approving what he is performing.[118] This they consider, however, to be a purely speculative argument which can never apply in practice; if man had not been corrupted by the Fall and had remained master of his passions the distinction between the two reactions would be valid; but since the opposite is the case, the first form of pleasure, derived from the art rather than from the object in itself, is too near the second to be safe.[119]

Bossuet, after condemning Lully's music for insinuating passion into the soul, refers to the possible objection that 'on n'est occupé que du chant et du spectacle, sans songer au sens des paroles, ni aux sentiments qu'elles expriment'.[120] That, he argues, is precisely the danger, for while we are spellbound by the beauty of the melody or taken with the spectacle we unknowingly assimilate and derive pleasure

[116] This is of course the position adopted by Boileau in *Art poétique*, Chant III, 1–4.
[117] *Nouvelles réflexions*, p. 83.
[118] *Décision faite en Sorbonne*, p. 6.
[119] Ibid., pp. 86–7.
[120] *Maximes et réflexions*, U/L, p. 174.

from the feelings expressed in the production.[121] Bossuet implies that all contact with art must be severed because we can find no way of approaching it without being corrupted.

There is one more problematical point in Lamy's argument, which is not unconnected with the previous question. Lamy has said that the spectator is in a state of total involvement with the principal character and is 'dans son imagination ce qu'est ce Heros, et ce qu'il voudroit être luy-même'; there is no passion the spectator does not feel himself.[122] But Lamy also concedes that one may weep for a hero persecuted by his enemies, to whom the poet attributes all sorts of black deeds.[123] We feel satisfied, he continues, because we embrace virtue and are not insensitive to misfortune; at the same time, however: 'La peine que l'on souffre en voyant les maux d'une personne que l'on juge digne d'une meilleure fortune, est liée par une union merveilleuse avec des sentimens contraires de joye et de douceur: On pleure avec plaisir des miseres que l'on ne souffre point . . . Ce n'est pas que la peine des autres qui donne de la satisfaction, mais on est bien-aise de s'en voir à couvert.'[124] We are now confronted with an argument which postulates on the one hand a state of total involvement and on the other hand a certain distance between character and spectator, for tears in our response to drama imply a total grasp of the situation. Moreover, Lamy himself quite rightly points out that because the spectator does not share the hero's fate in a tragedy the experiences of spectator and hero are not identical, especially if the former 'est bien-aise de s'en voir à couvert'. Lamy's view that we react to art in a purely passive and unthinking way, a view he shares with other religious moralists, is thereby heavily undermined by some of his own arguments.

Vraisemblance and the aesthetic presentation of drama in general induce us, then, through a psychological

---

[121] Ibid. Here Bossuet specifically mentions Racine's renunciation of the theatre, claiming that, since Caffaro denied that there was any danger in the spectator's experience of passion, Caffaro, given Racine's renunciation, '[le ramenait] à ses premières erreurs' (*Maximes et réflexions*, U/L, p. 175). For Racine's reaction, see Urbain and Levesque's note 1 to page 175.

[122] *Nouvelles réflexions*, p. 98.

[123] Ibid., p. 94.

[124] Ibid., p. 95.

enslavement which leads us to the abandonment of self, to become part of a substitute world, itself having all the appearance of our own. Some religious moralists express dismay at poets wishing to imitate a world which is in fact quite worthless. Nicole explains that one of the principal effects of grace is the revelation of the emptiness and instability of worldly things, and at the same time of 'la grandeur et la solidité des biens éternels'.[125] This in itself should produce aversion for drama and, advancing a nakedly platonist argument, he writes: 'si toutes les choses temporelles ne sont que des figures et des ombres, en quel rang doit-on mettre les Comedies qui ne sont que les ombres des ombres, puis que ce ne sont que de vaines images des choses temporelles, et souvent des choses fausses?'[126]

The attempt at realism in drama is seen by Yves de Paris as a means of coming to grips with time, which is at once too rapid and too slow 'pour l'amour que les hommes portent aux affaires de ce monde, car il n'en donne la joüissance, qu'apres beaucoup de remises, et puis il la reduit bien-tost au rang des choses passées'.[127] Now, however:

On a trouvé l'art d'adjuster aux desirs humains, ces deux mouvemens qui semblent contraires et en deux heures representer aux yeux sur les theatres, toutes les grandes actions avec les advantures d'une longue et celebre vie; comme si elles estoient presentes.[128]

Soanen emphasizes the futility of the whole exercise:

. . . comment n'êtes-vous pas frappés de tous ces morts qu'on fait en quelque sorte revivre, pour vous intéresser? Comment ne redoutez-vous pas un plaisir, qu'on ne vous fait sentir qu'en remettant sur la Scene des Empereurs, des Rois, des Héros, qui ne sont plus, c'est-à-dire des hommes dont la mémoire doit vous avertir de votre derniere fin, et vous dégoûter pour jamais de tout ce qui respire la mollesse et la vanité?[129]

Other writers point out that the world to which drama

---

[125] *Traité de la comédie*, p. 72.
[126] Ibid.
[127] Yves de Paris, *L'Agent de Dieu dans le monde*, Paris, 1656, p. 465.
[128] Ibid.
[129] Soanen, Mgr J., 'Sermon pour le 1er dimanche de Carême: sur les spectacles', in *Sermons sur les différents sujets prêchés devant le roy*, 2 vols., Lyons, 1767, i, 61-2. The sermon 'Sur les spectacles' was preached in 1686. The ability to bring historical figures to life is a reason for praise in Rotrou's *Véritable Saint Genest* (ll. 239 seq.).

introduces us is different from our own and resembles the
latter only superficially. Lamy, adding to his statement that
man contemplates eternal beauty only through its manifestation in creatures, claims that poetry maintains this illusion
in men 'en leur cachant la bassesse des creatures, leurs bornes
et leurs imperfections'; furthermore, the images of art are
more attractive and more capable of arresting our gaze than
creatures themselves; he explains that the sweetness to be
found in earthly pleasures always turns to bitterness since the
finest things of this world are not without imperfection;
'mais cela ne se trouve point dans les images que la Poësie
en fait'.[130]

Moreover, the poet's portrayal of passion is such that all
the thorns are removed and readers find perfect portraits
of what they themselves would like to be.[131] The poet
persuades us that 'c'est dans ces amours que consiste le
bonheur que cherche la Nature';[132] two lovers 'dans la disgrace
de la fortune' receive such consolation from each other that
even misfortune is sweet, thus giving rise to the false
assumption that 'de veritables amants ne peuvent jamais être
malheureux'.[133] For this reason the hero must have all the
finest qualities of mind and body, and the heroine herself
must be a 'chef-d'œuvre des Cieux' and 'plus belle que le
soleil'.[134] Poetry thus represents an extremely idealized
world where we are spared the consequences of reality.

The difference between the reordered world of the dramatic
theorists and that of writers like Lamy is one of aims, since
both agree that poetry conforms to some form of ideal
world. For the theorists, subjects treated according to the
rules of *vraisemblance* contribute directly to the improvement of man's conduct; the imaginary world refers us back
to the real one. The religious moralists consider *vraisemblance*
rather as a means of turning us away from the real world or
of investing it with the false values that lead to our corruption.

[130] *Nouvelles réflexions*, pp. 12-13.
[131] Ibid., p. 44.
[132] Ibid., p. 51.
[133] Ibid.
[134] Ibid., pp. 91-2. For Lamy's mistrust of poetry in the context of education,
see Snyders, G., *La Pédagogie en France au XVIIe et au XVIIIe siècles*, Paris,
1965, p. 79.

But the major point of difference between the two sides regarding the value of this ideal world is that for the religious moralists the world of drama is a world without God. One of the letters in Voisin's treatise declares that: 'C'est dans ces pieces où l'on reconnoist le destin et la fortune, comme donnant le bransle à tous les mouvemens du monde, et qu'on leur attribuë le gouvernement qui n'appartient qu'à Dieu seul . . .'[135] The characters themselves become the object of our worship and God is far from the spectator's mind. As Conti writes:

La creature y chasse Dieu du cœur de l'homme, pour y dominer à sa place, y recevoir des sacrifices et des adorations, y regler ses mouvemens, ses conduites, ses interests, et y faire toutes les fonctions de Souverain qui n'appartiennent qu'à Dieu, qui veut y regner par la charité qui est la fin et l'accomplissement de toute la Loy Chrestienne.[136]

[135] *Défense, Lettre I*, p. 475.
[136] *Traité de la comédie et des spectacles*, pp. 27–8.

VI

THE EFFECTS OF DRAMA ON SOCIAL AND RELIGIOUS CONDUCT

It was the considered opinion of the religious moralists that drama led directly and inevitably to the deterioration of our future conduct both social and religious. Conti describes for us the various stages in our moral decline: 'Quels effets peuvent produire ces expressions accompagnées d'une representation reelle: que de corrompre l'imagination, de remplir la memoire, et se répandre apres dans l'entendement, dans la volonté, et ensuite dans les mœurs.'[1] Pégurier comments that once a young girl has learnt all about passion and the conduct which accompanies it 'il faut bon gré mal gré qu'elle mette en pratique ce qu'elle a appris'.[2] Lamy points rather to the pleasure derived from the poetic experience in that we always imitate 'avec joye ce qu'on a vû representer avec plaisir'; just as when a woman accustomed to reading novels notices she is adored 'elle croit être une de ces beautez pour lesquelles les Heros se sont exposez à tant de dangers'.[3] The logical consequence of abandoning our own personality during the performance is to try and become the *other* in reality. In other words we live a fantasy life.

For Coustel age is important in the effect that drama has on the spectator: once a young man has been to the theatre to be inspired by 'l'amour des plaisirs ou du luxe, ou de l'ambition, ou de la vengeance, il est aprés cela bien difficile de l'en guerir'.[4] Not only the young are affected; Rivet refers to women and young girls on the stage 'lesquelles ne sont pas seulement capables d'esmouvoir une populace, mais aussi d'attirer et arrester les yeux des hommes, qui sont d'ailleurs graves et prudents'.[5] It is Bossuet's contention that

---

[1] *Traité de la comédie et des spectacles*, p. 17.
[2] *Réfutation des sentiments relâchés*, pp. 116-17.
[3] *Nouvelles réflexions*, pp. 101-2.
[4] *Sentiments de l'Église*, p. 84.
[5] *L'Instruction chrétienne*, p. 21.

adolescence and even childhood last longer among men, 'ou plutôt on ne s'en défait jamais entièrement'.[6] Hence man is susceptible to corruption throughout his life, despite the apparent maturity which comes with age.

In view of what has been said about the vulnerability of youth it is not surprising that the plight of young girls should be a particular object of attention. One of the letters in Voisin's treatise recounts that one result of allowing young ladies to frequent the theatre is that 'leur esprit s'éveille: la pudeur s'évanoüit, et fait place à l'effronterie: l'honneste liberté degenere en libertinage'.[7] They become such competent actresses that they surpass even those who appear on the stage; they tell their mothers to keep out of the way and 'font des personnages, pratiquent des intrigues, et joüent des pieces qui remplissent leurs maisons de scandales, leurs familles d'opprobres, et toute une ville de la mauvaise odeur de leurs deportemens'.[8] What we have earlier seen criticized as drama is now translated into reality.

But, as the last statement suggests, the individual has a responsibility to the family as a whole. Nicole considers how, in the case of a wife, drama produces disgust for the ordinary but none the less important things of life; because plays are concerned with love affairs or extraordinary events, where characters speak in a way quite different from normal speech, one unconsciously acquires 'une disposition d'esprit toute Romanesque'; women in particular find pleasure in the attentions of young men they meet 'dans les compagnies de divertissement', where they are called 'Nymphes et Deesses'; when they come home 'avec cet esprit évapore' they find everything to their distaste, especially their husbands who 'étant occupez de leurs affaires, ne sont pas toujours en humeur de leur rendre des complaisances ridicules qu'on rend aux femmes dans les Comedies et dans les Romans'.[9] Upon discovering the incompatibility of the substitute world of drama and the real world, we none the less reject the latter in favour of the former.

[6] *Maximes et réflexions*, U/L, p. 218.
[7] *Défense, Lettre II*, p. 487.
[8] Ibid.
[9] *Traité de la comédie*, pp. 61-2.

Coustel remarks that if a young girl marries, having been previously accustomed to frequenting the theatre, she is so preoccupied with herself that she neglects her family and the education of her children; she stays in bed till the late hours of the morning and goes from her bed to the gaming table, on visits and to the opera; all this, he adds, is the fault of drama.[10] For Soanen the theatre is responsible for many divorces which replace a legitimate wife with a wretched actress, thus ruining whole families.[11]

Other writers examine the financial consequences of going to see plays. Vincent recognizes that for some buying theatre tickets entails no hardship but in other cases there are certainly many who 'acheptent ce passe-temps au depens de leurs familles qui ont de la necessité, et auroient besoin de ce qu'ils y mettent pour se nourrir et se vestir'.[12] In the opinion of Lejeune it would be an ideal penance to renounce drama as a diversion, the more so since such abstinence does not damage one's health, diminish one's wealth, inconvenience one's family or disrupt one's business.[13]

Rivet uses the financial issue to refute the argument that drama is not only to be tolerated but is also useful politically in that 'il est bon de donner aux peuples de tels divertissemens, pour les tenir en debvoir, autrement qu'ils pourroient s'eschapper, et se porter à des conjurations ou seditions'.[14] This is in fact d'Aubignac's position some years later in *La Pratique du théâtre*.[15] In Rivet's view, however, such an argument is invalid because very often spectacles are organized not for the *peuple* but for the rich who can afford to pay. Furthermore, the *peuple*, far from being kept within the bounds of duty, are debauched by those who offer them this occasion for pleasure; at present, he continues, the *peuple* are drained of their money with the result that

[10] *Sentiments de l'Église*, p. 72.
[11] *Sermons*, I, 67.
[12] *Traité des théâtres*, p. 7.
[13] Lejeune, le Père J., 'Sermon LXII contre les bals, les danses, ou comedies et autres divertissements mondains qui sont les allumettes de luxure', in *Le Missionnaire de l'Oratoire, ou sermons pour les Avents, Carêmes et fêtes de l'année*, 10 vols., Toulouse, 1689, vol. ii, 483.
[14] *L'Instruction chrétienne*, pp. 75-6.
[15] *Pratique*, pp. 7-10.

families are left in need; spectacles accustom *le commun* to idleness and neglect, and 'empeschent le service de Dieu'; finally, it can be shown that peoples for whom public spectacles have become accepted practice 'ont degeneré de leur ancienne vertu'.[16] His solution is that anything must be prohibited which turns workers away from their tasks, which accustoms them to idleness and curiosity at the expense of their families, which dissuades children from obedience to their parents, turns them from their studies and other 'exercices honnestes', and finally anything which debauches servants and makes them negligent in their duty.[17] For Rivet, as indeed later for Rousseau, the whole social structure was undermined by drama's influence and could only be saved by its total prohibition.

Such are the social effects of drama for the individual and society as a whole. But we are not just social beings; we are also Christians. Firstly, the argument that drama was still tainted by pagan religion is important in the present context, since some religious moralists believed that the experience of passion in itself had pagan associations. Nicole writes that plays are nothing but 'de vives representations de passions d'orgueil, d'ambition, de jalousie, de vengeance, et principalement de cette vertu Romaine, qui n'est autre chose qu'un furieux amour de soi-même'.[18] Henri Lelevel develops this point in his *Entretiens* where poets who portray passion are described as more dangerous than it seems, for their thoughts still bear the marks of the pagan philosophy from which they are derived: 'Ils inspirent la confiance en soi-même, comme si l'homme tiroit la vertu de son propre fond; et l'ame enchantée par leurs vains discours se repaît de vaines idées, et prend un esprit tout Païen.'[19] Later he goes so far as to say that even the best in poets' writings is founded on 'la fierté Stoïque' or 'l'impieté Épicurienne'.[20] Admittedly these statements concern poets in general. But in his work

[16] *L'Instruction chrétienne*, pp. 76–7.
[17] Ibid., pp. 50–1.
[18] *Traité de la comédie*, p. 52. In the text of 1667 this referred exclusively to the tragedies of Corneille (see *Traité de la comédie*, ed. Couton, p. 9).
[19] Lelevel, H., *Entretiens sur ce qui forme l'honnête homme et le vray sçavant*, Paris, 1690, p. 194.
[20] Ibid., p. 201.

against Caffaro Lelevel again declaims against 'le stoïsme de nos Poëtes graves, tres-injurieux au Christianisme'.[21] Thus passion in drama is almost equated with pagan philosophy and its deliberate excitement is a direct affront to the superiority of Christianity, which we betray by the experience of passion.

But there are other reasons why drama is incompatible with our life as Christians. For Vincent one evil associated with drama is loss of time, for we must account for every hour of our lives before God: what, then, will happen to those who, in attending the theatre, abandon their duties and their domestic affairs?[22] Here social behaviour is placed more firmly in a religious context. Lejeune declares that we are wasting the time granted 'pour faire vôtre salut, tems que vous deviez acheter bien precieusement, tems dont un petit quart-d'heure seroit beaucoup estimé et utilement employé par tant de pauvres ames qui sont en enfer, ou en Purgatoire'.[23] Our attendance at the theatre is therefore seen in terms of our collective responsibility for sin. Coustel too tells us that our time is not our own but belongs to Christ; how shall we excuse ourselves before God if we use it in unnecessary activities?[24]

Drama also distracts us from our fundamental Christian practices. Nicole finds that drama is opposed to the state of continual prayer, which is an express commandment given that temptation is also continual. Christians must flee drama because there is nothing 'qui fasse plus sortir l'ame hors de soi, qui la rende plus incapable de s'appliquer aux choses de Dieu, et qui la remplisse davantage de vains fantômes'.[25] One consequence of the spectator's psychological enslavement is that our mind is 'tout occupé des objets exterieurs, et entierement enivré des folies que l'on y voit representer'; we are thus deprived of that state of Christian vigilance which is so necessary for the resistance of temptation.[26] Although Nicole admits that the state of prayer cannot be induced by ourselves, the least we can do is to put no obstacle in its way; God easily pardons

---

[21] *Réponse à la lettre*, p. 31.
[22] *Traité des théâtres*, p. 6.
[23] *Le Missionnaire*, ii, 480-1.

[24] *Sentiments de l'Église*, p. 22.
[25] *Traité de la comédie*, p. 64.
[26] Ibid., p. 44.

distractions born of the fragility of our nature but not those which are voluntary, drama of course being among the latter.[27] Lamy is also of the opinion that introspection is necessary for salvation: God has written in the heart of man truths which should instruct and enlighten him; these truths cannot be perceived by those whose eyes are 'entierement tournez vers les choses exterieures'.[28]

The question of man's eternal interests are not forgotten by religious moralists. Coustel writes that since life on this earth is but one long penance drama induces a spirit contrary to that of grace: '[la comédie] ne travaille qu'à étouffer dans ceux qui la frequentent le souvenir et le regret de leurs pechez, afin qu'ils ne pensent qu'à se divertir, à rire et à passer agréablement leur temps'.[29] Yves de Paris believes that we cannot be Christians and theatre-goers at the same time because our preoccupation with extravagant passions prevents us from serious study or from conducting our business; being strangers to ourselves and in our own country, how can we think of eternity and salvation? 'La lecture des bons livres est le contrepoison de son mal; mais c'est un de ses symptomes, d'en fuir les remedes, et d'aymer ce qui l'aigrit. Vous preniez ces Livres et ces Theatres pour des sujets de divertissements, et vous voyez qu'ils le sont de votre supplice, des égaremens de pensées, des affections illegitimes, qui sont des offences devant Dieu.'[30]

One particular aspect of our religious conduct which is allegedly undermined by drama and which was considered in the seventeenth century as necessary for our salvation is that of alms-giving. The general view was that wealth has been placed in our hands by God and does not belong to us as individuals. The unequal distribution of this wealth which occurs establishes a sacred commerce among men for, theoretically, all wealth which exceeds a reasonable living allowance, the exact amount depending on rank and station, is called *superflu* and destined for the poor. Refusal to

---

[27]   Ibid., p. 65.
[28]   *Nouvelles réflexions*, p. 27.
[29]   *Sentiments de l'Église*, pp. 12-13.
[30]   *Les Vaines Excuses*, II, 342-3.

comply with this is robbery and constitues a mortal sin.[31]

For many religious moralists the money spent on drama is counted among the *superflu*. Vincent is quite explicit: God did not entrust us with wealth in order to pay for amusements which offend him or to 'entretenir des Basteleurs, en une profession deshonneste, et prejudiciable à la Sociéte'.[32] Such actions, he adds, provide less money for the poor whose already great number increases daily.[33] Soanen emphasizes the extent to which drama turns us away from the real world by asking why we should weep at Caesar's death, or bewail the misfortunes of Iphigenia and other 'infortunes Romanesques', when we are insensitive to the ills of our neighbour and when 'on brusque les pauvres au lieu de les assister'.[34]

The question of alms-giving was raised during the *affaire Caffaro*, where it was rather particular members of the audience who attracted most attention. Caffaro himself had remarked upon the gaming activities of abbés, priests, bishops, and other ecclesiastics, complaining that the leniency applied in gaming should also apply to drama.[35] La Grange is by no means lenient to some of the above-mentioned figures: since the Gospel tells us to love our neighbour as ourselves and that we must give the excess of our income to the poor, are not these two precepts violated when 'un Abbé, pour donner du divertissement aux Dames, met par an quarante ou cinquante loüis d'or à la Comédie, dans un tems où les pauvres meurent de faim et de misere'?[36] Coustel too refers to 'Abbés, les jeunes fainéans, les Dames mondaines' and warns them that God will say in his judgement that 'Vous estes coupables de la mort d'autant de personnes que vous en auriez pû sauver en les assistant de ce que vous avez prodigué pour vôtre plaisir.'[37]

---

[31] For a fuller account see le P. Quarré, *Le Riche charitable, ou de l'obligation que les riches ont d'assister les pauvres, et de la manière qu'il faut faire l'aumosne*, Paris, 1653.
[32] *Traité des théâtres*, p. 7.
[33] Ibid.
[34] *Sermons sur differents sujets prêchés devant le roy*, I, 73.
[35] *Lettre d'un théologien*, U/L, p. 97.
[36] *Réfutation d'un écrit*, p. 7.
[37] *Sentiments de l'Église*, p. 87.

But one of the most important points made by religious moralists is that our attendance at theatrical performances is a renunciation of the vows given at our baptism. Vincent describes those who go to see plays as guilty of *perjure*, for they are supposed to have renounced all worldly pomp and the devil.[38] His arguments have added weight because he writes as a Protestant, addressing those who have promised to live 'selon la Reformation sainte qui nous distingue d'avec ceux que l'erreur tient encore dedans ses liens'.[39] Thus attendance at the theatre not only discredits us as Christians but also as members of the reformed religion: our conduct must be exemplary in all our acts. The question of baptism is not, however, limited to such historical circumstances. Nicole suggests that, while nobody would approve of a Carthusian at the theatre in view of the discrepancy between his presence and his holy status, one is not similarly shocked at seeing so many Christians there; the reason for this is that we are ignorant of the implications of our baptismal vow.[40]

This comparison is not without importance. Caffaro mentions that members of the clergy are forbidden to go to the theatre because of their obligation to despise all the vain amusements of the world in order to read and meditate upon the Holy Scriptures.[41] He implies of course that one standard exists for laymen and another for those in holy orders. But it is clear that no such distinction exists for religious moralists; we are bound to renounce the evils of drama because of our vows as Christians. Indeed, Varet, advising his sister on the education of her children, reminds her that marriage is the only difference between a priest and a layman and that otherwise the rigours of religious conduct are the same for both.[42]

There is no doubt that, for these writers, frequenting the theatre leads to an abandonment of our condition as Christians. Soanen's opinion is that we go as far as actively

---

[38] *Traité des théâtres*, p. 17.
[39] Ibid.
[40] *Traité de la comédie*, p. 69. See also Coustel, *Sentiments de l'Église*, p. 15.
[41] *Lettre d'un théologien*, U/L, p. 116.
[42] Varet, A.-L., *L'Éducation chrétienne des enfants selon les maximes de l'Écriture sainte et les instructions des saints Pères*, Paris, 1666, pp. 18-19.

damaging our religion. Too often, he cries, we have heard applauded those who dare insult God on the stage and furthermore 'sous prétexte de louer une saillie, on fait souvent l'éloge d'un blasphême'.[43] Again appreciation of style cannot be separated from approval of evil. And when it comes to going to confession we are reluctant to interrupt our visits to the theatre: 'on s'éloigne des Sacremens, et l'on finit par n'en plus recevoir'; in order to stave off remorse we seek excuses for our own lapsed belief in the works of unbelievers; from this horrifying state we begin to mock the Church, its ministers, and all it prescribes for us.[44] The influence of drama leads to lapsed Christians becoming anti-Christians.

The view that drama undermines the quality of our religious conduct is, however, strongly contested by Caffaro. He declares that through confessions he has been able to discover the real extent of the effects of drama. He contends that if the latter were the source of so much crime surely it would follow that the rich and others who can afford theatre tickets would be the greatest sinners; on the other hand, the poor, who never go, commit no fewer sins of vengeance, impurity, and ambition than the rich; he therefore concludes that 'ces pechez sont des effets de la malice ou de la foiblesse humaine, qui de toutes sortes d'objets indifferemment prennent occasion de pécher'.[45] Caffaro in fact denies drama any special status in the hierarchy of things leading to corruption.

The replies to this point produced more sarcasm than reason. Gerbais asks: 'Qui lui a dit que si ces riches qu'il a confessez n'avoient point du tout été à la Comedie, ils n'auroient pas moins peché que les pauvres, par la bonne éducation qu'ils ont au dessus des pauvres? Qui lui a dit de même que si les pauvres y avoient été comme les riches, ils n'auroient pas peché plus que les riches?'[46] Bossuet answers Caffaro by using a slightly different example, saying that you have only to claim that luxury, 'mollesse', idleness, excessive refinement at table, and the quest for pleasure in

[43] Sermons, I, 76.
[44] Ibid., 76–7.
[45] Lettre d'un théologien, U/L, p. 101.
[46] Lettre d'un docteur de Sorbonne, pp. 97–8.

all things do no harm to the rich because the poor, 'dont l'état est éloigné de tous ces attraits, ne sont point moins corrompus par l'amour des voluptés'.[47] Do you not feel, he asks, that there are things which, while their effect may not be immediate, 'mettent dans les âmes de secrètes dispositions très mauvaises'?[48] We find a more theological reasoning in Lelevel although he distorts Caffaro a little by implying that the latter's complaint is that the poor cannot afford to attend the theatre; Lelevel asks: 'Si la pauvreté ne sert plus à nous rendre vertueux, on n'a nul avantage en cela sur les richesses, à quoi pensoit JESUS-CHRIST d'appeler les pauvres *bien-heureux*, et de dire anathême aux riches?'[49]

But the most contentious point in Caffaro's work was his attitude towards the role of passion. For example Caffaro describes the religious moralists' dire warnings about the dangers of love intrigues and other passions in plays as 'Belles paroles pour un Orateur austère, mais peu solides pour un équitable Theologien.' What a difference there is, he exclaims, between an action and a word which always excite passion and those which do so only *by chance*. The former, he continues, are forbidden and we are obliged to avoid them on pain of mortal sin; but there is nothing more unjust than to condemn the latter; how indeed could we unless we flee to a desert in order to avoid them?[50] Caffaro thus ignores the argument that we go to the theatre expressly for the purpose of experiencing passion and that playwrights seek above all to help us achieve this aim. In order to strengthen his argument he asks whether we must never wear a sword for fear of committing a murder? That would be ridiculous, 'et bien que par malheur il arrive un scandale, et qu'on en prenne occasion de pecher, c'est un scandale passif, et non pas un scandale actif . . . c'est une occasion prise, et non pas une occasion donnée, qui est la seule qu'on ordonne d'éviter, car, pour l'autre, il est impossible de s'y opposer, et quelquefois même de la prévoir'.[51] Drama becomes just one more

[47] *Maximes et réflexions*, U/L, pp. 193–4.
[48] Ibid., p. 194.
[49] *Réponse à la lettre*, pp. 30–1.
[50] *Lettre d'un théologien*, U/L, p. 105.
[51] Ibid., pp. 105–6.

occasion in everyday life where sin is possible but never inevitable.

He concludes from this that plays are not in themselves dangerous and that although particular passions may be their subject they make no necessary impression on the spectator. Indeed he writes earlier in his letter that his information on the state of the theatre had come from '[des] personnes de poids et de probité, lesquelles, avec l'horreur qu'elles ont du peché, ne laissent pas d'assister à ces sortes de spectacles'.[52] He admits that there may be those who feel ill-effects but, he says, let them not return; must we prohibit drama because there are some people who cannot see plays without feeling in themselves the passions portrayed on the stage?[53] The onus is clearly on the individual conscience.

The answer to the point that passion is excited by chance and never by intent in drama has largely been given in the examination of the moral response to drama. Bossuet reminds us, however, that in the case of passion 'il n'y a rien de plus direct, de plus essentiel, de plus naturel à ces pièces, que ce qui fait le dessein formel de ceux qui les composent, de ceux qui les récitent, et de ceux qui les écoutent'.[54] Pégurier mentions that, given the aim of drama, it is rather by chance that passion is not aroused.[55] As for the assertion that drama is only one of a number of things which arouse passion in our everyday life Bossuet replies: 'Sans doute, la conséquence est fort bonne: tout est plein d'inévitables dangers; donc il en faut augmenter le nombre.'[56]

Caffaro's detractors also examine very closely the nature of the circumstances in which sin may be committed, especially with a view to casting doubt on Caffaro's claim that the 'personnes de poids et de probité' he had consulted leave the theatre none the worse for their experience. Here we are introduced to two concepts: firstly, the *occasion prochaine de péché* where sin is the immediate and inevitable effect of a cause; secondly, the *occasion éloignée* where sin

---

[52] Ibid., p. 98.
[53] Ibid., pp. 106–7.
[54] *Maximes et réflexions*, U/L, pp. 175–6.
[55] *Réfutation des sentiments relâchés*, p. 105.
[56] *Maximes et réflexions*, U/L, p. 200.

is possible but not inevitable. Pégurier observes that despite the horror with which these people regard sin they do not cease to attend the theatre; even if drama is not an *occasion prochaine de péché* for everybody, it is for some; furthermore, he tells Caffaro that the people he had consulted cannot hold sin in real horror for 'elles s'exposoient à l'occasion ou prochaine ou éloignée volontairement, avec temerité, et sans quelque necessité'.[57] Pégurier adds that people who really abhor sin would avoid all occasions where sin is even remotely possible, 'quoi-que je ne prétende pas les y obliger'.[58] This last statement appears at first sight to be a concession in that Pégurier has admitted sin not to be a necessary consequence for everybody: we are, however, swiftly disabused for it is sufficient that the occasion be *prochaine* for some and *éloignée* for others 'de sorte pourtant qu'elle les engage insensiblement dans le peché; cela suffit . . . pour que tout le monde la doive éviter'.[59]

Religious moralists are indeed quick to point to the dangers of exposing ourselves voluntarily to a situation where there is the slightest possibility of sin. Firstly, we completely alter our relationship with God. Bossuet comments that he will help us in those temptations which we cannot avoid but will abandon those who seek them.[60] Rivet's position is that, since people are always asking God to lead them not into temptation, what excuse can those who 's'y jettent de gayeté de cœur' give?[61] This attitude is also expressed in the work of Nicole when he tells us that there is presumption and folly in believing that God will always deliver us by his grace from a danger to which we willingly expose ourselves.[62] In Soanen's opinion certain impressions may be resisted 'lorsqu'elles ne sont qu'un sentiment passager excité par la violence de quelque tentation', but when they come from such a premeditated act as going to the theatre, then the soul is powerless to defend itself and we end up doubting

[57] *Réfutation des sentiments relâchés*, p. 71.
[58] Ibid., p. 72.
[59] Ibid., p. 73.
[60] *Maximes et réflexions*, U/L, p. 201.
[61] *L'Instruction chrétienne*, p. 43.
[62] *Traité de la comédie*, p. 46.

the most certain truths.[63] Finally, we return to Caffaro's notion of chance when Coustel tells us that, 'en allant volontairement à la comedie, l'on devient coupable de toutes les mauvaises pensées qu'on y peut avoir par hazard, et de tous les pechés qu'on n'auroit pas dessein de commettre'.[64] Remember Caffaro had said that we could not always foresee what was going to happen. Coustel suggests that we should never put ourselves in a position to find out.

But the strongest reaction greeted Caffaro's suggestion that people of a psychologically weak disposition should not return to the theatre. His detractors read into his statement the implication that there were people completely immune to corruption in the theatre. Lelevel exclaims, 'doit-il ainsi mettre les ames à l'épreuve?' Where, he adds, is he who can say that he will not be moved by spectacle? He cites a young man 'qui n'a que des sens' or a young woman with 'le cerveau tendre et délicat' as those most likely to acquire 'l'amour des grandeurs et des plaisirs'.[65] Sin for these, he suggests, is inevitable.

The *Décision*, however, points out that the knowledge we have of our weakness must lead us to beware not to expose ourselves to a situation where God is usually offended.[66] Indeed this is a problem envisaged some years earlier by Rivet: if someone says that he is resolved to feel no ill-effects at the theatre, 'Quand il seroit aussi dur et serré qu'il se propose', he should remember the saying that 'les esprits de fer, ne laissent pas d'estre domptéz et amolis par le feu de la concupiscence'.[67] It is Vincent's opinion that drama's advocates are forced to admit the half-truth that danger exists for those with an 'esprit foible'; but, he continues, the exemption from this danger of the 'esprits forts' is of no serious consequence and, moreover, sheer presumption; men are not angels and are all subject to the same passions.[68] Indeed, the apparent absence of effect is not proof that

---

[63] *Sermons*, I, 75.
[64] *Sentiments de l'Église*, p. 114.
[65] *Réponse à la lettre*, pp. 34–5.
[66] *Décision faite en Sorbonne*, pp. 89–90.
[67] *L'Instruction chrétienne*, p. 44.
[68] *Traité des théâtres*, pp. 61–2.

none at all has occurred. According to Nicole, just as God has sown the seeds of good in our heart, so the devil has sown those of evil, bringing them to fruition when he pleases; at first we may feel no perceptible temptation but after a long time 'il les excite et les réveille, sans même qu'on se souvienne comment elles y sont entrées, afin de leur faire porter des fruits de mort . . .'[69] Bossuet too maintains that we do not fall at once: sometimes corruption comes in large doses but at others it insinuates itself little by little; the sickness is in the blood before it breaks into fever.[70] Héliodore believes that even the good come to enjoy evil because it contaminates them unknowingly: it is only recognized as such when the damage is done and the heart has passed 'de la vertu à l'indifférence, de l'indifférence au peché, du peché quelque-fois à la coûtume, à l'insensibilité, à l'impudence'.[71] Coustel writes that we pay insufficient attention to the thoughts which insinuate themselves into our hearts and which are none the less 'fort criminelles devant Dieu'.[72] We are therefore judged for what we do not know nor perhaps ever find out. Finally, Conti considers that those who claim not to have been at all affected by drama are few or of bad faith; the only reason drama has not corrupted their morals is that it has found them already corrupt.[73]

An important question is raised by the suggestion that some people may attend the theatre not from choice but from duty. The author of one letter in Voisin's treatise allows for such a possibility, commenting that 'il se peut faire que quelques-uns y iront sans y avoir d'affection'.[74] Pégurier too makes such a concession when, in his remark about spectators who feel no ill-effects, he admits that some may go from obedience to a husband or a parent, or, as in the case of those attached to the court, as a duty; he adds that, since these people go to the theatre neither because it is their inclination, nor because they want to do so, it cannot be doubted that

---

[69]   *Traité de la comédie*, p. 47.
[70]   *Maximes et réflexions*, U/L, pp. 196–7.
[71]   Héliodore de Paris, le R. P., *Discours sur les sujets les plus ordinaires des désordres du monde*, 4 vols., Paris, 1684–6, i, 308.
[72]   *Sentiments de l'Église*, p. 126.
[73]   *Traité de la comédie et des spectacles*, p. 18.
[74]   *Défense, Lettre I*, p. 473.

God protects them from a danger to which they are exposed involuntarily.[75]

However, the author of the other letter in Voisin's treatise does not share the same lenient attitude and reproaches a mother for taking her daughter to the theatre in the company of a marquise when she had every reason to refuse.[76] The problem is indeed often seen in terms of parental conduct. Rivet speaks with disgust of fathers and husbands who permit their daughters and wives to attend the theatre, and to approve by their very presence everything that the actors do and say.[77] The anonymous preacher from Cologne refers to the responsibilities of public figures and 'gens de qualité', whose conduct must be as examplary before their own family as it is before the people; they must therefore forbid their wives and daughters to go and see plays.[78] It is Vincent's opinion that those who send or accompany their children to the theatre 'les remettent à de mauvais Maistres, et les adressent à une eschole tres dangereuse'.[79] Finally, according to the *Décision*, since drama is bad in practice, attendance is forbidden even in cases where parents oblige their children to accompany them; people must do what they can to be exempted from it because it could lead to the possibility of offending God.[80]

The most important consideration for many religious moralists, however, was the spectator's responsibility before the Church as a Christian. Bossuet complains that the people who claim no ill-effects from drama 'ignorent que quand ils seraient si forts et tellement à toute épreuve qu'ils n'auraient rien à craindre pour eux-mêmes, ils auraient

---

[75] *Réfutation des sentiments relâchés*, pp. 113-14.

[76] *Défense, Lettre II*, p. 483.

[77] *L'Instruction chrétienne*, pp. 46-7.

[78] Anon., *Instructions morales et populaires sur les spectacles et les dances recueillies de quelques sermons prêchés par un missionnaire*, Cologne, n.d., p. 35. The copy of this work in the Bibliothèque de l'Arsenal has no date. A reference to Molière's death 'depuis quelques jours' suggests 1673 or 1674 as possible dates of publication. But further evidence may be provided in Chappuzeau's *Théâtre françois* where he remarks upon finding people in Cologne who declaimed against drama. Perhaps his work, published in 1674, was a reply to these attacks, although it is equally possible that the *Instructions* may have been published later.

[79] *Traité des théâtres*, p. 11.

[80] *Décision faite en Sorbonne*, pp. 129-30.

encore à craindre le scandale qu'ils donnent aux autres'.[81] A definition of the term *scandale* is provided by Rivet's *Instruction chrétienne* where he writes that even those who feel no ill-effects are in a state of sin 'Car ils sont en scandale et en achopement aux infirmes, qu'ils attirent dans les filets par leur exemple.'[82] Thus we encourage others to sin by our example. Vincent considers the 'esprits forts' to be particularly guilty since, admitting as they do to the danger of drama for the 'esprits foibles', 'Combien sont esloignez ici de la charité, ceux qui ne font nulle consideration de l'achopement qu'ils y donnent à leurs prochains?'[83] But as in the case of baptismal vows Vincent is aware of the circumstantial importance of his arguments in that it is the Reformed Church that is mocked when others see its members rushing to the theatre.[84] The conduct of the individual is directly related to the reputation of the sect as a whole.

Therefore, even though a spectator may remain unharmed by the dramatic experience, his presence attracts and encourages others of a weaker disposition. But our presence at the theatre has other consequences: as shown in a later chapter the actor's profession was considered illicit in the eyes of the Church, for it debauched not only the actor but also the spectators. The actor, whose intention it is to corrupt, is in a state of sin. But we as spectators, Coustel writes, are responsible for maintaining him in this state and therefore answerable to God for the sin itself.[85] What is more, by our presence and applause, we *approve* of what happens on the stage.[86]

Drama was, however, thought particularly dangerous in its capacity as a collective experience, as the notion of *scandale* suggests. The spectator is considered subject to certain social pressures to which he is afraid of failing to conform. Bossuet observes a 'malignité spéciale' in such assemblies where the aim is to arouse the senses:[87] as a

---

[81]   *Maximes et réflexions*, U/L, p. 199.
[82]   *L'Instruction chrétienne*, p. 45.
[83]   *Traité des théâtres*, p. 63.
[84]   Ibid., p. 18.
[85]   *Seniments de l'Église*, p. 87.
[86]   Ibid., p. 25.
[87]   *Maximes et réflexions*, U/L, p. 209.

member of an audience we are afraid of being the odd man out:

on se fait comme un point d'honneur de sentir ce qui doit toucher, et on croirait troubler la fête, si on n'était enchanté avec toute la compagnie. Ainsi, outre les autres inconvénients des assemblées de plaisir, on s'excite et on s'autorise, pour ainsi dire, les uns les autres par le concours des acclamations et des applaudissements, et l'air même qu'on y respire est plus malin.[88]

Again the spectator loses control and constraint because of external factors: he cannot remain independent when surrounded by others who are in fact seeking the same enjoyment as himself. The *Décision* finds there is a sort of union or common accord in the audience, 'ce qui fait que le peché qu'il y a en cette occasion, devient celuy de chaque particulier'.[89] There is thus a complicity among the spectators and the mere fact of being together means that sin is inevitable. Rivet even believes that the more people there are the more effort is made by actors to debauch them.[90]

More specifically, it is the theatre as a social occasion which some writers consider alarming. According to the *Décision* the number of people found at the theatre is dangerous, particularly for the rendezvous made there.[91] In an argument inspired by St. Clement of Alexandria it is for Coustel 'le mélange des hommes et des femmes, qui ne viennent en ce lieu que pour s'entreregarder, et qui se parent à ce dessein', which gives rise to 'une infinité de pechez'.[92] Lamy remarks with Tertullian that everybody attends the theatre to see and to be seen.[93] It is not only the plays which offer possibilities of sinning but the mere fact of seeking to be part of a crowd.

Theatre-going, then, is the beginning of a long road to corruption for each person who attends. But it concerns not only the individual conscience. The soul of the collectivity, be it in a social or religious context, is endangered by our attendance at a public assembly where

[88] Ibid., p. 209.
[89] *Décision faite en Sorbonne*, pp. 92-3.
[90] *L'Instruction chrétienne*, p. 13.
[91] *Décision faite en Sorbonne*, p. 80.
[92] *Sentiments de l'Église*, p. 18.
[93] *Nouvelles réflexions*, p. 198.

the object is pleasure. The introspection so necessary to our salvation is to be found in the cohesion of the family or society regarded as one in their Christianity; attention must be turned inwards towards one's duty rather than outwards towards one's pleasure.

VII

MORAL INSTRUCTION
AND COMEDY

Against the religious moralists' conception of drama as morally and socially harmful the dramatic theorists held that drama fulfilled a didactic function and that man was led thereby to moral improvement. Not surprisingly, the moralists were highly sceptical of this claim. This was particularly so in the case of comedy where, according to dramatic theorists, the source of instruction lies in the correction of vice by its exposure to public ridicule. The moralists utterly reject comedy with its particular concern for ridicule and laughter as a means of moral improvement, especially when they consider *Le Tartuffe* which, in its portrayal of the hypocrite, is alleged to have a positively harmful effect on the spectator. The *Lettre sur la comédie de l'Imposteur*, in upholding the play as an important contribution to our protection against hypocrites, will therefore serve as an interesting contrast to the religious moralists' views. First of all, however, how do they regard the notion of moral instruction in general?

An important feature of moral instruction was the punishment of vice and the reward of virtue. Pégurier contests the very basis of this principle; 'le châtiment ou la recompense d'une action ou d'une parole n'en change pas la nature, et n'est pas une preuve de sa bonté ou de sa malignité'.[1] In other words, the punishment or reward of an act is not necessarily a moral guide to the value of that act. Moreover, Lamy believes that the poet's deference to his audience rules out the effectiveness of punishment and reward; since poets do all in their power to make us love and esteem a character it then becomes necessary to fulfil the spectators' expectations for that character, 'et qu'enfin il luy arrive le bien qu'ils luy souhaittent'.[2] Equally poets never fail to bring

---

[1] *Réfutation des sentiments relâchés*, p. 93.
[2] *Nouvelles réflexions*, pp. 179–80.

the vengeance of heaven upon their hero's enemies 'et de leur faire souffrir quelque peine extraordinaire'; they cannot allow the audience to leave without such consolation because they would then leave the theatre dissatisfied.[3] Here punishment has no moral foundation and is determined by the likes and dislikes of the spectator. One wonders to what extent Lamy was familiar with the theoretical writings of Corneille.

But for Lamy the very portrayal of vice is not conducive to moral improvement, especially when hatred and ambition are depicted so as to make them attractive.[4] Although some vices in drama may inspire our horror this is owing rather to their nature than to their portrayal; as far as Oedipus' parricide and incest are concerned 'La seule crainte des supplices rigoureux ordonnez par les Loix retient assez de ce côté-là.'[5] Poets can claim no virtue in such cases. Finally, the hero, as shown in an earlier chapter, embodies the false values propagated by drama in such a way that they call for emulation not rejection; although poets do not openly praise vice itself they praise the characters in whom it is found.[6]

The fact that punishment comes only at the end of a play is a further cause of concern to the religious moralists, who contend that by this time the spectators have already been corrupted. Gerbais remarks that even if crimes such as parricide and incest are finally punished on stage 'c'est aprés avoir laissé la liberté à des impies de blasphêmer, et d'insulter au Ciel et à ses foudres'.[7] Similarly, Coustel observes that although in *Dom Juan* the central character becomes in the end an example of divine justice his punishment makes much less impression on the heart of an evil spectator than 'les maximes detestables qu'on luy entend debiter, n'en font sur les esprits'.[8] What is more, punishment of this sort is ineffectual because men have made an amusement of heaven's wrath and even of hell; how can a man be moved by the truth of religion when he finds all this agreeable and can even

---

[3] Ibid., pp. 178-9.
[4] Ibid., p. 189.
[5] Ibid.
[6] Ibid.
[7] *Lettre d'un docteur de Sorbonne*, p. 56.
[8] *Sentiments de l'Église*, p. 69.

laugh at it?[9] The comic context in itself is sufficient to render the effect of punishment null and void.

Besides the element of punishment dramatic theorists also recommended the use of moral *sententiae*, although these were subject to many restrictions. They advised that if vice remains unpunished it must at least be condemned by one of the characters in the play. For Conti this is clearly insufficient: after spreading his poison throughout the play 'd'une maniere agreable, delicate et conforme à la nature et au temperament', the poet 'croit en estre quitte pour faire quelque discours moral par un vieux Roy representé, pour l'ordinaire par un fort méchant Comedien, dont le roole est desagreable, dont les vers sont secs et languissans, quelques fois mesme mauvais: mais tout du moins negligés, parce que c'est dans ces endroits que [le poète] se deslasse des efforts d'esprit qu'il vient de faire en traittant les passions'.[10] Moral instruction is thus far from being the main object of the poet and moral maxims are seen as a form of relaxation after the effort exerted in portraying passion. Moral instruction is an afterthought.

Bossuet's opinion of moral teaching in the theatre is that 'la touche en est trop legere' and 'il n'y a rien de moins sérieux, puisque l'homme y fait à la fois un jeu de ses vices et un amusement de la vertu'.[11] The fact that drama is an entertainment precludes the dramatist from any serious attempt to improve man's conduct in society. For Vincent the problem is more fundamental in that stories which are scripturally or historically authenticated are far more suited to teach than plays 'qu'on sçait estre de nuës fictions, et des contes forgés à plaisir'.[12] It is because drama is fiction that it cannot be used for moral instruction.

There are, however, certain attitudes among the spectators which in themselves render the moral instruction in drama useless. Yves de Paris is concerned about the audience's

---

[9] Ibid., pp. 71-2.
[10] *Traité de la comédie et des spectacles*, pp. 34-5. In the *Examen* to *Nicomède*, Corneille mentions this very point about the role of kings being given to poor actors (*Writings*, p. 85). It may well be that this is the source of Conti's remark.
[11] *Maximes et réflexions*, U/L, p. 276.
[12] *Traité des théâtres*, p. 44.

realization of the difference between the social status of the
characters and their own: he explains that compared with the
great crimes of political usurpers the sins of ordinary life
appear to spectators as inconsequential; 'leur conscience s'y
tient asseurée, et sans en concevoir des remords, elle se croyt
assez juste de n'estre point si meschante'.[13] For Héliodore
too the comparisons made by the spectators with the
characters have the opposite of a moral effect; the weaknesses
we recognize in ourselves seem more excusable 'dans la
multitude des complices' and slight alongside those which
make such an impression on the stage.[14] The spectator,
confronted with crimes beyond his capacity and with weaknesses shared by many others, sinks into a sort of moral
self-satisfaction.

But it is the concupiscent nature of man that is seen as
the major obstacle to the success of moral instruction. As
Lamy comments, evil makes a stronger impression than good
on a man's mind; for one person who imitates a hero's virtue
there are a thousand who imitate his vices.[15] Rivet refuses to
believe that the presentation of 'les sinistres evenemens des
amours mal entrepris' or other reprehensible acts are useful
when men are 'bien plus susceptibles du mal qui est enseigné,
qu'émeus par la peine qui le suit; se promettant tousjours
qu'ils seront plus fins et plus advisés, et [ils] se garderont bien
de l'evenement, contre lequel ils semblent estre premunis'.[16]
Again the opposite of a moral effect is achieved because we
learn to be more cunning in committing sinful acts rather
than learning never to commit them.

One point arising from this discussion is that, if man is
more receptive to evil than to good, it follows that to give
moral instruction by portraying evil is a contradiction in
terms. Yves de Paris writes that: 'Quand le dessein principal
seroit de condamner la tyrannie, en faisant voir ses progrez
tousjours orageux, et sa fin ordinairement miserable, ces
noires pratiques salissent tousjours l'esprit des assistances:
elles y laissent les idées d'un mal, dont la passion se peut

---

[13] *L'Agent de Dieu*, p. 467.   [15] *Nouvelles réflexions*, p. 190.
[14] *Discours*, i, 279-80.   [16] *L'Instruction chrétienne*, p. 23.

servir en mille rencontres, et qu'il estoit meilleur d'ignorer.'[17]
Héliodore sees the inclusion of evil characters in certain plays
as not necessarily leading to evil but as none the less
obstructing the efforts of virtue; the spectator feels move-
ments of virtue and vice according to the different roles; he
hesitates between the two when actors recite something
morally indifferent and is moved to neither virtue nor vice.[18]
Vincent states quite simply: 'Il ne faut pas faire une plaie
sous esperance de la guerir.'[19]

An important aspect of man's concupiscent nature is his
inclination for pleasure; moral instruction in drama runs
directly counter to this inclination and is therefore greatly
attenuated in its effect. In the words of Godeau 'Le remede
y plaist moins que ne fait le poison.'[20] Voisin seems in no
doubt that pleasure and amusement rather than moral profit
are what the spectator seeks in the theatre.[21] Lamy suggests
that, far from being dissuaded from vice, the corrupt indulge
in the pleasure of seeing and hearing what they are particularly
inclined towards: furthermore, we are not able to suffer those
who are of the opposite opinion to ourselves and we look
upon them as censors.[22] Moral instruction is repugnant to the
very people who need it because it interrupts their pleasure.

Some writers refuse to believe that there is any intention
of instructing in the first place. The poet in fact models his
characters on the corrupt nature of his audience precisely
in order that they should derive the maximum pleasure from
their own corruption. Voisin says that the sole aim of drama
is to 'plaire au peuple, dont le plus grand nombre estant
vitieux, il faut necessairement que la Comedie ait quelque
chose de vitieux pour luy estre agreable'; this must be so, he
adds, because one of the greatest playwrights of the century
is obliged to admit that the aim of drama is not to 'avoir
égard aux bonnes mœurs'.[23] Nicole refers to the way a poet

[17] *L'Agent de Dieu*, p. 467.
[18] *Discours*, i, 304.
[19] *Traité des théâtres*, p. 44.
[20] *Poésies chrétiennes*, p. 464.
[21] *Défense*, p. 216.
[22] *Nouvelles réflexions*, p. 38.
[23] *Défense*, pp. 357–8. The reference is to Corneille in the *Épitre* of the *Suite du Menteur*.

defers to his audience when he mentions that since the poet's aim is pleasure, he flatters the inclinations of his audience, which tend towards the most harmful passions. Consequently, he adds, there is nothing more pernicious than 'La Morale Poëtique et Romanesque' which is but a mass of false opinion derived from man's concupiscent nature and pleasurable only in so far as it flatters the spectator's corrupt instinct.[24] Senault points out that poets are men like any others and subject to the moral disorder which spares no man; moreover, they are able to express violent and unjust passions better than their opposites, so well in fact that they unintentionally encourage the sin they wish to destroy and help the fight against the virtue they wish to defend.[25] Corrupt playwrights cannot improve corrupt spectators with corrupt maxims.

In the earlier discussion of the dramatic theorists it was observed that despite their admission that man was reluctant to be taught, they were none the less optimistic regarding the possibility of man's correction through the dramatic experience. It is, however, clear that the religious moralists considered such optimism to be totally unfounded. Theory does not coincide with practice; as Conti remarks, it is only in books of poetics that moral instruction is the aim of drama: this aim exists 'ny dans l'intention du Poëte, ny dans celle du spectateur. Le desir de plaire est ce qui conduit le premier, et le second est conduit par le plaisir d'y voir peintes des passions semblables aux siennes: car nôtre amour-propre est si delicat, que nous aimons à voir les portraits de nos passions aussi bien de ceux de nos personnes'.[26] The vanity produced by our own corruption encourages us to admire rather than to eradicate it.

From the religious moralists' rejection of the general claim of drama to instruct, the more specific question of comedy which is alleged to correct vice by exposing it to public ridicule can be considered. Dramatic theorists regarded comedy as much less worthy of attention than tragedy and as a result tended to dismiss it in a few brief sentences. Scudéry's manner is certainly condescending when he writes that 'quelque

[24] *Traité de la comédie*, pp. 54–5.
[25] *Le Monarque*, pp. 233–4.
[26] *Traité de la comédie et des spectacles*, pp. 23–4.

facetieuse que soit la Comedie pure, elle ne laisse pas de servir aux mœurs et d'enseigner en divertissant',[27] although evidently he does not deny its usefulness. Similarly, La Mesnardière says that comedy 'n'est pas tellement inutile à l'institution du peuple, bien qu'elle semble estre formée pour son divertissement, qu'elle ne corrige ses mœurs, lors mesme qu'elle les expose'.[28] But Rapin is more explicit: the purpose of comedy is to 'corriger le peuple par la crainte d'estre moqué',[29] and he defines comedy as 'une image de la vie commune' which corrects 'les defauts publics, en faisant voir le ridicule des défauts particuliers'.[30] Furthermore, comedy is worthless 'dés qu'on ne s'y reconnoist point, et dés qu'on n'y voit pas ses manieres et celles des personnes avec qui l'on vit'.[31] We must therefore be able to recognize ourselves in the stage character or we shall not be in a position to correct the faults which expose us to public ridicule. The claim for comedy as a useful moral corrective is made by Molière in his preface to *Le Tartuffe* where he holds that 'rien ne reprend mieux la plupart des hommes que la peinture de leurs défauts';[32] he goes on: 'C'est une grande atteinte aux vices que de les exposer à la risée de tout le monde. On souffre aisément des répréhensions, mais on ne souffre point la raillerie. On veut bien être méchant; mais on ne veut point être ridicule.'[33]

D'Aubignac, however, is not at all sure that comedy is a suitable vehicle for moral instruction, although admittedly he is writing about pre-Molière comedy where the emphasis on intrigue reduced the possibilities of instruction in any case. But, d'Aubignac explains, if the playwright does introduce moral maxims or 'les nobles mouvements de la Vertu' he runs the great risk of boring the spectator 'parce qu'on sort du genre Comique pour passer dans un autre plus élevé'.[34] Moral instruction has no place in comedy because it is not appropriate to the lowly rank and station of the characters. Indeed 'méme il faut souvent y corrompre les beaux sentimens de la Morale, et les traiter en burlesque, c'est-à-dire,

[27] Gasté, p. 461.
[28] *Poétique*, p. K.
[29] *Réflexions*, xxv, p. 154.
[30] Ibid., x, p. 94.
[31] Ibid., xxv, p. 155.
[32] *Œuvres*, iv, 377.
[33] Ibid., 377-8.
[34] *Pratique*, p. 285.

Comiquement'.[35] Instruction is undesirable in comedy because, in order to maintain the tone of the genre, moral sententiae would have to be burlesqued.

The *Lettre sur la comédie de l'Imposteur* is the only work of any length which does full justice to comedy in the seventeenth century as a serious dramatic form. This document (which, if we accept René Robert's arguments,[36] was written either by Molière himself or by someone directly inspired by him) was provoked by the adverse reactions to the 1667 version of *Le Tartuffe*, which had as title *L'Imposteur*, and in which the principal character was not Tartuffe but Panulphe. The *Lettre* offers not only an extended and intelligent analysis of the play itself but also contains a detailed argument regarding the moral function the play serves in striking a blow against would-be seducers. The author particularly stresses the positive effect the play has on the spectator which derives from the experience of seeing the ridicule of vice in action. The most important feature of the *Lettre*, however, is a theory of comedy which, while based on a single play, has far-reaching general implications, particularly as regards the concept of the ridiculous, and the manner in which the spectator responds to its presentation in a play.

The author begins his argument with the general proposition that we are all possessed of Reason and hence able to follow it. But in addition Nature has provided Reason with 'quelque sorte de forme extérieure et de dehors reconnoissable'.[37] When we see this we experience 'une joie mêlée d'estime'; equally, when we see something that departs from the reasonable we experience 'une joie mêlée de mépris'. The latter is none other than the means we use to recognize *le ridicule*. The author's precise definition of *le ridicule* is the 'forme extérieure et sensible' which Nature in her providence has attached to 'tout ce qui est déraisonnable'.[38]

But in order to appreciate fully what is ridiculous we must, the author considers, first understand the reasonable. The

[35] Ibid., p. 286.
[36] Robert, R., 'Des commentaires de première main sur les chefs-d'œuvre les plus discutés de Molière', *Revue des sciences humaines*, 1956, pp. 19–49.
[37] Molière, *Œuvres*, iv, 559.
[38] Ibid., 559–60.

latter has as its 'marque sensible' the *quod decet* of the
Ancients, which he translates as *bienséance*; this in turn
is a concrete manifestation of *convenance*, i.e. that which
is congruous. Thus 'ce qui sied bien' is always founded
on 'quelque raison de convenance'. The ridiculous is thus a
matter of *disconvenance*. Panulphe's attempted seduction
of Elmire is, according to the author, incongruous for two
reasons: firstly, because his public image of piety does not
conform with his *galanterie* in private; secondly, because the
means he chooses do not succeed — in other words, they are
inappropriate to his design.[39]

There now follow more precise indications as to the value
of our experience of Panulphe for our future conduct. The
spectator cannot fail to recognize what is ridiculous in
Panulphe because of the playwright's exaggeration of
Panulphe's technique of seduction and his failure to succeed.
The author of the *Lettre*, however, foresees the possible
objection that what is made to look 'extremely' ridiculous
in Panulphe will not appear so to the same degree in other
such persons we may encounter elsewhere.[40] His reply is
that on any other occasion that a man like Panulphe attempts
to seduce a woman she will be warned because she will
experience the same pleasure (i.e. 'une joie mêlée de mépris')
as when she saw the play.[41] Moreover, this experience of
pleasure will prevent her, in her initial reaction at least, from
distinguishing between Panulphe and her would-be seducer.[42]
The existence of pleasure in her reaction derives only from
the features shared by the two persons. The author makes the
general (and unwittingly controversial) point that since we
are reluctant to change our attitude towards things we have
considered ridiculous, we can never treat them seriously
again.[43] This remark assumes great importance when
considering the religious moralists' objections to the way
true and false piety are allegedly confused in *Le Tartuffe*.

But while the experience of the ridiculous is pleasurable

[39] Ibid., 560.
[40] Ibid., 561.
[41] Ibid.
[42] Ibid.
[43] Ibid., 563

for the woman who is the object of an attempted seduction, it is certainly not so for the person who is the object of ridicule. The author of the *Lettre* explains that the 'sentiment du ridicule' is the coldest of all responses for a person making amorous advances.[44] In this sense the feeling that one has been found ridiculous, especially by the woman one is trying to seduce, is enough to make anyone stop in their tracks.[45] And indeed it is not merely by reference to *L'Imposteur* that such would-be seducers are ridiculous; they are so absolutely speaking, since any *galant* who adopts this kind of approach must, given that he could not honourably avow his motives publicly, be in some degree 'dissimulé et hypocrite', and 'tout mensonge, déguisement, fourberie, dissimulation, toute apparence différente du fond, enfin toute contrariéte entre actions qui procèdent d'un même principe, est essentiellement ridicule'.[46]

The 'joie mêlée de mépris' we experience before the ridiculous thus serves to warn us of certain types of behaviour. But there is another feature of our response to *le ridicule*: 'la providence de la nature a voulu que tout ce qui est méchant eût quelque degré de ridicule, pour redresser nos voies par cette apparence de défaut de raison, et pour piquer notre orgueil naturel, par le mépris qu'excite nécessairement ce défaut, quand il est apparent comme il est par le ridicule'.[47] Pride, then, is an additional factor in our response and is an integral part of 'une joie mêlée de mépris'. Indeed our scorn for the person who is ridiculed derives from the conviction that we are his moral superiors, since we do not share the fault which leads to his exposure as ridiculous.

But there is a little more to it than this. Comedy is seen as a means of actively persuading ourselves and others of our moral superiority; the author explains that the soul 'se défiant, à bon droit, de sa propre excellence depuis le péché d'origine, cherche de tous côtés avec avidité de quoi la persuader aux autres et à soi-même par des comparaisons qui lui soient avantageuses, c'est-à-dire par la considération

---

[44] Ibid., 562.
[45] Ibid., 564.
[46] Ibid., 564.
[47] Ibid.

des défauts d'autrui'.[48] Comedy is a monument to our vanity,
a fact which will not be overlooked by the religious moralists.

The author of the *Lettre* is in no doubt that the notion of
le ridicule, as he outlines it, is 'une des plus sublimes matières
de la véritable morale'.[49] But it is clear from our analysis that
the author of the *Lettre* does not envisage the moral value
of comedy in the same way as Scudéry, La Mesnardière, or
even Molière in the preface to *Le Tartuffe*. There is in the
Lettre not one word about the value of comedy as a corrective
of vice; at the very most the suggestion is that the Panulphes
of this world will, because they find being ridiculed disagreeable, desist from their immediate efforts at seduction. The
spectator is not corrected in any way because he is from the
start convinced of his own moral perfection. Comedy in the
Lettre is seen rather as a means of arming us against certain
types of conduct which we may encounter on future
occasions. The person instructed is not the person who
practises vice but the person who might otherwise become
its victim.

Those writers who believe that comedy may correct faults
talk in very general terms without at the same time specifying
the limitations of the genre. Certain religious moralists,
however, are firm in the belief that comedy's powers are
limited and that ridicule is an inadequate weapon for its
supposed task. Lamy points to the restricted nature of the
faults comedy may correct when he remarks that poets
effectively condemn by ridicule only minor defects such as
the moodiness of old men, their meanness, their harsh
treatment of young people, and the ease with which they allow
themselves to be deceived.[50] On the other hand, 'l'impudicité
regne dans leurs Ouvrages, quoy qu'elle y paroisse sous les
habits de la vertu', for the idol of comedy is still a young man
'brûlé d'un feu criminel'.[51] Bossuet too considers that the
most important vices are left untouched; Molière has shown
how little advantage is to be gained from moral teaching in the
theatre which attacks only 'le ridicule du monde, en lui

[48] Ibid., 565.
[49] Ibid., 559.
[50] *Nouvelles réflexions*, p. 187. See also Coustel, *Sentiments de l'Église*, p. 73.
[51] *Nouvelles réflexions*, p. 187.

laissant cependant toute sa corruption'.[52]

Lamy too denies the usefulness of ridicule in the war against vice: he comments that certainly avarice is ridiculed, and the debauchery and love life of young men condemned; but it is not 'par des railleries que l'on détruit le vice, particulierement celuy de l'impureté; such a vice is too important to be cured by such a feeble remedy, 'et même souvent on prend plaisir à s'en voir raillé'.[53] Ridicule is too weak to combat vice, especially when combined with the pleasure of the experience, for, as remarked on earlier, the vanity of man leads him to derive pleasure from his own corruption. It is Lamy's contention that our inclination for pleasure is too strong for restraint by shame alone and in any case 'on espere toûjours la pouvoir eviter par le secret, dont on tâche de couvrir ses desordres aux yeux des hommes'.[54] Comedy is thus considered to have the opposite effect of that desired by Rapin and others in that public exposure of our vices leads us to be more secretive.

There are some writers who attack comedy not on the grounds that it is inadequate to instruct but on the grounds that it provides lessons in the very things it is supposed to eradicate. Vincent refers to portraits of filial disobedience and seduction.[55] Coustel considers not only that Sganarelle in L'École des maris is talking sense,[56] but that many young people will learn how to act the passionate lover from Arnolphe's example![57] Moreover, Lamy and Lebrun believe that the values which are most often ridiculed should rather be proposed as exemplary; for the latter, quoting the author of the République des lettres, Molière's plays are dangerous because 'on y tourne perpetuellement en ridicule les soins que les peres et les meres prennent de s'opposer aux engagemens amoureux de leurs enfans'.[58]

What, according to the religious moralists, is the spectator's response to comedy? An analysis of the Lettre sur la comédie

---

[52] *Maximes et réflexions*, U/L, p. 185.
[53] *Nouvelles réflexions*, p. 186.
[54] Ibid., pp. 186-7.
[55] *Traité des théâtres*, pp. 9-10.
[56] *Sentiments de l'Église*, p. 77.
[57] Ibid., p. 79.
[58] *Discours*, p. 29. See *Nouvelles réflexions*, p. 188.

de l'Imposteur showed that comedy was based on man's attempt to affirm his moral superiority by magnifying the ridiculous in the faults of others. Lamy attacks comedy for this very reason: comedies where man's faults are brought to our notice are a source of pleasure for us either because we are 'bien aise dans le desordre où on est, d'avoir des compagnons avec qui on partage la honte du peché', or because we derive a secret satisfaction from seeing that we are exempt from the faults of others: 'On s'élève au dessus d'eux, et on les meprise. Outre cela, on attribüe facilement les fautes qui sont exposées à la risée de tout le monde, à quelqu'un sur lequel on seroit bien-aise qu'en tombât l'infamie.'[59] Lamy sees our response as something approaching active malice and far from the objective experience described by the author of the *Lettre*.

Lelevel views the problem in a more precisely theological context, explaining comedy in terms of the Fall, where reason was taken from man, leaving him with only ridicule.[60] But, he continues, reason was not so totally extinguished that man could not perceive the faults of others, although nobody was able to recognize his own; consequently, feeling, on the one hand, the need for perfection, yet, on the other hand, not knowing how to find it, 'on a pris le parti de s'observer et de se critiquer les uns les autres; et non seulement on a sçû se réjoüir par cette voye, mais encore chacun a sçû tirer de là comme un témoignage de son excellence, parce qu'il ne se peut que celui qui critique ne s'imagine être plus parfait que celui qui est critiqué'.[61] The faults of others become the yardstick of our own perfection. The author of the *Lettre sur la comédie de l'Imposteur* could not have put it better.

There is of course the suggestion here that we do not recognize ourselves in the characters portrayed on the stage. For Lelevel this is often an unwitting act on the part of the spectator; in his reply to Caffaro he defines the audience at a comedy as 'une assemblée de railleurs où personne ne se connoît, et où chacun rit des defauts, qui les rendent tous

[59] *Nouvelles réflexions*, pp. 180–1.
[60] *Réponse à la lettre*, pp. 15–16.
[61] Ibid., p. 16.

également coupables et ridicules'.[62] In Lelevel's *Entretiens* Théodore is made to say that according to some people Molière and Harlequin 'representoient au naturel bien des gens', but that 'personne ne s'y reconnoissoit, et ce qu'on apprenoit avec eux, c'étoit à se moquer les uns des autres'.[63] How can we correct our faults if we fail to recognize ourselves in the characters?

Pégurier considers the rather different case where a particular individual may indeed be recognized in the character of a play: although people are not named when some vice or other is condemned portraits are often so natural that the originals are not difficult to recognize.[64] He continues: 'Et quand une fois on a par ce moyen perdu quelqu'un de reputation, si dans la suite touché de Dieu il change de sentimens, s'il quitte le vice qu'on luy a reproché pour embrasser la vertu; tout cela n'est pas pour l'ordinaire capable de détruire la méchante idée qu'on en a donné au public.'[65] Not surprisingly, Molière is cited as guilty in this respect.

A similar criticism is envisaged by Molière himself in the *Critique de l'École des femmes*, where in scene vi Climène complains of offensive satire of women contained in *L'École des femmes* itself, thus implying that she feels herself to be personally attacked. Uranie's reply is delicately barbed: these satires 'tombent directement sur les mœurs' and 'ne frappent les personnes que par réflexion'; she remarks that we might profit from the lesson of comedy 'sans faire semblant qu'on parle à nous'; moreover, the 'peintures ridicules' are 'miroirs publics où il ne faut jamais témoigner qu'on se voie', and 'c'est se taxer hautement d'un défaut que de se scandaliser qu'on le reprenne'. In other words, comedy aims at presenting an image of behaviour which is applicable to no one individual, but corresponds to an objective truth which is independent of the play. The similarity of this idea with that found in the *Lettre sur la comédie de l'Imposteur* is obvious. Furthermore, if the individual concerned recognizes the

---

[62] Ibid., p. 17.
[63] *Entretiens*, pp. 194–5.
[64] *Réfutation des sentiments relâchés*, p. 97.
[65] Ibid., pp. 97–8.

similarity between himself and the comic character it is better that he remain silent, for should he protest, he becomes his own accuser. One may, however, feel uneasy at such a reasoning: many vices or faults have in reality extremely recognizable features and it is possible that the audience will indeed point an accusing finger 'par réflexion'. Equally, it is possible that a person may be publicly ridiculed for a fault which is but a small part of his or her personality, whereas comedy makes the part represent the whole. Pégurier's doubts about comedy may indeed possess a measure of justification.

All this leads the reader to the problem of *Le Tartuffe* itself, where the main point of contention is the possible confusion arising from the portrayal of a hypocrite who has all the attributes of a real *dévot*. In the *Lettre* the author had written that once we had considered something ridiculous in a play it would be difficult to take it seriously in the future. This is precisely the objection made by some religious moralists regarding the portrayal of Tartuffe as a *dévot*; they argue tht real piety will suffer because of the similarity of certain of its features with those exhibited by the hypocrite. In the words of Coustel, 'sous pretexte de ruiner la fausse devotion, il represente les brutalitez de son Tartuffe avec des couleurs si noires, et il luy fait avancer des maximes si detestables, que la corruption du cœur humain ne manquera pas de les faire appliquer, non à un Tartuffe de Theatre: mais à un véritable homme de bien'.[66] It is interesting that Coustel should base his criticism on man's inability to distinguish between truth and falsehood, when this is the very thing denied in the *Lettre*.

But the controversy over *Le Tartuffe* involves many complex issues, and H. P. Salomon has provided a revealing discussion of them in his *Tartuffe devant l'opinion française*. He shows for example that at the time of the play and before it there were many moralists, including St. Vincent de Paul and le P. Lejeune, who bitterly attacked the fashion of employing a *directeur de conscience*.[67] Professor Butler also

[66] *Sentiments de l'Église*, p. 66.
[67] Salomon, H. P., *Tartuffe devant l'opinion française*, Paris, 1962, pp. 15-17.

remarks upon this phenomenon and suggests that if the Lamoignons and the Péréfixes of this world were outraged it was not because Molière had been spreading untruths but because 'il a visé trop juste et . . . toute vérité n'est pas bonne à dire'.[68] M. Salomon's other major contribution to the problem of *Le Tartuffe* in the seventeenth century is his demonstration that the controversy is directly linked with certain attitudes towards the immodest dress of women, parts of whose bodies were exposed for all to see. Thus Tartuffe's outburst in II, ii was seen by the predominantly Jansenist clergy of Paris as a parody of their rigorist attitudes.[69]

The subversive nature of the play is a prominent theme in the work of the authors under consideration. Two developed criticisms of *Le Tartuffe* by Massillon and Bourdaloue deserve special attention here for they both consider in detail the play's effect on other Christians and on Christianity as a whole. Massillon, in his sermon on *Les Gens de bien*, while agreeing that the hypocrite deserves 'l'exécration de Dieu et des hommes' and that his abuse of religion is the greatest of crimes, refers to the inadequacy of ridicule in this particular case; 'les dérisions et les satires sont trop douces pour décrier un vice qui mérite l'horreur du genre humain; et qu'un théâtre profane a eu tort de ne donner que du ridicule à un caractère si abominable, si honteux et si affligeant pour l'Eglise, et qui doit plutôt exciter les larmes et l'indignation que la risée des fidèles'.[70] In other words, ridicule and laughter have no serious connotation and as a result no effect on such a serious vice.

But, Massillon goes on, these continual outbursts against virtue, the confusion of *l'homme de bien* with a hypocrite, the spitefulness which 'en faisant des éloges pompeux de la justice, ne trouve presque aucun juste qui les mérite' (presumably a reference to Cléante's speech in I, v), all this 'anéantit la religion et tend à rendre toute vertu suspecte';

---

[68] Butler, Ph., 'Tartuffe et la direction spirituelle au XVIIe siècle', in *Modern Miscellany presented to Eugène Vinaver*, ed. T. E. Lawrenson *et al.*, Manchester, 1969, pp. 48–65, p. 60.

[69] *Tartuffe devant l'opinion française*, pp. 29–39.

[70] Migne, l'Abbé J.-P., *Collection intégrale et universelle*, vol. 42, col. 885.

consequently the impious are offered more arguments against religion at a time when so many other scandalous occurrences 'n'autorise que trop l'impiété'.[71] Although Tartuffe is recognized for what he is, Massillon seems to be criticizing the play for not publicizing the ways of orthodox religious conduct; Cléante in particular would not appear to be the right person to oppose the hypocrite.[72] But Le Tartuffe is attacked not so much for being a libertine play itself, but for giving libertins an excuse for attacking religion. Massillon adds to the above statement that when we think we are laughing at false virtue we are in fact blaspheming against religion: 'en vous défiant de la sincérité des justes que vous voyez, l'impie conclut que ceux qui les ont precédés et que nous ne voyons pas leur étaient semblables'.[73] Even martyrs would not be exempt from such treatment.[74]

Massillon is, however, particularly concerned that Molière should have dealt with a subject pertaining to religion at all: these scandalous things should not be exposed in public with an air of triumph, but effaced from the memory of man; the Law condemned 'celui qui découvrait la honte et la turpitude de ceux qui lui avaient donné la vie' but 'c'est la honte et le déshonneur de l'Église votre mère, que vous exposez avec plaisir à la dérision publique'.[75] This is no doubt a reference to the notion of sexual taboo found in Leviticus 18: 7, where the Law forbids one to uncover the nakedness of one's mother; here the latter is the Church and the act of introducing religion into comedy is seen as an act of defilement.

Bourdaloue devoted some time to the question of Le Tartuffe in his sermon on hypocrisy and he too sees it in terms of the libertin: if the latter is forced to admit that not all piety is false he will at least maintain that it is suspect, and as a result all piety will be weakened in its effect. Indeed this is what the libertin hopes to gain 'en faisant de ses entretiens et de ses discours autant de satyres de l'hypocrisie

[71] Ibid.
[72] Just as, indeed, Sganarelle is seen by some as an inadequate and blasphemous defender of religion in Dom Juan (see Rochemont, Observations in Molière, Œuvres, v, 425-6).
[73] Migne, Collection intégrale et universelle, vol. 42, col. 885.
[74] Ibid.
[75] Ibid., col. 889.

et de la fausse dévotion'.[76] Bourdaloue continues by saying that since real and false piety have much in common it is more or less inevitable that 'la mesme raillerie qui attaque l'une, interesse l'autre', and that 'les traits dont on peint celle-cy defigurent celle-là',[77] unless, of course, one takes 'toutes les precautions d'une charité prudente, exacte, et bien intentionnée, ce que le libertinage n'est pas en disposition de faire'.[78] Such, according to Bourdaloue, is not the aim of the 'esprits prophanes' when they undertake the censure of hypocrisy, for they in no way have the interests of God at heart; they do not wish to reform the abuse of religion, which they cannot do in any case, but to 'faire une espece de diversion dont le libertinage pust profiter, en concevant, et en faisant concevoir d'injustes soupçons de la vraye pieté par de malignes representations de la fausse'.[79] Molière is therefore condemned for spreading impiety just as he is for providing lessons in vice. But, as M. Salomon points out, Bourdaloue's argument marks a new phase in the debate. He does not dispute the fact of Tartuffe's hypocrisy; as Bourdaloue says, the comedy exposes 'à la risée publique un hypocrite imaginaire, ou mesmes, si vous voulez, un hypocrite réel'.[80] Bourdaloue's reproach is not that Tartuffe is not hypocritical enough but, in the words of M. Salomon, '[il] ne veut pas d'un hypocrite sur la scène'.[81]

For Bourdaloue, however, the *libertins* revel in an already established impiety: his great concern is the effect of such a play as *Le Tartuffe* on weak-minded Christians: firstly, they become afraid to pass for hypocrites, this fear arising from the similarity of conduct in real and false devotion, and they are prevented from performing their Christian duties;[82] secondly, they conceive 'un degoust de la pieté' for, although piety is 'solide en elle-mesme, et estimable devant Dieu', it is subject to men's censure and to the spitefulness of their

---

[76] Bourdaloue, le Père L., 'Sermon pour le septième dimanche après la Pentecoste: sur l'hypocrisie', in *Sermons . . . pour les dimanches*, Paris, 1716, III, 58-9.
[77] Ibid., 59.
[78] Ibid.
[79] Ibid.
[80] Ibid., 60.
[81] *Tartuffe devant l'opinion française*, p. 95.
[82] *Sermons pour les dimanches*, III, 70-1.

judgements;[83] thirdly, 'ils tombent par là dans un abattement du cœur, qui va souvent, jusqu'à leur faire abandonner le parti de Dieu, plutost que de s'engager à soutenir la persecution, c'est-à-dire, à essuyer la raillerie, qu'ils se persuadent que ce reproche odieux, ou mesmes que le simple soupçon d'hypocrisie leur attireroit'.[84] Molière is accused of turning people away from religion by his exposure of those who ill use it.

Thus, while *Le Tartuffe*, an isolated example, is considered an anti-Christian play it is clear that laughter in itself achieves the opposite of a moral effect. Some religious moralists go so far as to suggest that laughter is an un-Christian act, thereby attacking comedy in its fundamental aim. Bossuet relies mainly on the authority of the Fathers for his views on the subject. He reports St. Thomas as putting *bouffonneries* among the vices: 'la plaisanterie', he says, is forbidden to Christians because it is 'une action légère, indécente, en tout cas oisive . . . , et indigne de la gravité des mœurs chrétiennes'.[85] Another of his sources is St. Basil, who is reported to have said that men may ' "égayer un peu le visage par un modeste souris"; mais pour ce qui est de "ces grands éclats et de ces secousses du corps", qui tiennent de la convulsion, selon lui elles ne sont pas d'un homme "vertueux et qui se possède lui-même", ce qu'il inculque souvent, comme une des obligations du christianisme'.[86] As in the experience of passion, so laughter leads to the spectator's losing control. A modern scholar, however, assures us that, contrary to what Bossuet says, the Fathers were moderate in their condemnation of laughter; it was rather the excess with which they found fault.[87]

But comedy in its use of ridicule and sometimes in its choice of targets, sins against charity; this is indeed implicit in the statement of Pégurier quoted earlier, where a man ridiculed in a comedy later changes his ways but remains the object of ridicule because people remember only his portrayal

[83] Ibid., 71.
[84] Ibid.
[85] *Maximes et réflexions*, U/L, p. 232.
[86] Ibid., pp. 262-3.
[87] Ériau, *Pourquoi les Pères de l'Église*, p. 17.

in the play. Bourdaloue's argument that by including religious
elements in comedy one exposed the whole Church to
public ridicule has also been mentioned before. Lejeune
implies that the ridicule of individuals is no less a sin against
the very founder of Christianity; 'quel est le Chrestien . . .
qui se moque de Jesus-Christ? il faudroit estre barbare et
athée. Saint Paul vous répond, quand vous pechez contre
votre frére Chrestien vous pechez contre Jesus-Christ'.[88]
Comedy, given this definition of relationships between men,
is the ultimate act of profanity.

[88] *Le Missionnaire*, x, 506.

VIII

DRAMA AS DIVERTISSEMENT

The wholesale condemnation of drama by religious moralists and their rejection of its influence for good has profound consequences for drama's status as *divertissement*, one of the areas of social life of particular concern in rigorists' works. Indeed, given the importance of this subject in seventeenth-century thought as a whole, it is worth outlining the general considerations which underpin the religious moralists' attitudes to drama in this context.

The dramatic theorists had no doubts regarding the value of drama as *divertissement*: plays aimed to *instruire en divertissant*, which meant that at the same time as profiting morally from dramatic performances one should also derive pleasure from the dramatic experience. Pleasure, however, was not the sole aim for most writers but had, in order to be considered fit for drama, to conform to certain rules. *Divertissement* in the theatre was thus a strictly controlled phenomenon. Theorists, moreover, saw no moral objections to *divertissement* in the theatre: d'Aubignac, in his *Dissertation sur la condamnation des théâtres*, considers drama 'le plus beau des divertissemens publics',[1] while for Corneille it is 'un divertissement si honnête et si utile'.[2] Molière, in the preface to *Le Tartuffe*, declares that if respite is required amid 'les exercices de la piété' and if it is true that men need recreation none can be found 'qui soit plus innocent que la comédie'.[3]

The religious moralists, however, do not share the same optimism regarding the phenomenon of *divertissement* itself. The most celebrated discussion of the question is undoubtedly that in Pascal's *Pensées*, where it forms part of his apology for Christianity as a whole. Pascal's principal theme is that

---

[1] *Dissertation*, p. 245.
[2] *Writings*, p. 170.
[3] *Œuvres*, iv, 383.

man cannot bear to consider his own wretchedness but cannot find happiness in himself without God. Various activities thus become a means of turning his attention from his state of *misère*: indeed *divertissement* has much of its etymological force in Pascal's notion that: 'L'unique bien des hommes consiste donc à être divertis de penser à leur condition ou par une occupation qui les en détourne ou par quelque passion agréable . . . et nouvelle qui les occupe, ou . . . par le jeu, la . . . chasse, quelque spectacle attachant, et enfin par ce qu'on appelle divertissement . . .'[4] Or again, 'c'est le tracas . . . qui nous en détourne d'y penser et nous divertit'.[5] It is interesting to observe his specific reference to spectacle.

The notion of *détournement* is not entirely alien to dramatic theorists although, of course, in a slightly different sense. Profit is an 'indirect' result for the spectator who is promised only pleasure and it is d'Aubignac's contention that public spectacle turns people away from criminal activities.[6] But the most interesting statement comes from Saint-Évremond in his essay *Sur les plaisirs*: in order to be happy, he recommends, we must reflect little upon life 'mais sortir souvent comme hors de soy; et parmi les plaisirs que fournissent les choses étrangeres se dérober la connoissance de ses propres maux'.[7] He explains further that 'les divertissements ont tiré leur nom de la diversion qu'ils font faire des objets fâcheux et tristes, sur les choses plaisantes et agréables'.[8]

Pascal, of course, could not concede the validity of the former statement: man cannot be happy through *divertissement*, 'car il vient d'ailleurs et de dehors'; thus 'il est dépendant, et partout, sujet à être troublé par mille accidents, qui font les afflictions inévitables'.[9] We are toys of chance, of things outside us. Furthermore, man does not choose just any type of amusement: 'un amusement languissant et sans

[4] Pascal, B., *Pensées*, ed. L. Lafuma, 3 vols., Paris, 1947 (136**–269**), i, 92. See Mesnard, J., 'De la *diversion* au divertissement' in *Mémorial du 1ᵉʳ Congrès international des études montaignistes*, Bordeaux, 1964.

[5] Pascal, ibid.

[6] *Pratique*, p. 10.

[7] *Œuvres*, iv, 12–13.

[8] Ibid., 13.

[9] *Pensées* (132**–265**), i, 91.

passion l'ennuira'.[10] The whole of Pascal's discussion centres on the theme that man should be seeking God.

Pascal's thesis is similar in many respects to the views of certain opponents of drama recorded earlier. For example, Lamy mentioned that although there is a natural movement within us towards God, whose beauty is expressed in that of his creatures, we are turned from him by concupiscence towards creatures; drama encourages this attraction even more. Both Lamy and Nicole stress that drama, in its emphasis on passions and on involvement with the hero (we remember that 'l'esprit est tout occupé des objets exérieurs'[11]), is diametrically opposed to the state of introspection necessary to Christian life. Furthermore, Pascal's remark that man is bored by 'un amusement languissant et sans passion' reminds us of the contention of some religious moralists that an audience could never be satisfied with Christian humility on the stage; they need 'quelque chose de vif et d'animé'.[12] It is no accident that this phrase comes from Nicole who so often shares the spirit of Pascal's work.

Writers other than Pascal express four main attitudes to *divertissement*; two concern the conditions which determine our need for it; the others concern the nature of the activities which keep us amused. Regarding man's need of *divertissement*, Senault comments that, while work is in some way natural to man, he has need of relaxation because his mind is too weak to sustain constant occupation and would succumb if work were not followed by some form of recreation.[13] But the anonymous preacher from Cologne warns us that permission for recreation is a concession to man's weakness and not a right that he has earned.[14]

In the eyes of some religious moralists the activities which constitute *divertissement* are in themselves suspect. Senault, in his *L'Homme criminel*, explains that whereas before the Fall man's recreational activities were not divorced from his devotion, the corruption of sin has since separated

[10] Ibid. (136*–269*), i, 95.
[11] Nicole, *Traité de la comédie*, p. 44.
[12] Ibid., p. 53.
[13] *Le Monarque*, p. 235.
[14] *Instructions morales et populaires*, p. 31.

divertissement from duty with the consequence that man 'ne trouva plus son plaisir que dans son offense'; furthermore all the remedies applied to this disorder have failed and our most innocent recreations 'peuvent devenir criminelles'.[15] Thus, for Senault *divertissement* contributes little to our well-being since our pleasure is sought in sinful activities. Bourdaloue is of a similar opinion in his references to 'les divertissements du monde'; his sermon is intended to demonstrate that 'ils sont presque tous, ou impurs et defendus dans leur nature, . . . ou excessifs dans leur étenduë, . . . ou enfin scandaleux dans leurs effets'.[16] Finally, for La Colombière, our recreational activities are an obstacle to Christian life: 'Les divertissemens [du monde] font un contretemps dans des jours destinés au travail, ils deviennent importuns dans des jours de larmes et d'affliction';[17] moreover, all the days of a Christian's life are 'des jours de travail' and 'des jours d'affliction et de larmes'.[18]

Is there, then, a permissible form of recreational activity? First of all it is important to understand what the religious moralists saw as the aim of *divertissement*. Frain du Tremblay argues that, while man is made for work,[19] which indeed forms part of our penitence,[20] we must use *divertissements* only to renew the strength we need when we take up our work again, for they are but 'des remedes inventez pour le soulagement des hommes'.[21] Nicole explains that the word *divertissement* itself tells us that 'on ne s'y doit porter que pour se divertir, et se distraire des pensées et des occupations laborieuses, qui causent dans l'ame une espece de lassitude qu'on a besoin de reparer'.[22] Since the sole use of recreation is the renewal of our spiritual and bodily strength wearied through work, clearly 'il n'est permis de se divertir tout au plus, que comme il est permis de manger'.[23]

---

[15]　*L'Homme criminel*, pp. 684–5.
[16]　*Sermons pour les dimanches*, II, 67–8.
[17]　Migne, *Collection intégrale et universelle*, vol. 7, col. 992.
[18]　Ibid.
[19]　Frain du Tremblay, J., *Conversations morales sur les jeux et les divertissements*, Paris, 1685, p. 19.
[20]　Ibid., pp. 14–15.
[21]　Ibid., p. 29.
[22]　*Traité de la comédie*, p. 60.
[23]　Ibid., p. 59.

It is clear, therefore, that, in Frain du Tremblay's words, '[les divertissements] ne doivent point être aimez ni recherchez pour eux-mêmes'.[24] Nicole considers that once a Christian has renounced through his baptismal vow the world, its pomp, and its pleasure he may not seek pleasure or *divertissement* for its own sake; his recommendation is that: 'Il faut afin qu'il en puisse user sans péché, qu'ils lui soient necessaires en quelque maniere, et que l'on puisse dire veritablement qu'il s'en sert avec la modération de celui qui en use, et non avec la passion de celuy qui les aime.'[25] Pleasure is thus an indirect product of *divertissement* and not its prime aim. On the question of pleasure it is interesting to note that, while Voisin makes much of St. Francis's condition that 'Pour honneste que soit une recreation, c'est vice d'y mettre son cœur et son affection',[26] he chooses to gloss over the saint's qualification that 'Je ne dis pas qu'il ne faille prendre plaisir à joüer pendant qu'on joüe; car autrement on ne se recreeroit pas.'[27]

But not all religious moralists were as rigorous in their view of *divertissement*. In Le Moyne's *Dévotion aisée* a moderate view of *divertissement* is taken since it is regarded as wholly compatible with worship.[28] Le Moyne's major assumption is that 'cette severité si generale, qu'on impute à la Devotion est une imposture' and 'il est faux qu'elle soit ennemie de toute sorte de divertissemens'.[29] Indeed, somewhat curiously, he says of *la Dévotion* that: 'Toute severe qu'on la fait, elle a un Theatre tousjours ouvert et tousjours paré; et sur ce Theatre, elle a ses jeux, ses concerts; elle a ses danses et ses spectacles. Mais ce sont des jeux instructifs et divertissans; ce sont des concerts d'esprit et d'intelligence; ce sont des danses serieuses et modestes; ce sont des spectacles plus utiles que les leçons des Philosophes.'[30] Thus worship, in contrast with Senault's view, is itself a form of *divertissement* and is indeed described in a manner most *mondain*.

[24] *Conversations morales*, p. 29.
[25] *Traité de la comédie*, p. 59.
[26] *Défense*, p. 464.
[27] Ibid.
[28] Le Moyne, le Père P., *La Dévotion aisée*, Paris, 1652.
[29] Ibid., p. 96.
[30] Ibid., pp. 96-7.

But the need for *divertissement* outside devotion is recognized just as is the need for food and rest.[31] Such a concession, moreover, is, according to Le Moyne, authorized both by the general policy of the State 'qui a donné des festes aux Peuples, des vacations aux Magistrats, des spectacles à toutes les conditions et à tous les âges', and by the practice of the Church 'qui mesle à ses plus augustes mysteres, les parfums, la musique, et le son des instrumens'.[32] Even the most rigorously minded saints did not always carry crosses and skulls; nor were they always 'dans la plus haute region du Ciel' for they sometimes came down to earth 'avecque les Anges et les Aigles'.[33]

Le Moyne's attitude towards the various forms of recreational activity is not, however, entirely laxist. Just as they are not all rejected they are not all haphazardly and indiscriminately accepted; certain rules must be obeyed.[34] The first is that all recreational activities 'qui blessent la conscience et donnent la mort à l'âme' are forbidden; his example is the 'jeu des Soldats de Joab et d'Abner, qui s'égorgerent mutuellement'.[35] Secondly, devotion does not permit 'les divertissemens qui laissent des taches, quoy qu'ils ne laissent point de playe; qui souïllent la reputation, quoy qu'ils ne blessent point la conscience'.[36] Thirdly, devotion cannot suffer those *divertissements* which disturb domestic life and which sow division among families.[37] For other religious moralists this would apply directly to drama; but Le Moyne himself is not explicit on this point. There is, however, another restriction imposed by Le Moyne: although recreational activities must have 'un temps reglé', 'ce temps-là ne doit pas revenir tous les jous ny à toute heure'; in this case they change their name and nature, and instead of being pastimes become 'des vacations et des emplois'.[38]

---

[31] Ibid., p. 101.
[32] Ibid., pp. 102–3.
[33] Ibid., p. 103.
[34] Ibid., p. 104.
[35] Ibid., pp. 105–6. The reference is obscure: a possible explanation is that duelling is forbidden, but this is, admittedly, hardly a recreational activity.
[36] Ibid., p. 107.
[37] Ibid., p. 108.
[38] Ibid., pp. 118–19.

Divertissement is also considered by Le Moyne in its social context. One quality of *divertissement* is *bienséance*, which is defined as 'la Loy du Monde civilisé' and which requires that we contribute 'au divertissement honneste des compagnies, où l'on se trouve engagé par civilité ou par devoir'; further-more, 'ce ne seroit pas tendresse de conscience, ce seroit foiblesse d'esprit, à celuy qui se retirant d'une partie faite regulierement et selon les formes, romproit par la bizarrerie une feste de famille, et déconcerteroit la réjouyssance d'une Assemblée'.[39] *Divertissement* therefore becomes a form of social duty. It is even more instructive to read that charity, another quality of recreation, is discussed in similar terms to *bienséance*.[40] The last consideration mentioned by Le Moyne is *coustume*. There are, he explains, times when 'le serieux seroit l'impertinent, et le chagrin seroit de mauvais augure'; it is then just to make some concession to custom because '[il] n'est pas toujours bon de contredire le Public, et de s'inscrire en faux contre les modes';[41] one may sometimes follow the crowd 'quand elle ne se detourne qu'un peu, et qu'il est aisé de revenir du détour où elle est portée'.[42] Finally, the *sage* will not only be temperate for 'la veille des Roys' and moderate in his pleasure during the Carnival, but 'il sera sobre sans austerité, il sera modeste sans estre de mauvaise humeur; et ses joyes justes et compassées, ses divertissements moderez et retenus, seront une plus douce, et plus efficace censure de la débauche et des Baccanales, qu'une severité importune, qui viendroit à contre-temps, et hors de sa place'.[43]

There are, therefore, two opposing attitudes towards *divertissement*. On the one hand, there are those who regard its necessity as indicative of weakness and who wish to restrict it to the absolute minimum; and, on the other hand, there is Le Moyne, whose outlook is to say the least conciliatory, since he stands opposed to 'une severité importune'.[44] In his

[39] Ibid., p. 122.
[40] Ibid., pp. 122-3.
[41] Ibid., p. 124.
[42] Ibid.
[43] Ibid., pp. 124-5.
[44] *La Dévotion aisée* is interestingly enough one of the works Pascal attacks in the ninth *Lettre provinciale*.

views on *divertissement* we see to what extent religious
conduct need not be divorced from a social context. Charity
to one's neighbour means living with him sociably. Most of
Le Moyne's work is inexplicit in its reference: but from this
it derives its greatest virtue because the question is left open-
ended. The lack of strict definitions regarding any particular
form of *divertissement* means that each must be judged on its
merits according to circumstance. *La Dévotion aisée* is a fine
example of moral pragmatism.

What, then, is the status of drama in the context of
divertissement? The most sustained attempt to justify drama
as a legitimate recreation is found in Caffaro's letter where
the author uses arguments regarding 'games' from St.
Thomas's *Summa*, which at times resemble very closely
those used by Le Moyne in a more general perspective. Since
Caffaro is for the most part faithful to the text of the *Summa*
it is quoted in the English edition, indicating any deviation
on the part of Caffaro.

His first reference to the *Summa* is to the second article of
Question 168 in which St. Thomas recognizes the need for
the soul to rest, commenting that 'the soul's rest is
pleasure'.[45] A little earlier Aquinas quotes St. Augustine
(*Music*, ii, 15) as saying that 'it becomes a wise man sometimes to relax the high pressure of his attention to work', and
St. Thomas adds that the relaxation of the mind consists
in 'playful words or deeds wherein nothing further is sought
than the soul's delight'.[46] It is on the definition of the
expression 'playful words and deeds' that Caffaro's argument
will depend.

Caffaro now moves on to St. Thomas's more socially
orientated justification of recreation contained in the fourth
article entitled *Whether there is a sin in lack of mirth*. Again
he quotes directly from the *Summa*:

In human affairs whatever is against reason is a sin. Now it is against
reason for a man to be burdensome to others, by offering no pleasure
to others, and by hindering their enjoyment. Wherefore Seneca says . . .:
'Let your conduct be guided by wisdom so that no-one will think you
rude, or despise you as a cad.'[47]

[45] *Summa*, IIa. IIae, 168, a.2, ad. 3, vol. 13, p. 296.
[46] Ibid., pp. 296–7.
[47] Ibid., a. 4, ad. 3, vol. 13, p. 302.

Caffaro, however, extends this a little when he writes:

Comportez-vous dans les compagnies avec tant de sagesse et de discretion que personne ne vous trouve fâcheux ou ne vous méprise comme un homme de rien qui ne sauroit pas vivre, car c'est un vice d'être fâcheux à tout le monde, et l'on s'attire avec sujet le nom de sauvage et de grossier.[48]

There then follows the optimistic conclusion that the words of St. Thomas refer to the theatre when he says that the relaxation of the mind, which is a virtue, 'se fait par des paroles et par des actions divertissantes. Qu'y a-t-il de plus propre et de plus particulier à la Comédie, qui ne consiste qu'en des paroles et en des actions risibles et ingenieuses qui font plaisir et qui délassent l'esprit?'[49] This is a fair assumption, especially when St. Thomas answers the objection that *histriones* would seem to sin through excess of mirth. But while the above statement seems to refer exclusively to comedy Caffaro adds that St. Thomas's answer to this objection legitimizes plays and other spectacles as forms of *divertissement*.[50] Caffaro's general conclusion is hotly contested by Bossuet who keeps to the literal wording of the *Summa*, saying that the latter speaks only 'en général des jeux necessaires à la récréation de l'esprit' and that there is not one single word about drama.[51]

St. Thomas's lenient views on *divertissement* are not, however, entirely unqualified for he is careful to ask that recreational activities fulfil three basic conditions. Caffaro, having now justified drama as a legitimate recreation, is firm in his belief that the plays of his day conform to these conditions, although his detractors think decidedly otherwise. Following a discussion of theory it is appropriate to embark on a more pragmatic discussion which places drama in its contemporary context.

The first condition according to the *Summa* is that 'the pleasure in question should not be sought in indecent or injurious deeds or words'.[52] Caffaro's evidence that such a

---

[48] *Lettre d'un théologien*, U/L, p. 73.
[49] Ibid.
[50] Ibid.
[51] *Maximes et réflexions*, U/L, p. 227.
[52] *Summa*, IIa. IIae, 168, a.2, ad. 3, vol. 13, p. 297.

precept was followed by the plays of his time is based
on the fact that plays are tolerated at all; for this reason
he says, they must of necessity be exempt from any indecent
words or deeds; he further states that no such examples are
to be found in printed plays.[53] It is unfortunate that a
defence of drama which is in many ways sound should be
marred by excessive *naïveté*, for it seems a legitimate assumption that Caffaro's contact with printed plays was limited to
the ones sent to him by Boursault.

The second condition of St. Thomas was that 'one lose
not the balance of one's mind altogether'; quoting St.
Ambrose he adds that 'We should beware lest, when we seek
relaxation of mind, we destroy all that harmony which is
the concord of good works.'[54] The usual French translation
for *balance of mind* was *la gravité de l'âme*. Caffaro's main
point here is that drama constitutes a relaxation from work;
thus implicitly it cannot be considered to disrupt the soul's
harmony. Indeed he reaffirms man's need of relaxation and
offers the orthodox argument that without such rest man
would succumb through work,[55] although he judiciously adds
that nothing is more sinful than to enjoy oneself continually
and without moderation.[56] In his final statement on St.
Thomas's second condition Caffaro states that neither those
who attend plays, nor those who write or perform them
'ne relâchent point leur esprit jusqu'à la dissolution de
l'harmonie de l'âme'. In the case of spectators they are free
to go or not to go to the theatre and are not forced to attend
against their conscience; moreover, after a day's work, an hour
or two of pleasure and relaxation is not excessive.[57]

Caffaro's remarks on St. Thomas's third condition were
the most controversial of all. The Saint says that 'we must be
careful, as in all other human actions, to conform ourselves
to persons, time and place, and take account of other

---

[53] *Lettre d'un théologien*, U/L, p. 103.
[54] *Summa*, IIa. IIae, 168, a.2, ad. 3, vol. 13, p. 297.
[55] *Lettre d'un théologien*, U/L, p. 108.
[56] Ibid., p. 109. U/L write on the term *criminel*: 'Autrefois, on qualifiait crime
tout peché mortel, c'est-à-dire méritant la damnation; aujourd'hui, ce mot est
pris dans un sens plus restreint, et est réservé pour certains péchés d'une gravité
exceptionnelle, tels que l'homicide, la trahison etc. . . .' (p. 253).
[57] Ibid., p. 110.

circumstances, so that our fun "befit the hour and the man", . . ."[58] To begin with, Caffaro regards this condition as fulfilled because theatrical performances take place after the hour of divine office,[59] a point made some years earlier by Chappuzeau.[60] Caffaro's mistake, however, was to justify performances on Sundays by arguing that even God rested on the seventh day.[61] Another contentious point centres on his recommendations for the Christian's conduct during Lent; he quotes St. Thomas as saying that the penitent, although he must conduct himself differently from others, may none the less make moderate use of games (which for Caffaro includes drama) 'comme d'une honneste recreation de l'esprit, ou pour entretenir la société entre ceux avec qui l'on est obligé de vivre'.[62] Caffaro's only restriction is that during Lent Christians must frequent the theatre less often than usual.[63]

Each of these arguments received detailed replies from those who joined in the controversy against Caffaro. Pégurier, however, is considerably in advance of St. Thomas regarding the number of conditions imposed upon recreational activities, since he mentions no less than six. It is therefore convenient to base a discussion on Pégurier's division and to deal with the three basic conditions when they occur within it. The arguments of religious moralists not involved in the *affaire Caffaro* are also included in this discussion.

Pégurier's first condition, that the aim of *divertissement* is the relaxation of the mind,[64] is in fact the general principle of recreation as a whole in the *Summa*. It allows Pégurier to attack members of the audience whom he considers in no need of rest since they spend their time on nothing else. Who, he asks, seeks this 'délassement du corps ou de l'esprit', what have these affected young people and society women

---

[58] *Summa*, IIa. IIae, 168, a. 2, ad. 3, vol. 13, p. 297.
[59] *Lettre d'un théologien*, U/L, p. 111.
[60] *Le Théâtre françois*, p. 132.
[61] *Lettre d'un théologien*, U/L, p. 113.
[62] Ibid., p. 112. The reference to St. Thomas is *D. Th*, in 4, dist. 16 quaest. 4, art. 2, in corpore.
[63] Ibid., pp. 112-13.
[64] *Réfutation des sentiments relâchés*, p. 39.

done that is so tiring?[65] The former, tired of all sorts of pleasure, 'ne cherchent dans la volupté que de nouveaux ragousts'.[66] As for the aforementioned ladies, who live in continual idleness, how can their intention be to rest when they spend all their time in idolizing their body and parading their vanity from morn till night; what of these coquettes 'dont l'esprit n'est rempli que d'intrigues ou de commerces, qu'elles cherchent ou à commencer ou à entretenir à la Comedie'?[67]

The audience is also an object of Nicole's wrath in his *Traité*. That *divertissement* is merely a means of renewing the strength of body and soul, and must not be sought for its own sake, manifestly condemns those who attend the theatre and who clearly do not do so 'pour se délasser l'esprit des occupations serieuses', particularly when they are never seriously occupied anyway. He explains their predicament when, in a truly Pascalian phrase, he says that: 'Leur ennui est un dégoût de satieté, pareil à celui de ceux qui ont trop mangé, et il doit être guéri par l'abstinence, et non pas par le changement des plaisirs. Elles se doivent divertir en s'occupant, puis que la faineantise et l'oisiveté sont la principale cause de leur ennui.'[68] Thus the roles are reversed: *divertissement* should consist of work.

Pégurier's second and third conditions really divide the first rule of St. Thomas, that pleasure be not sought in indecent or injurious words or deeds, for he deals with the indecent in the second and the injurious in the third. Pégurier also widens the scope of his second rule when he speaks of diversion at the expense of innocence and purity, by which he means the way plays instruct in vice rather than provide examples of virtue.[69] As for *words* he here remarks upon those 'saletez' which are concealed by more 'refined' expressions for the sake of 'good taste',[70] and comments that most spectators would be bored if there were no disreputable

[65] Ibid., p. 64.
[66] Ibid., p. 65.
[67] Ibid.
[68] *Traité de la comédie*, p. 60.
[69] *Réfutation des sentiments relâchés*, pp. 67–8.
[70] Ibid., pp. 85–6.

words or deeds.[71] Gerbais refers to scandalous dialogue in this context,[72] while Coustel mentions love, anger, and vengeance, as well as *équivoques*,[73] for presumably words which express passion must of their nature be indecent. Pégurier's remarks on injurious words and deeds concern generally the attitudes in plays to God and to one's neighbour. Naturally, *Le Tartuffe* and *Dom Juan*, in their references to religion, are considered to offend against God.[74] In the case of one's neighbour Pégurier makes the point about comedy that on the occasions where the person who is the target for ridicule has in fact changed his ways, he is none the less marked for ever as ridiculous in the eyes of public opinion.[75] Ridicule, which is an essential feature of comedy, can never therefore be reconciled with any idea of *divertissement*.

Passion is the object of Pégurier's fourth condition, that the harmony of good works must not be dissipated by the destruction of the soul's *gravité*, and here he coincides with St. Thomas's second condition. Pégurier's explanation is based on the standard theory of the passions where, as he says, the harmony of the soul consists in the *accord* and subordination found in its various faculties, in the submission of the lower to the higher part, 'et de la superieure à la Foy et à Dieu'.[76] Christians are persuaded that this subordination and submission cannot be perfect in this life while the soul is imprisoned in the body; there is no victory unless the passions are suppressed.[77] All that excites passion destroys the harmony of the soul, which is in reality the victory of Christianity over the passions.[78] It is in this part of his work that Pégurier sets out to prove that drama is contrary to this principle.

Passion interests other writers in this same context. Gerbais asks how the gravity of the soul may be maintained

---

[71] Ibid., p. 92.
[72] *Lettre d'un docteur de Sorbonne*, p. 100.
[73] *Sentiments de l'Église*, p. 103.
[74] *Réfutation des sentiments relâchés*, pp. 93-4.
[75] Ibid., pp. 97-8.
[76] Ibid., p. 98.
[77] Ibid.
[78] Ibid., p. 100.

while heroes and heroines cry out their passion to the greatest excess, and while the horrible crimes of parricide and incest are displayed before us.[79] Although Coustel does not comment to any great extent upon passion in relation to St. Thomas's second condition, he does refer elsewhere in his work to the incompatibility of *divertissement* with the excitement of passion. Coustel's basic principle is that, even granted that *divertissement* is necessary to man, it does not follow that a Christian may propose as his aim the pleasure of the senses;[80] nor does it follow that one may attend the theatre for this purpose.[81] One evil effect of drama is 'une grande dissipation de l'esprit' where the latter becomes full of ideas seen and heard in the theatre.[82] In this case one must not be surprised to find people abandoning themselves 'à la mollesse d'une vie toute sensuelle'.[83] Thus, instead of indulging in recreation as a means to work more effectively, these people 'se divertissent incessamment, et ne travaillent jamais'.[84] Furthermore, people find nothing solid in such pleasures and pass from one to another.[85] The spiritual dissipation caused by drama is thus incompatible with what others, in the context of the *Summa*, call *la gravité de l'âme*.

Coustel is not alone in his concern that passion should be excluded from *divertissement*. For Nicole the excuse that drama constitutes relaxation is in no way valid 'puisqu'elle [i.e. la comédie] imprime . . . de mauvaises qualitez dans l'esprit, qu'elle excite les passions, et qu'elle y déregle toute l'ame'.[86] Drama is, then, the opposite of recreation. Frain du Tremblay tackles the question of *gravité* when he remarks that we must beware in all our diversions lest the pleasures of the senses 'ne precedent nôtre raison' and lest they weaken 'la vigueur de nôtre esprit, en excitant dans nôtre cœur des passions qui ne luy obeïssent pas'.[87] Finally, Bossuet

---

[79] *Lettre d'un docteur de Sorbonne*, p. 56.
[80] *Sentiments de l'Église*, p. 133.
[81] Ibid., p. 43.
[82] Ibid., p. 45.
[83] Ibid., p. 46.
[84] Ibid.
[85] Ibid.
[86] *Traité de la comédie*, p. 62.
[87] *Conversations morales*, p. 351.

comments that if our corrupt taste can no longer content itself with simple things and it is necessary to awaken 'les hommes gâtés, par quelques objets d'un mouvement plus extraordinaire', he will not hesitate to pronounce that we must find 'des relâchements plus modestes, des divertissements moins emportés'.[88]

Pégurier's fifth condition, that in relaxation one must not disobey the commandments of God or of the Church, is wholly a gloss on St. Thomas and is perhaps inserted in order to reconcile him with other traditional authorities. To this end Pégurier refers to Tertullian's interpretation of various passages from the Bible,[89] mentions a number of Councils,[90] and the importance of the ritual.[91]

His sixth condition, however, corresponds to the third rule of St. Thomas which concerns the appropriateness of time, person, and place, Pégurier adding *affaires*.[92] His initial argument is that since none of the other conditions have been observed there can be no suitable time or place, nor any person who may indulge in the pleasure of drama.[93] Most of the other replies, however, concentrate on the question of time, there being general consternation at Caffaro's comparison of attending plays on Sundays with God's rest on the seventh day of the Creation. Bossuet remarks that 'on nous vient donner le plaisir de la comédie, où les sens sont si émus, comme une imitation du repos de Dieu et une partie du repos qu'il a établi'.[94] He says that for ancient peoples relaxation was found rather in the contemplation of God's law.[95] Another of Caffaro's points, referred to earlier, was that performances begin after the hour of divine office. Gerbais asks whether, after giving ourselves to God, we are then entitled to give ourselves to the devil?[96] Bossuet wonders whether it matters very much what time performances begin,

---

[88] *Maximes et réflexions*, U/L, p. 211.
[89] *Réfutation des sentiments relâchés*, p. 135.
[90] Ibid., p. 139.
[91] Ibid., p. 161.
[92] Ibid., p. 41.
[93] Ibid., pp. 170-1.
[94] *Maximes et réflexions*, U/L, p. 249.
[95] Ibid., p. 248.
[96] *Lettre d'un docteur de Sorbonne*, pp. 112-13.

for would the spectators go to church anyway; 'songent-ils seulement qu'il y a des vêpres?'[97]

But the most daring of Caffaro's points was that according to St. Thomas penitents during Lent, although they must indulge less frequently in *divertissement*, may none the less make moderate use of recreation (which for Caffaro includes going to plays). Gerbais denies the acceptability of drama during a time of penitence, given the fact that drama is a bad thing in itself.[98] Bossuet, however, chooses to attack Caffaro's interpretation of St. Thomas and contends that in the passage concerned it is not a question of Lent at all; even giving St. Thomas's thought a broader frame of reference there is still nothing which comes to Caffaro's rescue.[99] Firstly, he explains, St. Thomas forbids penitents to 's'abandonner dans leur particulier aux jeux réjouissants, parce que "la penitence demande des pleurs et non pas des réjouissances" '.[100] All he allows (this is still quoting from St. Thomas) is moderate use of some games in as much as they relax the mind and 'entretiennent la société entre ceux avec qui ils ont à vivre'.[101] But, Bossuet continues, where St. Thomas speaks of spectacles, his decision is indisputably that penitents should avoid (again a quotation) not only those which are bad, 'dont ils doivent s'abstenir plus que les autres', but also those which are 'utiles et nécessaires à la vie'.[102] Thus, according to Bossuet, Caffaro has mistaken the first part of this quotation as a reference to games in general. Bossuet says earlier that we must not be surprised that spectacles are especially forbidden during Lent; even when they are perhaps innocent 'on voit bien que cette marque de la joie publique ne conviendrait pas avec le deuil solennel de toute l'Église'.[103] Bossuet's view is indeed supported by St. Thomas's statement in the fourth article of *Question 168* that: 'Mirth is forbidden the penitent because he is called

[97] *Maximes et réflexions*, U/L, p. 252.
[98] *Lettre d'un docteur de Sorbonne*, pp. 106-7.
[99] *Maximes et réflexions*, U/L, p. 243.
[100] Ibid.
[101] Ibid. Urbain and Levesque do not contest the validity of Bossuet's interpretation.
[102] Ibid., p. 244.
[103] Ibid., p. 242.

upon to mourn for his sins. Nor does this imply a vice in default, because this very diminishment of mirth in them is in accordance with reason.'[104]

The final word on the problem posed by the use of St. Thomas in justifying performances on Sundays and during religious festivals must, however, rest with Bossuet. Why, he asks, should St. Thomas demand that the time of recreation befit the hour and the man if he does not wish us to understand that some are forbidden on holy days 'quand ils seraient permis d'ailleurs'? As a final thrust Bossuet claims that in any case St. Thomas and other theologians of the past could not be explicit on this point because such a profanation of holy days was inconceivable in their time.[105] Arguments about the exact interpretation of St. Thomas are therefore no longer useful. Guidance can only be sought from the results of a pragmatic analysis of modern drama and prevailing theatrical conditions. For Bossuet and his like these indisputably militate against drama.

Another argument which arose in 1694 from the interpretation of the *Summa* concerns what St. Thomas regards as a virtue in recreation. Caffaro outlines the problem when he asserts that St. Thomas 'n'y croit point de mal, mais encore . . . il y trouve quelque bien, et cette vertu qu'Aristote appeloit *Eutrapelie'*.[106] Caffaro defines *eutrapelia* as 'une vertu . . . qui sait mettre un juste temperamment dans les plaisirs.'[107] Such a view would of course legitimize recreational activities which for Caffaro include drama. It is as well, however, to cast a glance in the direction of the source of Caffaro's view. St. Thomas, in his consideration of the virtue found in recreation, remarks that Aristotle 'assigns to games the virtue of *eutrapelia*, which we may call *pleasantness'*;[108] later he says of games that:

---

[104] *Summa*, IIa. IIae, 168, a.2, ad. 1, vol. 13, p. 302.
[105] *Maximes et réflexions*, U/L, p. 251.
[106] *Lettre d'un théologien*, U/L, p. 72.
[107] Ibid.
[108] *Summa*, IIa. IIae, 168, a.2, ad. 3, vol. 13, p. 296. The original text has *eutrapelia* in Greek letters.

these things are directed according to the rule of reason: and a habit
that operates according to reason is virtue. Therefore there can be a
virtue about games. The Philosopher gives it the name of wittiness
(*eutrapelia*) and a man is said to be pleasant through having a happy
turn of mind, whereby he gives his words and deeds a cheerful turn;
and inasmuch as this virtue restrains a man from immoderate fun, it
is comprised under modesty.[109]

Caffaro seems, therefore, to have understood the virtue to be
that of modesty rather than pleasantness.

Again Caffaro's application of St. Thomas's statements to
drama aroused much indignation among his opponents, La
Grange is adamant that the virtue of *eutrapelia* in no way
authorizes drama because St. Thomas means nothing more
by this term than 'un mélange de la joye et de la modestie
dans des paroles et des actions qui naissent naturellement
au milieu d'une conversation libre, et non pas des paroles
bouffonnes, des mensonges, des fables, et des expressions
d'amour, de vengeance ou d'orgueil, dont les Comedies sont
remplies'.[110] A man is said to have this virtue 'quand il est de
bonne conversation, qu'il sçait tourner d'une maniere bien
séante quelques paroles et quelques actions pour le soulagement de l'esprit'.[111]

Bossuet confines his discussion more to the implications of
Caffaro's statements for comedy in particular. He is indeed
more radical than La Grange in his attack since he wishes to
deny *eutrapelia* the status of a virtue at all: 'je ne sais aucun
des anciens qui, bien éloigné de ranger les plaisanteries sous
quelque acte de vertu, ne les ait regardées comme vicieuses',
although they are not always 'criminelles, ni capables de
damner les hommes'.[112]   The least evil the Ancients find is
that pleasantries are useless and, according to Christ, we must
account for them when the day of reckoning comes; we
should not therefore be surprised if the Fathers condemned
jokes; as for *eutrapelia* they scarcely knew of it.[113]

As his evidence Bossuet discusses the way the term
eutrapelia has been translated and used, particularly in the

[109] Ibid., pp. 297–8.
[110] *Réfutation d'un écrit*, p. 38.
[111] Ibid., p. 40.
[112] *Maximes et réflexions*, U/L, p. 253.
[113] Ibid.

work of St. Paul. Some translators, he says, have translated
the Greek term as *urbanité* or *politesse*; according to the
spirit of Aristotle's work (and according to Bossuet) it may
be rendered as 'plaisanterie, raillerie, et, pour tout com-
prendre, agrément ou vivacité de conversation, accompagné
de discours plaisants; pour mieux dire, des mots qui font
rire'.[114] St. Paul, however, gives the same name to a vice
involving 'paroles, sales ou déshonnêtes' and 'paroles folles';
St. Paul, he adds, does not say that one should never be
'plaisant', but that 'il est malhonnête de l'être toujours, et
comme de profession'.[115] Many moralists will see this as
grounds for condemning the actor, as will be shown in the
next chapter. But such words, in St. Paul's opinion, do not
become a Christian; St. John Chrysostom agrees, including
even the politest jokes in his censure[116] and is astonished that
eutrapelia has ever been regarded as a virtue. It is Bossuet's
claim that this particular Church Father was alluding to
Aristotle in his discussion of the matter.[117]

Bossuet now proceeds to the Latin Fathers who, he tells
us, were no less severe in their treatment of the pleasantries
he equates with *eutrapelia*. Ambrose is quoted as saying that
one must flee them all, and Bossuet remarks that St. Thomas
himself had some difficulty in making Ambrose agree with
Aristotle.[118] Indeed, Bossuet continues, St. Thomas tries to
argue that Ambrose wished to exclude pleasantries only from
doctrinal works, but, Bossuet writes, this cannot be so. Here
he warns us that we must not always expect from St. Thomas
an exact interpretation of the Fathers, 'surtout quand il
entreprend de les accorder avec Aristote, dont il est sans
doute qu'ils ne prenaient pas les idées'.[119]

At this stage of his argument, however, Bossuet tries to
temper the extreme rigour of his earlier statements: although
the Fathers never approved of making people laugh they
allowed in conversation 'la douceur, les agréments, les grâces'

---

[114] Ibid., pp. 253–4.
[115] Ibid., p. 254.
[116] Ibid., pp. 255–6.
[117] Ibid., p. 256.
[118] Ibid., p. 257.
[119] Ibid., p. 259.

and 'un certain sel de sagesse ... qui fait que l'on plaît à ceux qui écoutent'.[120] He adds that if St. Thomas seems to 'pousser un peu plus en avant ... la liberté des plaisanteries', he restricts them none the less to being a few, or, as he says, according to Aristotle 'il faut peu de délectation, comme peu de sel dans les viandes par manière d'assaisonnement'; he also excludes 'ce qui relâche entièrement la gravité'.[121] It must be said that this is relatively faithful to St. Thomas's statement in the relevant section of *Question 168*.[122]

It has already been mentioned that Bossuet equates the disputed virtue of *eutrapelia* with the pleasantries destined to make people laugh. In the context of the dispute this is sufficient for our purposes. But contrast Bossuet's view with another interpretation of *eutrapelia* in Aristotle which, if correct, means that once again Bossuet has overstrained his interpretative powers. Urbain and Levesque, in a note to their edition of Bossuet's *Maximes*, write that *eutrapelia* should rather be translated as 'enjouement, gaieté de bon aloi'; moreover, *eutrapelia* is 'une disposition, une manière d'être, ... et la *plaisanterie* en est seulement la manifestation'; according to Aristotle's definition, 'l'eutrapélie ne dépasse jamais la mesure; elle tient le milieu entre la *sauvagerie* ou morosité, qui, non seulement ne se déride jamais, mais s'indigne de toute plaisanterie, et la *bouffonnerie*, qui cherche à faire rire de tout et de tous, au risque de blesser ceux à qui elle s'en prend'.[123] Thus Caffaro's definition of *eutrapelia* as moderation is somewhat nearer the mark than Bossuet's.

The usefulness of St. Thomas in the justification of drama deserves mention here. Firstly, the relevant part of the *Summa* would seem, in its reference to 'playful words and deeds', to apply exclusively to comedy, and indeed much of the discussion of *eutrapelia* tends in this direction. But in Caffaro's *Lettre*, admittedly published in an edition of

---

[120] Ibid., p. 261.
[121] Ibid., pp. 261-2.
[122] *Summa*, IIa. IIae, 168, a. 4, ad. 3, vol. 13, p. 302.
[123] *Maximes et réflexions*, U/L, p. 300. The reference in the *Nicomachean Ethics* (in vol. ix of *The Works of Aristotle Translated into English*, Oxford, 1925) is Book IV, 8.

Boursault's comedies, the reference of the word *comédie* is
not always explicit, especially when he considers the theatre
of antiquity. His and others' use of the term *spectacles* also
falls into the same category. It is for this reason that I have
mostly preferred to use the term *drama*. Caffaro's detractors
do not themselves limit their replies to comedy, even when
they consider the problems posed by the *Summa*. La Grange,
in his consideration of *eutrapelia*, mentions both 'paroles
bouffonnes' and 'expressions . . . de vengeance, ou d'orgueil',
the latter being more associated with tragedy. St. Thomas is
therefore a spring-board for a discussion of the wider issues
involved.

   Turn the attention from the *Summa* to a complaint made
by Caffaro against what he sees as an unfair difference in the
treatment of drama and attitudes to games of chance which,
he mentions, are banned by rituals, canons, Councils, and the
Fathers without discrimination.[124] The same doctors who so
sonorously quote the Fathers and Councils of the Church are
not so intransigent when it comes to games of chance: abbés,
priests, bishops, and other ecclesiastical gentlemen find no
difficulty in gambling, offering as their excuse that the
Fathers condemn excess rather than the activity itself, which
is 'modéré, sans attache, et seulement pour passer un peu
de temps'. Why, he asks, can this reasoning not be applied
equally to drama?[125]

   Indeed throughout the century religious moralists are on
the whole far from categorical about the moral implications
of gaming as a recreational activity. Senault, in his *Monarque*,
at the same time as finding drama 'le plus charmant' and
consequently the most dangerous *divertissement* of all,
remarks that gambling is not 'entierement criminel', although
it has its excesses and disorders.[126] A similar view is found in
La Dévotion aisée where Le Moyne writes that devotion
condemns 'les jeux où l'on hazarde des sommes excessives'
because such games are neither 'd'honnestes exercices pour
le corps', nor 'd'agréables divertissemens pour l'esprit'.[127]

[124] *Lettre d'un théologien*, U/L, p. 96.
[125] Ibid., p. 97.
[126] *Le Monarque*, p. 238.
[127] *La Dévotion aisée*, p. 113.

Despite the final qualification the emphasis is clearly on the excessive sums involved.

Two of Caffaro's opponents reply directly to his point and draw our attention to the different natures of drama and gaming. Gerbais contends that among the items condemned by traditional authorities and mentioned by Caffaro 'l'on peut garder quelque moderation supportable', whereas drama is something which 'n'ayant ni necessité ni bienséance, mais étant un plaisir purement mondain, n'est susceptible d'aucune moderation'.[128] La Grange offers us a somewhat more detailed explanation. For him, the essential difference between the two forms of *divertissement* is that the evil in gambling has not become so contagious as that present in drama: individuals who like games of chance indulge in them for a short time and it is rather a passing fancy than a constant source of pleasure; furthermore, there is no place appointed for gaming as there is for drama which seems to 'dresser Autel contre Autel, et avoir des Palais fixes, qui sont comme les Temples du Prince des tenebres, dont il se sert pour faire insulte à Dieu'.[129] Another point of La Grange is that there are no assemblies of young men and women involved in gambling.[130] Of course, both points are difficult to substantiate in reality. But the most important difference for La Grange is in the dimension of the two activities: gambling 'n'a qu'une malice successive', which is to say that ordinarily it starts 'par quelque chose de si léger, qu'on ne peut pas toûjours l'accuser de crime'.[131] The theatre-goer, however, 'a dessein d'en goûter le plaisir tout entier, il y abandonne son ame' while 'on voit souvent se retirer du jeu par prudence, ceux qui s'apperçoivent qu'ils sont prêts d'y faire mal leurs affaires'; but 'on ne voit point sortir de la Comedie ceux qui commencent à en goûter le plaisir fatal'.[132] Le Grange adds that although he does not condone gambling others have no right to complain because it is not treated harshly.[133] One activity, to whatever degree permitted, does

---

[128] *Lettre d'un docteur de Sorbonne*, pp. 69–70.
[129] *Réfutation d'un écrit*, p. 78.
[130] Ibid.
[131] Ibid.
[132] Ibid., p. 79.
[133] Ibid.

not justify another. It is all a question of degree but a degree not applicable to drama because a single experience is sufficient to sow the seeds of the corruption which must inevitably follow.

The most serious obstacle, then, to considering drama as a legitimate recreation is that it is incompatible with Christian life. The 'grande dissipation d'esprit' induced by drama can in no way be accommodated with the spirit of prayer which, in Coustel's words, requires 'beaucoup de recüeillement et d'attention', and which is obstructed by the 'divers phantômes des choses qu'on a vûës'.[134] Nicole shows us that drama is useless as recreation because, far from returning us fresh to our Christian duties, it dissipates our minds even further.[135] He concludes that drama is necessary only to those who indulge all the time in *divertissement* and who feel the need to remedy the 'degout' which is the natural accompaniment of 'la continuation des plaisirs': 'Et comme cette nécessité ne vient que de leur mauvaise disposition qu'ils sont obligez de corriger, on peut dire qu'elle n'est necessaire à personne, et qu'elle est dangereuse à tout le monde.'[136]

[134] *Sentiments de l'Église*, p. 45.
[135] *Traité de la comédie*, pp. 62-3.
[136] Ibid., p. 63.

IX

THE ACTOR

So far drama has been discussed as an essentially aesthetic phenomenon and in terms of its effects on the spectator, with some reference made to the physical circumstances of its performance. Among the latter must be counted the presence of actors. Dramatic theorists, however, apart from polemical considerations, hardly discuss the actor's art and regard a play's success in terms of its purely poetic qualities. This is not altogether surprising in cases where poetry is regarded as a fabric of rhetorical figures simply awaiting enunciation. D'Aubignac speaks only of 'combien il faut d'adresse, de suffisance, et de precautions pour achever des Ouvrages qui ne donnent à nos Comédiens que la peine de les reciter'.[1] The actor is seen as an instrument rather than as a creator: hence the emphasis in theoretical writings is on composition rather than on acting.

The religious moralists on the other hand see the actor as directly responsible for what takes place on the stage; he is accused of moral irresponsibility for performing what is corrupt, and making corrupt by means of gesture and tone of voice plays or parts of plays which would otherwise be considered harmless. The actor thereby embodies, in the most literal sense of the word, the corruption of drama; he is the tangible and visible instrument of corruption, and consequently his condemnation often entails that of drama as a whole. But concern for the actor is not limited to his purely theatrical activities, since the time he devotes to these is considered to have adverse effects on his personality, which in turn affect his social and religious status. This last fact makes his position similar to that of the spectator; the latter, however, does not exercise a profession in the theatre, nor is his corruption public to the same extent. Moreover, the actor

[1] *Pratique*, p. 18.

is regarded as the main agent of the spectator's corruption. The actor is thus seen as a very special individual who, by the power he exercises through his art, becomes a danger to the moral welfare of society.

The situation of the author is somewhat different in that, unlike the actor, he is 'absent' from the performance of his creation. Consequently he does not attract the same amount of attention as the actor, especially when the aims of the author and drama itself are often confused; in other words, the author is in many respects the agent of poetry, which is seen to have an independent existence.[2] The author and actor as individuals do, however, share a number of similar features, for example their common need to 'become' the characters they portray, and in such cases the author will be included.[3]

One reason, then, for the actor's unfortunate reputation in the seventeenth century is derived from historical prejudice; since the actor has been condemned for centuries past it follows that this must always be so. Such a view is made to seem respectable by the treatment of actors allegedly associated with Ancient Rome and by the notion of the actor's infamy which Roman law bequeathed to French law. L'Abbé d'Aubignac, in his *Dissertation sur la condamnation des théâtres*, sought to undermine this notion by an analysis of the exact extent of the Romans' discrimination against members of the acting profession. His analysis rests on a number of distinctions of kind between mummers and actors, and between the various dramatic forms of the period. It is as well to emphasize here that this chapter is concerned with the actor's social, moral, and religious position from the purely theoretical standpoints expressed in writings for or against drama. Anecdotes and more general historical considerations are not relevant except where they qualify or contradict particular theories. This approach to historical arguments has regard solely to the interpretation of history

---

[2] For the development of attitudes to writers in the seventeenth century, see Dubu, J., 'La Condition sociale de l'écrivain de théâtre au XVII^c siècle', *XVIIe siècle*, 1958, vol. 39, pp. 149–83.

[3] Pégurier comments that 'il est inutile de recourir icy à la distinction, si c'est par accident ou non', *Réfutation des sentiments relâchés*, p. 120.

by various writers and not to the verification of that interpretation.

D'Aubignac's first point concerns the types of play current in Ancient Rome. He distinguishes between 'jeux de la scène' (mime, crude farce, etc.) on the one hand, and comedy and tragedy on the other; while the former were condemned in Roman law for their extreme licentiousness the latter were exempt from this fate in view of their conformity to certain moral standards.[4] Confusion has arisen between these different forms, he explains, because many subjects of tragedy were often used for mimes performed during the games dedicated to Flora, which were not usually known for their moral purity.[5]

D'Aubignac now turns to a discussion of terms. The actors of tragedy and comedy are not to be confused with those designated by the term *histrio*; the latter are defined as 'gens de Scene ou de Theatre, pratiquans l'art de joüer, bouffonner, et faire monstre de leur corps, par des postures insolentes, et par de ridicules plaisanteries',[6] and it was only in a later period that the word *histrio* was applied indiscriminately to all who appeared on the stage. Even Scudéry is taken to task for not having made such a distinction in his attempt to prove the good conduct of actors of antiquity.[7] D'Aubignac, however, does no good to his own case when in his dissertation on Corneille's *Sophonisbe* he refers to the actors of his own day as *histrions*;[8] admittedly, though, his defence is based on a difference of kind in that he abhors the return of the 'farces ridicules et malhonnestes' that Richelieu had banished from the stage.

[4] *Dissertation*, pp. 104–5.

[5] Ibid., pp. 117–18.

[6] Ibid., pp. 129–30.

[7] *Dissertation*, pp. 172–3. It is worth mentioning here the following statement of Urbain and Levesque: 'Il semble bien que le mot *histrio* est un terme général qui convient à toute personne prenant une part active à un spectacle quelconque. Saint Augustin s'en est servi pour désigner les mimes (*De Doctrina Christiana*, 1.II. cap. III)' (n.2, p. 227).

[8] Granet, i, 138. During the course of this chapter I have sometimes used the Latin form *histrio* and the French form *histrion*. *Histrio* occurs in the context of debates on the definition of the Latin term and is therefore best left in the original. *Histrion* is a term used by d'Aubignac in derogatory references to the actors of his day, for reasons I explain in the text.

In support of his claims d'Aubignac quotes numerous sources, including St. Jerome, St. Cyprian, and even St. Augustine who, he says, mentions that comedy and tragedy were the most reputable of the pagan spectacles.[9] D'Aubignac goes as far as to say that Tertullian, such a frequently quoted source among religious moralists, never charges actors with infamy.[10] This in fact is textually incorrect: in his *De Spectaculis* Tertullian, having said that all fiction is in God's eyes 'adultération du vrai', goes on to say that God could as a consequence never approve 'celui qui altère mensongère- ment la voix de son sexe et de son âge, qui feint l'amour, la colère, les gémissements, les larmes'; God in effect condemns 'tout faux semblant'.[11] The words *infamy* and *anathema* are not actually used but the implication is nevertheless quite clear.

The importance of d'Aubignac's distinctions become clearer in his assertion that 'les Acteurs du Poëme Dramatique ont toûjours esté maintenus dans tous les droicts et les honneurs de la Republique Romaine, et que les Sceniques seulement, les Histrions, les Mimes, et les Basteleurs, exerçans l'art de bouffonner, ont esté marquez de cette infamie, qui fait soûlever tant de gens par ignorance ou par scrupule contre le Theatre'.[12] He also claims that the Fathers' anathema was directed not against dramatic actors but against the 'Histrions' or 'Basteleurs' 'qui par la turpitude de leurs discours et de leurs actions avoient encouru l'indignation de tous les gens de bien, l'infamie des Loix, et l'anathème du Christianisme'.[13] Thus, if comedy and tragedy are in themselves morally sound so are they who perform them. This is to argue that the opinion of the Fathers is not applicable to the seventeenth-century stage.

A firm protest is made against this view by Jean de Voisin whose treatise more than matches d'Aubignac's for sheer weight of erudition. We are presented with the declarations

[9] *Dissertation*, pp. 232–3.
[10] Ibid., pp. 230–1.
[11] Tertullian, *De Spectaculis*, trans. Pierre de Labriolle, Paris, 1937, p. 26.
[12] *Dissertation*, pp. 192–3.
[13] Ibid., pp. 216–17. For a less optimistic view of the actor's status under the Roman Republic, see J. P. V. D. Balsdon's *Life and Leisure in Ancient Rome*, London, 1969, pp. 274–88.

of various councils, parliamentary decrees, and quotations from every conceivable source from the Fathers to the Spanish Jesuit, Mariana. We are even treated to detailed criticisms of d'Aubignac's interpretation of the Latin. Voisin of course rejects d'Aubignac's distinction between 'jeux de la scène', and comedy and tragedy, considering the latter two as occupying only a different place in the hierarchy of pagan spectacles. He thus infers that they both share the infamy accorded to other dramatic forms. Later he attacks d'Aubignac for seeing in the term *ars ludicra* a reference to buffoonery only and with a mass of quotations concludes that it is the *genre* of which tragedy and comedy are *espece(s)*.[14] Voisin also refuses to acknowledge d'Aubignac's distinction between actors and *histriones*. Although he challenges d'Aubignac's categories in great detail, the principle of his dismissal of these distinctions is that 'cette distinction des differens Acteurs de Theatre, ne regarde point la morale, qui ne les distingue que selon la difference de leurs vices, et qui les condamne tous selon qu'ils sont plus ou moins vicieux'.[15] The difference in kind is in other words an aesthetic and not a moral difference.

Turning for a moment to the broader historical perspective could it not be asserted that actors have changed over the centuries? D'Aubignac, in his brief discussion of the theatre of his day, had been content to refer to Richelieu who had re-established the reputation of comedy and tragedy 'en n'y laissant rien de ce qui les avoit exposées justement à l'indignation des personnes d'honneur, et à la peine des Loix'.[16] This is also a clear reference to the edict of 1641 which absolved actors from the charge of infamy. But Voisin manages to use the edict in his own argument by stating that the very need for such an edict proved that actors were still considered infamous during the early years of the century.[17] It is clear, however, that ultimately Voisin does not think that erudite discussion is of any great value since 'Il suffit

[14] *Défense*, p. 150 et seq.
[15] Ibid., p. 134.
[16] *Dissertation*, p. 243.
[17] *Défense*, p. 317. The first ritual of Paris to deviate from the Pauline model of 1614 was published by Jean-François de Gondy, Archbishop of Paris in 1654.

donc de ... dire que l'Église de Paris a déclaré que les Comediens sont notoirement infames et excommuniez. C'est une affaire jugée, il ne faut plus chicaner.'[18]

Church tradition was, however, by no means unanimous in its condemnation of the actor. St. Thomas's *Summa* once again provides ample material for controversy in its apology for those who appear on the stage. St. Thomas considered that the soul's rest is found in pleasure, moreover, that this rest may consist in 'words or deeds wherein nothing further is sought than the soul's delight'.The place of the actor in our recreation is firmly established in the fourth article of *Question 168*:

As stated (A. 2) play is necessary for the intercourse of human life. Now whatever is useful to human intercourse may have a lawful employment ascribed to it. Wherefore the occupation of play-actors, the object of which is to cheer the heart of man, is not unlawful in itself: nor are they in a state of sin provided that their play-acting be moderated, namely that they use no unlawful words or deeds in order to amuse, and that they do not introduce play into undue matters and seasons.[19]

He continues:

And although in human affairs, they have no other occupation in reference to other men, nevertheless in reference to themselves, and to God, they perform other actions both serious and virtuous, such as prayer and the moderation of their own passions and operations, while sometimes they give alms to the poor. Wherefore those who maintain them in moderation do not sin but act justly, by rewarding them for their services. On the other hand, if a man spends too much on such persons, or maintains those comedians who practise unlawful mirth, he sins as encouraging them in their sin.[20]

Earlier in the same *Question* St. Thomas also approaches the problem of the actor's profession making of recreation a full-time occupation, something frowned upon in other circumstances: he remarks that:

---

[18] Ibid., p. 243.
[19] *Summa*, IIa. IIae, 168, a. 3, ad. 3, vol. 13, pp. 300–1.
[20] Ibid., p. 301.

Comedians especially would seem to exceed in play, since they direct their whole life to playing. Therefore if excess of play were a sin, all actors would be in a state of sin; moreover all those who employ them, as well as those who make them any payment, would sin as accomplices of their sin. But this would seem untrue; for it is related in the Lives of the Fathers (ii, 16; viii, 63) that it was revealed to the Blessed Paphnutius that a certain jester would be with him in the life to come.[21]

In the *Summa*, therefore, the justification of the actor follows logically from that of recreation itself. He is certainly not condemned outright. It is interesting too that St. Thomas can conceive of a morally upright actor since the spectator sins only if he encourages 'comedians who practise unlawful mirth'. Moreover, the actor does no injury to his chances of salvation by the simple fact of being an actor so long as he observes his spiritual obligations.

There are, however, implied a number of points which qualify any over-optimistic conclusions. What is the interpretation of 'words and deeds' and what exactly constitute 'unlawful words and deeds'? What is the definition in practice of 'the moderation of their own passions and operations'? Is St. Thomas's actor in any way similar to the actor in seventeenth-century France? Can the tragic actor be included among St. Thomas's *histriones*, especially since he seems to limit his discussion to the question of mirth? Caffaro, who refers extensively to the parts of the *Summa* we have quoted, casts all such doubts aside and refers to all actors without distinction when he claims that 'il ne faut pas croire en état de peché les Comédiens qui passent toute leur vie sur le Theatre, et moins par conséquent les Auteurs qui leur donnent des pieces à représenter'.[22] Thus, in adding authors, Caffaro even makes a complete gloss on the *Summa*.

The religious moralists were not impressed by Caffaro's enthusiasm for St. Thomas's view of the matter. Bossuet denies that there is any question of drama in the *Summa*; the definition of the pleasurable words and deeds provided by St. Thomas's *histriones* is rather '[des] discours facétieux, accompagnés de gestes plaisants, ce qui est encore bien

---

21 Ibid., p. 299.
22 *Lettre d'un théologien*, U/L, p. 75.

éloigné de la comédie'.[23] Allied to this is the question of
whether the actor St. Thomas describes is the same as the
actor in seventeenth-century France. Lebrun explains that in
the saint's time playwrights did not mount the stage, but
simply added 'quelques voix ou quelques instrumens de
Musique à la récitation de leurs Vers dans des maisons
particulieres'; this is very different from an established
theatre with daily performances where, like today, one sees
'des femmes avec les ajustemens les plus recherchez'.[24]
Voisin argues similarly that St. Thomas is speaking only of
jongleurs or of those who play the flute.[25] As for those
who had sought the vindication of the actor in the story of
Paphnutius, Voisin and La Grange emphasize that the man
who accompanied the saint was a musician and, moreover,
had renounced his profession after meeting Paphnutius.[26]
They suggest, therefore, that the actor is in a permanent
state of sin until he too renounces his profession.

As in the case of the more general considerations of drama
the value of St. Thomas's views is held by religious moralists
to be greatly reduced by his method of argumentation.
Voisin maintains that St. Thomas does not state the actor's
freedom from sin as a fact, since he does not consider drama
'dans la pratique commune et ordinaire'; because actors never
fulfil the conditions required by St. Thomas 'dans la pratique
commune, et ordinaire le mestier des Comediens tel qu'ils
l'exercent, et qu'ils l'ont toujours exercé est vitieux'; furthermore, they must give up their profession if they care anything
at all for their salvation.[27] A similar attitude is adopted by
Bossuet in his *Maximes*: St. Thomas excuses *histrions*
(Bossuet is careful to avoid *comédiens* in this context) only
'en supposant que leur action *de soi*, n'a rien de mauvais ni
d'excessif', whereas the seventeenth-century theatre is
'revêtu de circonstances nuisibles'.[28] He strengthens his
attack by a reference to another part of the *Summa* where

---

[23] *Maximes et réflexions*, U/L, p. 230.
[24] *2ième Discours*, pp. 202-3.
[25] *Défense*, p. 362.
[26] Voisin, *Défense*, p. 362, and La Grange, *Réfutation d'un écrit*, pp. 59-60.
[27] *Défense*, p. 365.
[28] *Maximes et réflexions*, U/L, p. 234.

St. Thomas regards the actor's wages as 'ill-gotten'.[29] From this Bossuet concludes that when St. Thomas excuses the actor, 'ou si l'on veut, qu'il l'approuve', he is arguing 'selon une idée générale, abstraite et métaphysique'; but 'lorsqu'il le considère naturellement de la manière dont on le pratique, il n'y a point d'opprobre dont il ne l'accable'.[30]

One final argument concerning the *Summa* commands our attention. In the chapter on *divertissement* it was observed how the denial of *eutrapelia* as a virtue could be prejudicial to the actor. While the earlier discussion was more concerned with the nature of the pleasantries themselves and whether they were fitting for Christian ears, clearly, the discussion must embrace not only the joke but also the joker. Bossuet has the latter in mind in his comment that 'il ne faut pas croire que saint Thomas ait été capable d'approuver les bouffonneries dans la bouche des chrétiens',[31] especially when in St. Thomas's commentary on St. Paul's Epistle to the Ephesians it is explained that included as vices are 'les paroles *par lesquelles on veut plaire aux autres*'.[32]

It is impossible to deny the implications of such a view for the comic actor. We are presented with a similar argument to d'Aubignac's; if the jokes are evil then so must be the joker. Indeed Bossuet adds that although St. Paul allows one to be sometimes *plaisant* 'il est malhonnête de l'être toujours, et comme de profession'.[33] But the words of St. Paul and St. Thomas Bossuet uses to support his argument are of use to him only in the context of the *comic* actor. A little-known comment of Charpentier serves as an interesting contrast to Bossuet's opinion that the nature of the performance condemns the performer. Charpentier first of all denies that all actors are bad and adopts the Thomist line that if actors perform 'des choses honnêtes' then their profession is equally 'honnête'. Indeed 'ce reproche de faire rire les autres, ne regarde que les Acteurs Comiques; il ne touche point les Acteurs Dramatiques'; the latter 'divertissent, non en faisant

---

[29] This passage is found in *Summa*, IIa. IIae, 87, a. 2, ad. 2, vol. 11, p. 99.
[30] *Maximes et réflexions*, U/L, pp. 235-6.
[31] Ibid., p. 231.
[32] Ibid., p. 232. Bossuet's emphasis.
[33] Ibid., p. 254.

rire, mais en donnant de l'admiration'.[34] Charpentier therefore
makes a distinction similar to d'Aubignac's but this time
firmly situated in a contemporary perspective.

Consider, then, the actor in his contemporary setting. The
major work by a layman in the defence of the actor in our
period was Chappuzeau's *Théâtre françois*. Here he attempts
to show how the actor in fact fulfils a moral function in his
intention to instruct. The didactic orientation of drama is
not therefore something simply handed down through the
tradition of poetics but becomes embodied in the very being
of the actor.

According to Chappuzeau the actor's profession is based
on two principles, 'l'honneste divertissement' and 'l'utile
instruction des Peuples'.[35] Moreover, actors set out to bring
men to hate vice and to cherish virtue.[36] He then invokes
the inevitable historical argument that following the example
of the Greeks, who thought that drama could only do good,
other people introduced drama and supported actors.[37] We
even find that French actors are more or less alone in maintaining the moral standards required by the dramatic art.[38]
The existence of actors is also regarded by Chappuzeau as a
force against the corruption of youth so much feared by
religious moralists; many fathers would agree that without
actors many young people would spend their time in places
of debauchery, whereas in the theatre they can at the same
time 's'instruire et se divertir'.[39] Thus actors provide a
morally sound alternative to more corrupt forms of entertainment and as such perform a social duty.

The claim that the actor's aim is to instruct his audience
is greatly contested by religious moralists. In Pégurier's
opinion 'Le desir et le dessein de plaire, est ce qui conduit
l'Auteur et qui anime l'Acteur.'[40] For Rivet the actor's aim
is 'donner du plaisir et du passetemps, aux spectateurs, et

---

[34] Charpentier, Fr., *Carpentariana, ou Remarques d'histoire, de morale, de
critique, d'érudition et de bons mots de M. Charpentier*, Paris, 1724, pp. 388-90.
[35] *Le Théâtre françois*, p. 50.
[36] Ibid., p. 8.
[37] Ibid., pp. 4-5.
[38] Ibid., p. 50.
[39] Ibid., pp. 140-1.
[40] *Réfutation des sentiments relâchés*, p. 107.

en tirer du gain et du proffit',[41] and the actor's greatest wish is to penetrate the hearts of men in order to corrupt their morals.[42] The poet often comes under the same suspicion as the actor regarding his claim to instruct. Lamy describes the author's sole aim as 'plutôt rendre le vice aimable que honteux'.[43] and the *Décision* declares that all who co-operate in the organization of the theatre 'd'une maniere prochaine et determinée' are in a state of sin, particularly authors, because 'leur action tend d'une maniere déterminée à une chose mauvaise'.[44]

One specific reason for denying the actor's claim to fulfil a moral function is that his very art corrupts the text even when the latter is not morally reprehensible in itself. Pégurier writes that 'plus une Piece est modeste et honnête dans la Poësie, plus on la gâte et plus on la corrompt dans la representation par les gestes et les postures'.[45] Moreover, because the moral teaching contained in plays would have quickly bored the spectators, 'les Comediens crurent être obligez de suppléer par l'immodestie des gestes à la modestie de la Poësie'.[46] Even for those actors who do not indulge in the extravagant forms of gesture or posture, Lelevel is uncompromising since 'Une expression ménagée, et un peu de retenuë dans la posture agit plus sûrement', and the actor or actress 'par ses manieres délicates, et sous ses apparences de pudeur ne manque point de porter le coup mortel'.[47] It is easy to see why the actor attracts more attention than the author as an individual; the actor animates the written word and sometimes adds to it. He thus physically embodies the corruption of drama.

Since, according to the religious moralists, an important part of drama's corruption was its arousal of passion in the spectator, it is not surprising that the actor's assumption of the various passions does not stand in his favour. It is, of course, a fundamental dictum of dramatic theory that both

---

[41] *L'Instruction chrétienne*, p. 12.
[42] Ibid., p. 87.
[43] *Nouvelles réflexions*, p. 187.
[44] *Décision faite en Sorbonne*, p. 127.
[45] *Réfutation des sentiments relâchés*, p. 87.
[46] Ibid.
[47] *Réponse à la lettre*, p. 10.

author and actor should themselves experience the passion
they are meant to portray. La Mesnardière declares that the
poet will not produce the necessary effect if he does not
himself feel the 'sentimens interieurs qu'il doit inspirer à
ses Juges'; furthermore, the poet 'se les figure avec tant de
réalité durant la composition, qu'il ressent la jalousie . . . et
la vengeance avec toutes leurs émotions'.[48] But the author
must be none the less absent from his work in that 'le Poëte
dramatique ne parle jamais de soy-mesme' and that 'toutes
ses Productions sont des discours perpetuels des Personnes
introduites'; thus he is obliged to 'entrer dans leurs sentimens,
de se vestir de leurs passions' and to 'espouser leurs interests,
pour les faire passer ensuite dans l'esprit de ses Acteurs, et
enfin par leur ministere, dans l'ame de son auditeur'.[49] It is
precisely this transformation of personality that Scudéry
demands from actors in his *Apologie*: 'Il faut s'il est possible,
qu'ils se metamorphosent, aux personnages qu'ils representent:
et qu'ils s'en impriment toutes les passions, pour les imprimer
aux autres; qu'ils se trompent les premiers, pour tromper le
Spectateur ensuite; qu'ils se croyent Empereurs ou pauvres.'[50]
The theorists' demands in fact amount to an abdication
of self.

Lelevel similarly believes that the actor's experience of
passion is total; he speaks of the actor as one who 'par ses
mouvemens mesurez et par ses expressions sensibles allume
dans le cœur d'un autre le feu criminel dont il est embrasé
lui-même'.[51] Other religious moralists, however, vary in the
degree to which the actor is supposed to deliver himself over
to the experience. Conti remarks that actors 'ne diront que ce
qui est dans leur roole, parce qu'il n'y a que leur memoire qui
s'en mesle'.[52] There is for him no necessary indication of
emotion on the actor's part. Lamy suggests that 'Un
comedien lascif émeut les passions des autres, *en feignant*
d'en avoir luy-mesme.'[53] Passion is thus a question of

---

[48] *Poétique*, p. 73. Corneille has some interesting remarks on the degree to which
actors are involved in their roles in *L'Illusion comique*, ll. 1617–24.
[49] Ibid., p. 364.
[50] *Apologie*, p. 85.
[51] *Réponse à la lettre*, p. 6. See also *Décision faite en Sorbonne*, p. 76.
[52] *Traité de la comédie et des spectacles*, p. 26.
[53] *Nouvelles réflexions*, p. 191. My emphasis.

pretence. Equally Coustel writes that a good actor makes such an impression on his audience because 'il paroist ressentir luy-même cette passion'.[54]

In any case, the actor's assumption of passion to whatever degree can serve only to deny his claim that he fulfils a moral function. For Bossuet the actor's portrayal of passion is harmful because he is communicating his own corruption. What, Bossuet asks, does the actor do but 'rappeler autant qu'il peut [les passions] qu'il a ressenties'?[55] The actor's art is based on his past experience of sin for these passions should have been forgotten and drowned in tears of repentance.[56] Moreover, 'il faut que [les passions] lui reviennent avec tous leurs agréments empoisonnés, et toutes leurs grâces trompeuses'.[57] The actor must therefore relive his life of sin if he is to perform successfully; his performance becomes an exteriorization of his inner corruption.

Certain religious moralists strongly contend that the acting of passion can of itself have an adverse effect on the actor's personality. Even La Mesnardière tells us that some actors, so moved by their roles, find it impossible not to collapse in tears 'et de n'estre point abattus d'une longue et forte douleur après avoir representé des Avantures pitoyables'.[58] Whether this is true or not, it is significant enough that La Mesnardière can believe it. Nicole, affirming that actors really experience the passions they portray, warns that 'il ne faut pas s'imaginer que l'on puisse effacer de son esprit cette impression qu'on y a excitée volontairement, et qu'elle ne laisse pas en nous une grande disposition à cette même passion qu'on a bien voulu ressentir'.[59]

The implications for the actor's life outside the theatre are clear. Indeed for some writers there is no necessary divorce between the actor's life on and off the stage. La

[54] *Sentiments de l'Église*, p. 41.
[55] *Maximes et réflexions*, U/L, p. 180.
[56] Ibid.
[57] Ibid., pp. 180–1.
[58] *Poétique*, p. 74.
[59] *Traité de la comédie*, p. 42. Louis Jouvet says of the actor that 'L'illusion de vouloir être ou d'être un autre lui fait ignorer ce qu'il est lui-même, au moins trouble sa personnalité, son existence' (quoted by Duvignaud, *L'Acteur: esquisse d'une sociologie du comédien*, Paris, 1965, p. 153).

Grange comments that acting demands the total absorption
of the actor even off-stage:

Un personnage à faire, occupe tout entier celui qui en est chargé; il
remplit tout son tems, et ne souffre plus qu'il soit le maître de son
imagination, pour l'arrêter à point nommé: Si un acteur a le personnage
d'un Amant disgracié, ou d'un autre qui réüssit dans ses poursuites;
il y pense jour et nuit; et il songe aux moyens de s'exprimer d'une
maniere vive et touchante.[60]

Moreover, the actor feels passions we should never admit
willingly to our minds 'sans nous croire coupables devant
Dieu'.[61] The actor thus transfers control of his own mind to
an exterior agency to the point at which the alienation of
personality that occurs during the performance is perpetuated
through every hour of the day. Pégurier even sees an inter-
action between the theatre and the actor's domestic life:
those who continually conduct secret intrigues in their own
homes learn to perform them better on stage; or perhaps
'à force de les representer sur le Theatre, [ils] s'accoûtument
et apprennent à les mieux conduire ailleurs'.[62] This points
not to an alienation but to a perversion of the personality.

The connection between the stage and loose morals is
most clearly seen in views concerning the appearance of
women on the stage. Pégurier comments that once a girl
becomes an actress she is lost forever, since there is no
profession where 'on avale plus l'iniquité comme l'eau
que dans celle-là'.[63] The greater part of the religious
moralists' censure regards the unsuitablility of the acting
profession for a woman. Is it not, Coustel asks, an offence
against 'la pudeur du sexe' and 'l'honneur de la virginité'
to see a Christian woman appear on the stage to act the part
of 'une femme passionnée, coquette, effrontée, emportée
ou furieuse selon les diverses passions qu'exige son rollet'?[64]
He evokes the effrontery and impudence of a woman who
is prepared to perform in front of two thousand people, all
of whom are looking only at her. How much, he asks, must

[60] *Réfutation d'un écrit*, p. 64.
[61] Ibid.
[62] *Réfutation des sentiments relâchés*, p. 121.
[63] Ibid., pp. 124-5.
[64] *Sentiments de l'Église*, p. 39.

she 'se fortifier contre la retenuë, si bienseante et si naturelle
à son sexe, pour pouvoir parler avec assurance'?[65] Another
source of indignation is the manner in which the actress, by
her whole act and dress, encourages the rapt attention of her
audience. In one of the letters in Voisin's treatise we read
that: 'La nudité de son sein, son visage couvert de peinture et
de mouches, ses œillades lascives, ses paroles amoureuses, ses
ornemens affetez, et tout cet attirail de lubricité, sont des
filets où les plus resolus se trouvent pris.'[66] Gerbais too feels
distaste at actors appearing 'avec des ajustements mondains
et peu modestes'.[67] Costume also becomes an outward sign
of an inner moral disorder.

The scandal is even greater if the actress is married.[68] Is
she not offending the honour due to the sacrament of
marriage, Coustel asks, by doing everything to appear beautiful in the eyes of so many spectators? Is she not afraid of
appearing before God as guilty of all the sinful thoughts she
inspires in her audience's mind?[69] Bossuet complains that
actresses are disobeying their baptismal vow and is concerned
that such women should be the centre of so much attention,
especially when 'l'infirmité naturelle demandait la sûre
retraite d'une maison bien réglée'.[70] An actress, then, sins
against the natural state of her sex; she is not only responsible
for the thoughts of lust she provokes in her audience but is
guilty of mass adultery!

The life of the acting profession is therefore but 'une vie
molle et sensuelle, une vie de gens qui ne cherchent qu'à
se procurer des commoditez temporelles'; it is a life entirely
opposed to that of a Christian, which is one of mortification,
a refusal of vain pleasure and of the world's false joys.[71]
According to Pégurier actors are more corrupt than others
because 'portant eux-mêmes le poison dans le cœur des autres,
comment pourroient-ils s'en garantir sans des préservatifs

---

[65] Ibid.
[66] *Défense, Lettre I, p. 477.*
[67] *Lettre d'un docteur de Sorbonne,* p. 41.
[68] In this context see d'Aubignac's *Projet pour le rétablissement du théâtre françois* in *Pratique,* pp. 394–5.
[69] *Sentiments de l'Église,* p. 39.
[70] *Maximes et réflexions,* U/L, p. 192.
[71] Coustel, *Sentiments de l'Église,* p. 34.

extraordinaires qu'ils n'ont pas?'[72] Indeed, he says, actors join the profession only 'par la vûe d'un interêt sordide ou par le libertinage'.[73]

There can no longer by any doubt as to the reason why religious moralists regard actors as unfit to fulfil any sort of moral function, for it is a logical conclusion to their views on the gap between the actor's personality and his moral pretensions. Vincent comments that 'Posé qu'un Harlequin prononçast de dessus le Theatre tous les plus graves dits de Seneque, ceste bouche ridicule les exposeroit à la risée', it is:

une absurdité entre les plus grandes, de croire que quelcun deviendra plus chaste, ou plus temperant, pource qu'un Comedien l'y aura exhorté, luy qu'il voit est dissolu, et d'une vie abandonnée.[74]

Rivet too feels that:

ce n'est pas le faict des yvrognes et gourmands de faire des leçons de la sobrieté: et les hommes infames et fripons ne sont pas des precepteurs propres pour enseigner la probité, r'appeler les hommes du vice à la vertu, ... Il faut que celui qui enseigne les bonnes mœurs commence par soy-mesme.[75]

But this last condition is, for Coustel, never translated into reality:

C'est un commandement de Dieu qui regarde generalement tous les Chrestiens de travailler à leur propre sanctification ... Les Comediens en ont-ils jamais eu le moindre dessein? et demeureroient-ils dans un employ qui est condamné par l'Église, s'ils avoient une telle pensée?[76]

Not only are the actors' moral aims denied in practice but they can never by nature fulfil them.

The religious moralists' view of the acting profession as being by its very nature corrupt was not accepted by either Chappuzeau or Caffaro, both of whom suggested that this profession was in many ways indistinguishable from others and thereby constituted no special moral case. Caffaro remarks that actors are:

[72] *Réfutation des sentiments relâchés*, p. 122.
[73] Ibid., p. 62.
[74] *Traité des théâtres*, p. 43.
[75] *L'Instruction chrétienne*, p. 79.
[76] *Sentiments de l'Église*, p. 33.

d'honnestes Gens qui se sont destinez à cet employ et qui s'en acquit-
tent sans scandale et avec toute sorte de bienséance, à moins que parmy
eux il ne s'en trouve de malhonnestes, de même qu'en toute autre
Profession; alors leur malice naist de leur propre corruption, et non pas
de leur état ny de la Profession dont ils se meslent, puisque tous ne leur
ressemblent pas.[77]

In other words, actors are unlikely to be more corrupt than
people in any other profession. Chappuzeau too insists on the
actor's respectability and the idea that actors are in some way
reprehensible is a popular misconception. He is, however,
careful to distinguish between certain types of actor and
drama. He understands by *Comedie* 'celle qui est purgée de
toutes sales equivoques et de mechantes idées', and by actors
'ceux qui vivent moralement bien, et qui parmy les devots . . .
passeroient pour fort honnestes gens dans le monde'; he does
not regard highly an actor who leads a dissolute life but
equally he would scorn anybody from whatever profession
who overstepped the bounds of decency; 'L'honneste homme
est l'honneste homme partout.'[78] Firstly, Chappuzeau
implies in his definition of drama that if it is morally sound,
then so must be the actors who perform it; secondly, he
assimilates the actor to the rest of society, all of whose
members are equal so far as moral judgement is concerned.

Such an argument carries no weight with Pégurier who
draws a distinction between conduct according to the rules of
society and conduct according to Christianity; he too knows
actors who, outside the theatre, give every appearance of
virtue, 'ayant en un mot, tout ce qui fait l'honnête homme
selon le monde', but 'tout ce qui fait l'honnête homme selon
le monde, ne suffit pas pour faire le Chrétien'; it is among
these 'honnêtes gens selon le monde' that corruption is
greatest, although it is not always apparent.[79] The assimilation
of the actor with the rest of society may mean respectability
but not moral probity.

Chappuzeau, however, utterly rejects the argument
according to which the actor's private life does not differ
significantly from his life on the stage. Although, he says,

[77] *Lettre d'un théologien*, U/L, p. 115.
[78] *Le Théâtre françois*, pp. 129-30.
[79] *Réfutation des sentiments relâchés*, pp. 121-2.

acting often obliges actors to perform love intrigues, to laugh
and romp about on the stage, when they return home they
are possessed of 'un grand serieux et un entretient solide';
and in the conduct of their domestic life we find the same
virtue and decency as in any other respectable family.[80]

Gougenot, in his *Comédie des comédiens*, performed in
1631 or 1632, and thus coming at the very beginning of the
movement to raise the status of the professional theatre, is
concerned to demonstrate the actor's knowledge of his
responsibility to society. One actor in the play declares that
as a profession they have observed 'toutes les regles de la
vertu pour parvenir à l'honneur qui doit affranchir le theatre
de blasme et de reproche'.[81] He further remarks that the
intelligence required to become a good actor may be acquired
in time by those who do not possess it through education,
but, he adds to the two aspirants to the profession, 'Puis
donc . . . que vous estes tous deux tres-capables du Theatre
soiez soigneux aussi de son honneur qui consiste en la bonne
conduite.'[82] Gougenot is obviously aware that the theatre's
reputation depends on the behaviour of its actors, and that
the need is for good conduct as much as acting ability. This
is very far from the opinion of those who believe theatrical
life to be but 'une licence au vice'.[83]

Chappuzeau, too, is in no doubt regarding the actor's
responsible position in society. He mentions the fact that in
the past actors had been chosen for many types of public
service,[84] and concludes that the examples he cites are
sufficient proof that actors may be admitted to positions at
court, in society, or in the church 'sans que la profession
qu'eux ou leurs peres ont suivie, et qu'ils quittent alors, leur
serve d'obstacle'.[85] The principal theme of Chappuzeau's
apologia is the attention paid to actors at Court; one reason
given for their favour is 'le plaisir qu'ils donnent au Roy
pour le delasser quelques heures de ses grandes et heroïques

[80] *Le Théâtre françois*, p. 131.
[81] Gougenot, *La Comédie des comédiens*, Paris, 1633, Prologue, p. 2.
[82] Ibid., I, i, pp. 18–19.
[83] Ibid., ii, p. 38.
[84] *Le Théatre françois*, p. 138.
[85] Ibid., p. 139.

occupations'.[86] The King, according to Chappuzeau, is even responsible for the actor's existence: as fathers of the people monarchs have found it appropriate that there should be people devoted to serve the public good 'pour nous representer bien naïvement un avare, un ambitieux, un vindicatif, et nous donner de l'aversion pour leurs defauts'.[87] Moreover, the King authorizes no profession 'qui ne soit juste et utile, et qui n'ayt pour but le bien public'.[88] A position analogous to Chappuzeau's is of course adopted by Corneille in *L'Illusion comique*.

Although Caffaro mentions the positive fact that Floridor had not been deprived of his noble status for acting,[89] he chooses rather to complain that attitudes towards the actor have failed to change in the same way as they have done for other professions formerly viewed as undesirable. A short time previously, he says, innkeepers were considered most infamous but they are now respected as wine merchants and fill the front ranks of the 'Bourgeoisie'. Were not doctors expelled from Ancient Rome? Their children now occupy considerable positions in the Church, 'dans l'Epée et dans la Robe'. What remains of their infamy? Why is the actor's profession still prejudicial to his social status when this is no longer so for other professions?[90]

An answer to Caffaro's first argument is supplied by Gerbais who describes innkeepers and doctors as fulfilling a function necessary to the state, thereby earning praise.[91] Pégurier makes a more important point when he indicates how the actor finds himself torn between civil and religious law: 'Les loix peuvent à la verité décharger et purger d'infamie des gens qu'elles en auroient notez dans un autre temps; mais le public ne reforme pas toûjours l'idée qu'il a une fois conçûë lorsque les Loix s'adoucissent à leur égard; et l'Église

---

[86]   Ibid., pp. 138–9.
[87]   Ibid., p. 10.
[88]   Ibid., p. 129.
[89]   For details of Floridor's case see Maugras, *Les Comédiens hors la loi*, Paris, 1887, pp. 104–5, and Mongrédien, *Les Grands Comédiens du XVIIe siècle*, Paris, 1927, p. 156.
[90]   *Lettre d'un théologien*, U/L, p. 94.
[91]   *Lettre d'un docteur de Sorbonne*, pp. 79–81.

ne reçoit pas toûjours ces adoucissements.'[92] This is a clear reference to the edict of 1641. The law is therefore not necessarily regarded by the Church as an arbiter of morals. La Grange writes on this point that 'la tollerance de plusieurs choses qui seroient à retrancher, inseparable de la Politique, n'excuse point de peché devant Dieu dont la Loi sainte ne flechit jamais, parce qu'elle est la souveraine équité'.[93] Thus the actor performs a social function whereby he provides entertainment which prevents men from committing further evil. (Let us note here that Richelieu's edict states that the actor's activity 'peut innocemment divertir nos peuples de diverses occupations mauvaises'.)[94] This does not, however, bring him the same credit afforded to the innkeeper. The activity in itself is still evil.

But the actor's place in society is further complicated by the relation of his profession to his status as a Christian. It has already been demonstrated that drama is said to be, from the spectator's point of view, incompatible with any sort of Christian life. Is the same true of those who perform it? St. Thomas did not feel that play-acting precluded the possibility of a healthy spiritual existence; he simply requires that actors 'perform actions both serious and virtuous, such as prayer . . . , while sometimes they give alms to the poor'.[95] While Caffaro is content to repeat the words of St. Thomas, Chappuzeau studies the question in some detail.

His first concern is to show that actors perform their spiritual duties, and he mentions the attendance of actors at holy office on Sundays and feast-days, the fact that they assiduously perform acts of devotion, and that the theatre is closed on solemn holy days and during the two weeks of Christ's passion. Moreover, he quotes some actors as saying that since they had embraced a way of life which is most worldly they thought it their duty to 'travailler doublement à s'en detacher, et cette pensée est fort Chrétienne'.[96] Here

---

[92] *Réfutation des sentiments relâchés*, p. 126.
[93] *Réfutation d'un écrit*, p. 83.
[94] *L'Église et le théâtre*, p. 10.
[95] *Summa*, IIa. IIae, 168, a. 3, ad. 3, vol. 13, p. 301.
[96] *Le Théâtre françois*, p. 133. Some Catholic commentators on *Le Tartuffe* in the present century eagerly point to Molière's having observed the Easter devotion the year before his death.

Chappuzeau seems to use as a redeeming feature the actor's own recognition that his profession has some special quality, a fact he has earlier denied. Finally actors 'font des aumônes et particulieres et generales'.[97]

The religious moralists, on the other hand, vehemently deny the possibility of any positive qualities in the actor's religious observances. The general basis for such a view is supplied by Nicole: when one considers that the actor's life is wholly occupied by the excitation of passion, 'qu'ils la passent toute entière à apprendre en particulier, ou à repeter entre eux, ou à representer devant les spectateurs, l'image de quelque vice; qu'ils n'ont presque autre chose dans l'esprit que ces folies; on verra facilement qu'il est impossible d'allier ce metier avec la pureté de nôtre Religion'.[98] But two items of religious observance are particularly deserving of attention, namely attendance at mass and the giving of alms.

Pégurier implies that the actor's participation in the mass is valueless because, 'n'ayant pas la véritable pieté dans le cœur, et ne la pouvant avoir, tandis qu'ils persisteront dans cet employ, qui est condamné par l'Église, toutes les actions qu'ils font par une pieté apparente, ne peuvent plaire à Dieu'.[99] Moreover, the actor is not regarded as a sincere penitent if a basic requirement of his profession is that he be in a constant state of sin, something which St. Thomas specifically denies.[100] Caffaro argues that the inclusion of actors among those forbidden to receive the sacraments is only for those who perform in an indecent fashion.[101] This, as many religious moralists point out, is false and is an interpretation which ignores the intention with which the insertions into the Pauline ritual were made. Moreover, since the whole of drama is condemned by most religious moralists 'acting decently' is void of meaning.

The question of alms-giving is more complex since the matter centres on the moral acceptability of the money

[97] Ibid., p. 134.
[98] *Traité de la comédie*, p. 42.
[99] *Réfutation des sentiments relâchés*, p. 55.
[100] For the historical details of the practice of the Church regarding actors and the sacraments see Mongrédien, *La Vie quotidienne des comédiens au temps de Molière*, Paris, 1966, p. 15 et seq.
[101] *Lettre d'un théologien*, U/L, p. 96.

actors offer as alms. A hint of this problem was given earlier when Bossuet quoted a passage from the *Summa* which clearly condemns profit made from the stage as ill-gotten. Such a view is implicit in the following statement of Voisin: 'Le mestier donc de Comedien qui de sa nature n'a point d'autre fin que de gagner de l'argent par la representation des jeux quels qu'ils soient indifferemment honnestes ou deshonnestes, ne peut estre bon de sa nature, parce qu'il n'exclud pas la volonté de faire le mal, mais l'enferme au contraire, s'il en vient un plus grand profit.'[102] The inference is that actors are spurred on to greater evil if they think a greater profit will come of it. Coustel, while conceding the need for the actor to earn his living, states quite categorically that profit is an evil end and that actors are free to choose a more honourable profession.[103]

In his *Apologie* Scudéry utterly rejects the view that 'la honte pretenduë des Comediens, vient du Salaire qu'ils exigent';[104] it is after all quite normal to be paid for one's work, a point indeed sanctioned by the *Summa*. One of the most remarkable statements on profit comes in the final scene of Corneille's *L'Illusion comique* when Alcandre says:

D'ailleurs, si par les biens on prise les personnes,
Le théâtre est un fief dont les rentes sont bonnes;
Et votre fils rencontre en un métier si doux
Plus d'accommodement qu'il n'eût trouvé chez vous.[105]

Thus profit becomes a justifiable motive for entering the acting profession, a powerful argument indeed for a bourgeois such as Pridamant.

The fact remains that profit from theatrical performances was not acceptable to religious moralists as alms.[106] Gerbais warns actors to beware of boasting about their 'aumônes pretenduës', and doubts whether they are any more acceptable to God than those of a certain cobbler who stole leather to make shoes for the poor; actors 'ne peuvent faire des

---

[102] *Défense*, pp. 270–1.
[103] *Sentiments de l'Église*, p. 42.
[104] *Apologie*, p. 73.
[105] *L'Illusion comique*, V, v, 1665–8.
[106] The regular clergy of Paris were not as reluctant as their secular counterparts in accepting and even begging alms from actors. See Maugras, *Les Comédiens hors la loi*, pp. 167–71.

aumônes que d'un gain sordide et honteux . . . que l'Église
n'approuvera jamais'.[107] Even in the case of their money
being accepted as alms the predicament of actors is not significantly lessened: Lelevel explains that the poor may well
benefit from them but the Church counts them for nothing
'parce qu'elle sçait que demeurant Comédiens, ils ne peuvent
être touchez des biens qu'elle propose à ses enfans'.[108]
La Grange writes that even actors giving all their money to
the poor is to no avail 's'ils n'ont pas la charité'. Alms-giving
requires a certain spiritual predisposition which actors do
not possess. St. Paul, La Grange continues, teaches us that
charity seeks to help others at the expense of one's own
interests, whereas actors 'cherchent leur interêt temporel aux
dépens du salut éternel de leurs freres'.[109] The suggestion is
that since the very profession of the actor is sinful in that he
corrupts others there can be no question of money made
in the theatre serving a purpose sanctified by the Church.

One other criticism arising from the actor's financial
situation is that his standard of living is conspicuously high
compared with that of the less privileged members of the
community. Coustel points to the discrepancy between 'les
pauvres, pâles et decharnez comme des squelettes' dying of
hunger in the streets, and 'des Comediens gros et gras [qui
ne songent] qu'à rire et à divertir des faineans'.[110] Costume
is singled out as symbolic of this indulgent life, Coustel
referring to 'habits magnifiques' and Rivet to 'des femmes et
des filles, parées et desguisées d'habits somptueux'.[111]

Chappuzeau does not agree that the actor's life is one of
over-indulgence: in his experience their table is 'bonne sans y
avoir rien de superflu'.[112] He also justifies the sporting of
fine costume; since actors are often obliged to be constantly
in the presence of 'personnes de qualité', especially at court,
they have of necessity to follow fashion and 'faire de
nouvelles dépences dans les habits ordinaires'.[113] An

[107] *Lettre d'un docteur de Sorbonne*, p. 121.
[108] *Réponse à la lettre*, p. 37.
[109] *Réfutation d'un écrit*, p. 62.
[110] *Sentiments de l'Église*, p. 63.
[111] Ibid., p. 51, and Rivet, *L'Instruction chrétienne*, p. 21.
[112] *Le Théâtre françois*, p. 135.
[113] Ibid., pp. 171-2.

interesting statement on this subject is again found in
L'Illusion comique: uncovering a magnificent array of actors'
costumes, Alcandre says to Pridamant:

Jugez de votre fils par un tel équipage:
Eh bien! celui d'un prince a-t-il plus de splendeur?
Et pourrez-vous encor douter de sa grandeur?[114]

Pridamant's first reaction is to comment upon the discrepancy
between his son's rank and the splendour of the clothes. In
the final scene of the play Pridamant is disabused by the
magician's explanation that:

Le gain leur [i.e. actors] en demeure, et ce grand équipage
Dont je vous ai fait voir le superbe étalage,
Est bien à votre fils, mais non pour s'en parer
Qu'alors que sur la scène il se fait admirer.[115]

It none the less remains true that Alcandre has deliberately
used the splendour of costume in order to illustrate the
actor's glory, just as he has dangled the possibility of profit
before Pridamant's eyes. But costume is also symbolic of the
actor's elevated status in society, enhanced moreover by the
fact that drama is a favourite recreation of the King and his
nobles. The actor, by virtue of his profession, may accede to
a position otherwise impossible for him. He can even imitate
a king, be it only for a few hours.

The actor was of course rehabilitated in law by the edict of
1641 which absolved him from the charge of infamy and
opened the way for him to assume public office and to enter
religious orders. How did the religious moralists view this
move? Basically they regarded it as ineffectual. Lebrun
considers that Richelieu ordered actors to do precisely what
they were incapable of, that is, to perform plays which
contained nothing 'qui ne fût dans la bienséance'.[116] Rivet,
two years before the publication of the edict, contends that
no reform of actors can be possible: who, he asks, could
contain people so accustomed to 'bouffonneries, brocaads,
paroles impudiques, et gestes dissolus' once they are allowed
to set up their theatres and appear in public, 'en sorte qu'ils

---

[114] L'Illusion comique, I, ii, 134-6.
[115] Ibid., V, v, 1637-40.
[116] 2ième Discours, p. 257.

se tiennent és limites de la raison et de l'honnesteté'?[117] His answer is, of course, negative: undertake the reform of actors 'et vous les chasseréz du tout, ou ils ne vous obeiront point, et se rendront plus coupables et de plus mauvais exemple, par le mespris de vos ordonnances'.[118] Lebrun is equally uncompromising: even if actors did not always sin against the prescribed rules and occasionally performed decent plays 'il suffit qu'ils en representent quelquefois d'indécentes, pour être jugez toujours criminels'.[119]

The most categorical refutation of the edict's efficacy is found in Coustel's *Sentiments de l'Église*. He compares actors to poisoners, explaining that if the latter are exterminated, with what execration must we not treat actors who, 'faisant doucement avaller le venin des passions dans les comedies, ostent la vie de la grace, qui est incompatible avec elles'.[120] Moreover, we cannot expect actors to reform because they would cease to be what they were 'et ne pourroient plus divertir le monde, s'ils n'esmouvoient les passions', adding that innocence is something quite incompatible with such a profession.[121] His position on the edict itself is unequivocal: let no actor cite it in his favour: 'Car cet Arrest ne leur peut servir (qu'en cas qu'ils reglent tellement les actions du Theatre, qu'elles soient entierement exemptes d'impureté) ce qui ne doit pas seulement s'entendre de l'amour impudique, mais aussi de toutes les autres passions qui soüillent l'ame, et la rendent desagreable à Dieu.'[122] Now since actors have never fulfilled such a condition and are simply unable to do so because drama cannot be reformed on this point, it follows that they themselves render the edict void and consequently must always be held as 'des gens infames'.[123] The edict is regarded, therefore, as a superficial reform and unworkable because of the actor's fundamental corruption.

The actor is clearly established as an undesirable figure in

---

[117] *L'Instruction chrétienne*, p. 84.
[118] Ibid., p. 83.
[119] *2ième Discours*, p. 202.
[120] *Sentiments de l'Église*, p. 84.
[121] Ibid.
[122] Ibid., p. 40.
[123] Ibid.

society because of the nature of his profession. Some writers
do not understand, however, why a similar condemnation is
not extended to boys who act in their schools. One defence
of drama in d'Aubignac's *Dissertation* is that is still constitutes
'l'exercice de la jeunesse studieuse', and he mentions that the
Jesuits compose and produce an enormous number of plays
using their pupils as actors.[124] Caffaro is much more specific
in his reference: if actors are infamous through performing
plays, by what criterion may young people in schools portray
dramatic characters 'pour se divertir et sans scandale'.[125]

The replies to Caffaro's complaint distinguish a number of
elements in the comparison of the public theatre with school
drama. In the first place they are seen to have completely
different aims. Coustel explains that the aim of school plays
is to equip young people with 'une loüable hardiesse de
paroistre et de parler en public avec grace et bienseance',[126]
(although pure enjoyment is not absent, for Bossuet writes
that plays may also constitute 'quelque honnête relâchement'
at the end of the year).[127] Similarly, Vincent, many years
before the *affaire Caffaro*, remarks upon the difference
between verse recited by children 'en un *College privé*, pour
leur façonner la grace' and a theatre 'dressé en un lieu *public*
sans utilité quelconque, et tout au contraire avec peril
evident'.[128] While the intention of the public theatre is to
corrupt, school drama has a good and useful aim, being no
more than a rhetorical exercise.

The content of school drama was in fact strictly regulated
by the *Ratio Studiorum* of 1583. This document, frequently
mentioned by the religious moralists under discussion,
forbade secular plays, ruling that dramatic subjects should be
in Latin and have a sacred theme. Vincent remarks that 'une
composition sur quelque belle histoire, diligemment examinée
par un Colloque' is very different from plays performed by
professional actors, where one finds mostly 'des fictions,
dont le theme est un amour sale, et dont la representation

---

[124] *Dissertation*, pp. 237-8.
[125] *Lettre d'un théologien*, U/L, p. 92.
[126] *Sentiments de l'Église*, p. 110.
[127] *Maximes et réflexions*, U/L, p. 266.
[128] *Traité des théâtres*, p. 49. Vincent's emphasis.

prejudicie à la Societé'.[129] The *Décision* says more simply
that 'Les sujets en sont bien plus purs.'[130]

The religious moralists also deny any possibility of
comparison between the circumstances of school performances and those which generally accompany performances in
the public theatre. Vincent comments that the infrequency
of plays in schools prevents the waste of time encouraged by
the actor's theatre.[131] Gerbais claims that school plays take
place 'sans scandale' and 'hors certaines circonstances qui ne
s'ajustent pas avec la Modestie chrêtienne, et qui sont
inseparables des representations pompeuses et mondaines'.[132]
The *Décision* asserts that 'la modestie du Theatre est bien
plus grande, les passions en sont moins vives et moins
violentes; les circonstances enfin du lieu, du temps auquel les
Tragédies se joüent, et encore des personnes qui s'y trouvent
fournissent bien moins d'occasions d'offenser Dieu'.[133] It is
interesting to note that passion is not absent from these
exercises; it is present to a lesser degree.

Finally, there is a difference in the moral implications of
acting for schoolboys and actors. The major distinction
between the performers is that the actor exercises a profession
in the theatre. Voisin contrasts boys who perform only
'choses honnestes' for practice in public speaking with actors
'qui font un mestier honteux de ces spectacles pour gagner de
l'argent, à qui il est indifferent de representer des choses
honnestes ou mal honnestes'.[134] Thus schoolboys make no
money from acting and perform only what is morally good.

The special case made out for school drama by the religious
moralists is unacceptable to Chappuzeau. Although the
Théâtre françois appeared some twenty years before the
affaire Caffaro Chappuzeau dealt with many of the arguments
advanced in 1694. In contrast to the rule that forbids the
acting of secular plays, Chappuzeau claims to have witnessed
performances in schools of Plautus, Terence, and Seneca.

[129] Ibid.
[130] *Décision faite en Sorbonne*, p. 83.
[131] *Traité des théâtres*, p. 48.
[132] *Lettre d'un docteur de Sorbonne*, pp. 76-7.
[133] *Décision faite en Sorbonne*, p. 83.
[134] *Défense*, p. 277.

Moreover, even in religious communities there are constructed every year 'de superbes Theatres pour des Tragedies, dans lesquelles par un meslange ingenieux du sacré et du profane toutes les passions sont poussées jusqu'au bout'.[135] Chappuzeau suggests, of course, that in its content and setting school drama is taken much more seriously than a mere rhetorical exercise.

Chappuzeau sees the only difference between drama performed in schools and in the public theatre as being in the language used, and in the quality of the performers. School plays may very well be in Latin; since, however, Latin is understood by both actors and public the passions of love and ambition can have just the same effect as in a performance of *Cinna* or *Pompée*.[136] As far as the circumstances of school drama are concerned, although there are no women on the stage, there are a great number in the audience.[137] Chappuzeau is therefore using an argument commonly directed against the public theatre in the context of school drama; performances become a meeting-place for both sexes. Coustel's rhetorical exercises are opportunities for public enjoyment.

It is possible that Chappuzeau's argument is exaggerated for the sake of polemic. In many cases, however, the scholarship of Maugras, Boysse and many others largely substantiates his claims. Maugras writes of the nature of the occasion that:

> Ces représentations étaient assez fréquentes; elles n'avaient pas lieu, comme on pourrait le croire, dans l'intimité et en présence de quelques parents et amis; le public y était admis librement et il payait sa place tout comme au théâtre. On y accourait en foule, et les femmes particulièrement marquaient un goût des plus vifs pour ce genre de divertissements.[138]

Admittedly the source of his evidence is Loret who claimed he had paid fifteen *sols* for a seat, but the fears of excess recorded in the works of some religious moralists certainly suggest that these performances were much more than

---

[135] *Le Théâtre françois*, pp. 17–18.
[136] Ibid., pp. 18–19.
[137] Ibid., p. 20.
[138] *Les Comédiens hors la loi*, p. 110.

improvised affairs. Chappuzeau himself mentions 'de superbes Theatres' and it seems that schools provided quite sumptuous decors for their productions.[139] There is a lengthy passage in the work of the anonymous preacher from Cologne which criticises the income religious communities receive from such productions,[140] and many religious moralists complain of the time spent on them.[141] Finally, although the *Ratio Studiorum* forbade female roles there is abundant evidence from the programmes of performances produced for prize-givings that such roles did in fact exist.[142]

The fact remains, however, that the actor is for religious moralists a *personnage maudit*. Firstly, there is concern at the moral impunity of the actor when he is on the stage. Vincent complains that since plays sometimes tell the most horrible stories and re-enact the crimes of the past we must recognize this as a dangerous artifice of the Devil who has found a subtle means of pronouncing 'impunément dessus le Theatre, ce qui ailleurs seroit puny de mille gibets et de mille roües'.[143] The actor is here little more than a common criminal.

But most of all, as stated earlier, religious moralists disapprove of the ways plays suggest that there are forces in the world derived from a purely human source, of which the actor is the perfect illustration. In the first place, in his assumption of different roles, he suggests the possibility of a world different from the one we see around us and which is of man's making. It is no accident that disguise should be particularly attacked for this itself is seen to contravene the order of Providence. Vincent damns those who disguise themselves as women as wishing to 'sortir du rang où [leur] Créateur [les] a mis', and actors conceal by masks 'l'image de Dieu, que luy-mesme a empreinte dessus

---

[139] See Boysse, E., *Le Théâtre des Jésuites*, Paris, 1880, pp. 63–8.
[140] See *Instructions morales et populaires*, pp. 39–40.
[141] Ibid., pp. 40–1, and Coustel, *Sentiments de l'Église*, p. 110.
[142] See Boysse, *Le Théâtre*, p. 28. For a more detailed discussion of this topic, see my forthcoming article, 'Le Théâtre scolaire dans la querelle du théâtre au dix-septième siècle', in *Revue d'histoire du théâtre*.
[143] *Traité des théâtres*, p. 9.

nostre face'.[144] The suggestion is, then, that the actor appears
to derive strength from his person alone, thus dispensing with
the need for God. Lelevel comments that: 'Celui qui parle
comme n'appuyant que sur ses propres forces, comme tirant
de luy-même la plus pure vertu et le bonheur le plus parfait,
qui transporte à la Créature ce qui est dû au Créateur, est-il
exempt de blasphême et d'adultere dans l'école du Théologien
[i.e. Caffaro]?'[145] A similar idea is found in his remarks
concerning the Academy of Music which, given the last
statement, could equally well apply to the actor: here 'l'on
fait de l'orgueil et de la confiance en soi-même la plus sublime
vertu'; furthermore: 'De misérables créatures y affectent la
puissance et la majesté divine; elles veulent faire servir toute
la Nature à leurs passions; on n'y réveille que des idées
profanes, on n'y travaille qu'à enchanter les ames par les
sens.'[146] The actor, in showing the strength and possibilities
of the self, becomes a source of great danger to the Christian
religion. We may therefore apply more generally what Jean-
Marie Piemme finds implicit in Nicole's *Traité*, namely that:
'[il] dénonce l'autonomie du domaine artistique et ses con-
séquences esthétiques parce qu'il ne peut concevoir l'existence
d'un monde où Dieu serait absent . . . A un monde régi par
la loi divine, [le poète] en substitue un autre où domine la
volonté du dramaturge. Nicole ne peut accepter que l'artiste
soit "le singe de Dieu".'[147]

---

[144] Ibid., p. 8. It is against God's law as expressed in Deuteronomy 22: 5 that a
person of one sex should take the clothes of another. (See Rivet, *L'Instruction
chrétienne*, pp. 48-50.)
[145] *Réponse à la lettre*, p. 6.
[146] Ibid., pp. 18-19.
[147] Piemme, J.-M., 'Le Théâtre en face de la critique religieuse: un exemple,
Pierre Nicole', *XVIIe siècle*, vol. 88, Paris, 1970, pp. 49-59, p. 53.

X

THE THEATRE, THE CHURCH, AND THE STATE

The theatre in seventeenth-century France is clearly seen by most religious moralists as an undesirable and harmful institution. Indeed the extremity of the views presented in previous chapters poses the question whether the theatre can be allowed to exist at all; in other words, should the theatres be closed, as they were in England at the time of Cromwell? In France, however, the situation was slightly different: the secular and religious authorities did not combine in the exercise of power. Moreover, they were not of one mind in questions of morals and this was particularly the case with drama. Certain sections of the Church may indeed declaim against the theatre from their pulpits and in their rituals, but Richelieu, the Court, and Louis XIV liked and encouraged it. Those who defended drama were not slow to point this out.

The most celebrated attempt to defend the theatre by the quality of its supporters is found in Corneille's *L'Illusion comique*, where drama is described as:

Le divertissement le plus doux de nos princes,
Les délices du peuple, et le plaisir des grands.[1]

Moreover;

Même notre grand Roi, ce foudre de la guerre,
Dont le nom se fait craindre aux deux bouts de la terre,
Le front ceint de lauriers, daigne bien quelquefois
Prêter l'œil et l'oreille au Théâtre françois.[2]

Two things are implied here: firstly, if it is legitimate for those who govern to attend performances of plays, it is equally so for the ordinary individual; secondly, the theatre is given an important role in the well-being of the State.

Caffaro introduces a more controversial argument into the discussion when he mentions the attendance of bishops,

---

[1]   *L'Illusion comique*, V, v, 1650–1.
[2]   Ibid., 1657–60.

cardinals, and papal nuncios at court performances, adding that it would be madness to assume that all these great prelates 'sont des Impies et des Libertins, puisqu'ils autorisent le crime par leur présence'.[3] The implication is that drama cannot be as bad as some writers suggest, even though he says later that he would have difficulty in absolving the people he has mentioned from the charge of mortal sin, since priests are forbidden to attend the theatre.[4]

Caffaro's detractors are quick to point to this apparent contradiction in his argument.[5] How, they ask, can one use the presence of prelates as proof of a play's decency when, at the same time, they commit a mortal sin in watching it? Caffaro means, however, that those in holy orders are bound by a different set of standards from other men because they have renounced the world and its pleasures. But it has already been shown that Varet and Nicole reject any such distinction between the rigours of Christian duty for the lay and ordained members of the Church.

Most of all, the replies to Caffaro's arguments do not agree that the practice of some members of the Church in any way invalidates their teaching. Lebrun distinguishes between act and advice: even if we admit that some prelates have attended plays, we should regulate our conduct according to what they preach in public, in their Councils and Synodal statutes rather than according to their actions as private individuals. The authority of the Church as a body is, then, more important than the conduct of its individual representatives. Gerbais, however, seeks a more equitable judgement than Caffaro's upon the dignitaries of the Church, saying that if prelates do attend performances at court 'c'est qu'ils sont entraînez par le torrent des Courtisans, et non pas qu'ils y aillent avec inclination et de leur gré'.[6]

The most fully developed thesis rejecting the argument that an audience which includes high-ranking members of the social hierarchy either excuses the institution of theatre or its

---

[3] *Lettre d'un théologien*, U/L, p. 99.
[4] Ibid., pp. 115-16.
[5] See Coustel, *Sentiments de l'Église*, p. 106, and Gerbais, *Lettre d'un docteur de Sorbonne*, pp. 88-90.
[6] *1er Discours*, p. 32 and *Lettre d'un docteur de Sorbonne*, p. 90.

attendance by less distinguished individuals comes from Vincent in 1647. He reminds spectators that in the first place they are neither kings nor princes, and in the second that the important question is not whether a certain type of conduct is in vogue at court, but whether it conforms to God's teachings; thus, 'si la conscience de quelcun luy dit que Dieu y est offensé, et son Église scandalisée, l'exemple de tous les Princes de la terre ne le doit pas emporter dessus le devoir'.[7] The conduct of certain individuals is therefore no yardstick, especially when one is bound by the oath of the Reformed Church. The reputation of the latter plainly takes precedence over conformity with the rest of society in one's pleasure. But Vincent is careful not to attack (consciously, at least) the conduct of the King himself; the King's edicts, to which everyone owes unconditional obedience, are still sacred, and we have no right to question acts which are his private concern; moreover, the intentions of all kings 'sont à la vertu, et à ne rien faire où elles creussent que Dieu fust offensé'.[8] He further excuses the King's attendance at plays by suggesting that on such occasions actors are highly circumspect in what they perform.[9] His final comment is perhaps meant to placate the Jesuits when he says that if those who govern the conscience of kings allow such diversions he, Vincent, has no right to meddle in what is not his concern.[10]

Caffaro, however, adds further weight to his argument when he contends that by attending plays the King and other people of importance actively approve of drama; moreover, the Church can have no real objection to it because it too tolerates its existence by doing nothing to suppress it. Caffaro specifically mentions the toleration of posters which publicly invite people to attend forms of spectacle performed 'avec privilege du Roy et par des Troupes entretenuës par Sa Majesté'; if, on the other hand, one were invited by such means to eat meat on days when it is forbidden, it is certain that magistrates, far from permitting such publicity, would severely censure its authors 'qui abuseroient de l'autorité

---

[7] *Traité des théâtres*, pp. 60-1.
[8] Ibid., p. 60.
[9] Ibid.
[10] Ibid., pp. 59-60.

d'un Roy tres-Chrestien et tres-Religieux, pour inviter les fidelles à commettre des crimes si énormes'.[11] If they do not in the case of the theatre, then no argument exists for condemning it. Thus, he continues, drama as it exists cannot be so harmful since it is neither forbidden by magistrates nor opposed by prelates; furthermore plays are performed 'avec le Privilege d'un Prince qui gouverne ses Sujets avec tant de sagesse et de pieté, qui n'a pas dédaigné d'y assister luy-même, et qui ne voudroit pas par sa présence autoriser un crime dont il seroit plus coupable que les autres'.[12]

The position of Archbishop Harlay of Paris was vigorously defended by Caffaro's opponents. Gerbais,[13] Pégurier,[14] and Coustel[15] all mention his conduct over Molière's burial and his invocation of the insertion of actors into the list of those forbidden the sacraments in the ritual. They even refer somewhat cruelly to Caffaro's own treatment, for he was deprived by the Archbishop of his functions as a priest for having written a defence of drama. The most important observation to be made, however, is that the reluctance to criticize the King in this matter is not limited to the Protestant Vincent. Pégurier is convinced of 'la droiture des intentions de Sa Majesté',[16] and Gerbais is confident that the King, in his toleration of the theatre, has 'raisons de politique' which are not our concern.[17]

This of course leads directly to the question of the relation of Church and State in the realm of moral responsibility. Gerbais has suggested that the King has a specific aim in view, which is no concern of the Church. Where, then, in the case of drama, does the Church's responsibility begin and end? Pégurier marks very clearly the limits of the Church's power when he says that 'L'Église n'est pas responsable de tous les desordres qu'elle ne détruit pas; et il y a bien des choses dont elle gemit sans y pouvoir remedier.'[18] The policy of the State

---

[11] *Lettre d'un théologien*, U/L, pp. 99–100.
[12] Ibid., p. 100.
[13] *Lettre d'un docteur de Sorbonne*, p. 86.
[14] *Réfutation des sentiments relâchés*, p. 165.
[15] *Sentiments de l'Église*, p. 108.
[16] *Réfutation des sentiments relâchés*, p. 167.
[17] *Lettre d'un docteur de Sorbonne*, pp. 95–6.
[18] *Réfutation des sentiments relâchés*, p. 165.

is to some extent independent of the Church because 'tout ce qui se fait dans la Police n'est pas examiné par les regles severes de la Morale, et que la Police ne prétend pas justifier tout ce qu'elle permet. En cela, la Police évite de plus grands maux par un moindre qu'elle tolere.'[19] The theatre is a necessary evil which prevents men from committing harmful acts. Coustel, replying to the possible objection that magistrates should close the theatres because it is their duty to defend God's majesty as it is reflected in the Christian faith, writes that 'la prudence et les maximes de la politique' often oblige magistrates to tolerate certain things despite their personal principles; he affirms that they know exactly what they owe to God and to their religion, and that if they sometimes appear to relax their code it is because of 'la crainte de voir troubler l'État et le repos public par des esprits inquiets et remuans'.[20] Thus both the Church and the magistrates must recognize the inevitable presence of evil in society and their relative powerlessness before it. As has already been said, the theatre exists as a relatively harmless outlet for evil inclinations, in that it does no ill to the body politic.

The distinction between the religious and civil domains, and its consequences for the spectator (and the actor), is dealt with at length in Lelevel's reply to Caffaro. He in fact emphasizes the king's position more than that of magistrates but the essential principles are the same. He admits that princes must work for the good of the Church but this does not necessarily mean that the rules of each always coincide; it is enough that kings 'fassent observer les loix divines et ecclesiastiques autant qu'il est en leur pouvoir, et qu'ils n'en fassent point de contraires'.[21] On seeing that most of his subjects have not the education befitting Christians, and believing that if they engaged in no form of activity at all they would commit excesses dangerous to the State, the prince must tolerate drama as we know it, 'accommodée aux sens et aux passions, comme un mal beaucoup moindre

[19] Ibid., p. 169.
[20] *Sentiments de l'Église*, p. 107.
[21] *Réponse à la lettre*, p. 26.

que ceux qu'il apprehende'.[22] The prince does all in his power to see that God's law is observed and 'il nous laisse instruire par l'Église';[23] if we do not follow the precepts of the Church, then 'c'est nôtre affaire'.[24] The limits of kingly and ecclesiastical power are clear: the king does not rule over individual conscience, just as the magistrates are not bound by uniquely moral considerations. Lelevel explains that the king's power is confined 'au bien et à la conservation de la societé civile'; here he replies to one of La Bruyère's comments on actors (in which the latter says that we must either treat actors more equitably or close the theatres)[25], saying that 'Si on ne ferme point le Théâtre, c'est par pure politique; et si on le condamne, c'est par principe de Religion.'[26]

Having then asked why so few people are intelligent enough to distinguish between 'un remede au corps politique' and 'ce que la Religion que nous professons peut souffrir',[27] he proceeds to develop his thesis:

On peut dans l'ordre civil permettre un mal dont les effets sont moins tumultueux, pour éviter des maux trop éclatans et sans reméde. Mais la Religion est toute pure et toute sainte; elle n'a jamais souffert et ne souffrira jamais aucun mal. Les deux mots de *remede* et de *divertissement* ne lui imposent point; elle déteste tout ce qui est un mal en soi, tout ce qui nous lie à autre chose qu'au Créateur.[28]

Lelevel continues:

La politique met l'ordre qu'elle peut dans les dehors, elle s'accommode à l'homme tel qu'elle le trouve; mais la Religion va droit à l'interieur, et tend à rendre l'homme tel qu'il doit être; l'une n'a pour but que la conservation d'une societé exterieure; l'autre établit entre Dieu et nous une communion parfaite de sentimens et de pensées; l'une et l'autre sont subordonnées, mais chacune a son objet déterminé.[29]

The moral latitude afforded the ruler by such a view — he

---

[22] Ibid. The edict of 1641 records a similar wish.
[23] Ibid., pp. 26-7.
[24] Ibid., p. 27.
[25] *Les Caractères*, ed. R. Garapon, Paris, 1962, 'De Quelques usages', no. 21, pp. 419-20.
[26] *Réponse à la lettre*, p. 27.
[27] Ibid., p. 28.
[28] Ibid.
[29] Ibid., pp. 28-9.

'uses' the sins of his subjects (and perhaps his own) for higher ends — is clearly very great. The same is not true of the subjects themselves who have no other end in view than their own pleasure. This is the concern of the Church which otherwise compromises with the needs of the absolutist state.

Caffaro had endeavoured to prove from the magistrates' toleration of the theatre that the latter is not harmful and may be attended without fear of corruption. His opponents argue that toleration is merely a political expedient and that the individual is still responsible to the Church, since he owes obedience to its rulings. Coustel writes that toleration is not the equivalent of approval, and that since drama has been condemned in the Scriptures and by the Councils and Fathers of the Church 'la dureté des hommes qui ne veulent pas deferer à ces loix de Dieu, qui sont immuables, sera sans doute tres-severement punie dans son Jugement'.[30] If the authority of the Church condemns drama, then we sin by watching it. The plays themselves may be politically necessary but are condemned according to immutable moral standards, the latter being the most important consideration for the individual. That drama is *legal* does not make it *moral*.

Since, then, according to some of its members, the Church is led to accept the fact of the theatre's existence in society, the question arises whether or not it is worthwhile to attempt some practical reform of drama, which would obviate the religious moralists' objections to it. Although Caffaro believes that the king's attendance at plays and their toleration by the Church proves that they contain nothing 'qui puisse empescher en conscience les Chrestiens d'y assister',[31] even some defenders of drama are not entirely happy with the moral quality of plays. D'Aubignac, while referring to Richelieu as having re-established the theatre's reputation in the eyes of the law and of honourable men,[32] at the same time deplores the reintroduction of farces, which have contributed formerly to the theatre's dishonour. In 1674 Chappuzeau still feels obliged to admit that actors and

---

[30] *Sentiments de l'Église*, p. 108.
[31] *Lettre d'un théologien*, U/L, p. 100.
[32] *Dissertation*, pp. 242-3.

plays have their defects.[33] But ridding society of the theatre altogether is no solution for him because, as he says, such an attitude would lead to the expulsion of other arts, like painting. His answer is reform; then theatre-goers might eventually be able to enjoy performances 'où il y eust un peu moins de bagatelles et plus de solide', and plays consisting of 'choses bonnes et honnestes' rather than farces.[34] It is particularly interesting to find that Leibniz, in what is left to us of a letter concerning drama and addressed to Caffaro's detractors in 1694, writes that 'il faut plus tost songer à la rectifier qu'à la rejetter'.[35]

In 1684 a remarkable and little-known work by Héliodore de Paris, a Capuchin preacher, proposed just this. But the main importance of his work lies in his views on the role of the magistrature in drama, for they stand in direct contrast to the views just expressed regarding the division of responsibility between the secular and the religious domains. His argument rests on the division of plays into three categories: plays are 'ou innocentes, ou criminelles, ou en partie innocentes et en partie criminelles',[36] the latter being plays where crime is concealed beneath a mask in order to protect the spectator's sensibilities, and where, despite frequent exhortations to virtue, the central character yields to evil while blinded by passion.[37] Some playwrights write these plays in such a way that 'les plus méchans y trouvent suffisamment de quoy se contenter, et que les bons, à moins d'estre bien eclairez, ont de la peine à y découvrir ce qui merite la censure, et sont presque contraints de suspendre leur jugement, et de dire ... [que] la chose n'est pas constante'.[38] Such plays are more dangerous than those which are thoroughly evil for three reasons; they maintain and increase disorder in a person who is already corrupt; they corrupt those who are in some way disposed towards vice, since there is too much poison present not to ruin a

[33] *Le Théâtre françois*, p. 30.
[34] Ibid., p. 48.
[35] Leibniz, Gottfried W. von., *Correspondance avec l'Électrice Sophie de Brunswick–Lunebourg,* ed. O. Klopp, 3 vols., Hanover, 1874, p. 307.
[36] *Discours*, i, 280.
[37] Ibid., 300.
[38] Ibid., 302.

weak and crumbling moral constitution; finally, 'les bons sont souvent perdus pour avoir osé les voir joüer'.[39]

But Héliodore does not categorically reject all drama merely because certain parts of it are corrupt. He finds, on the contrary, that some plays are 'des copies animées de l'innocence et de la sainteté'.[40] What he actually means here is not clear, but the reference cannot only be to religious drama, as suggested by the term *sainteté*, because he says that secular subjects are also a rich source of drama; 'les mœurs des siecles luy donnent d'amples matieres, et si le tout est traité avec la bienseance qui est convenable à la Religion, et à l'honnesteté publique; leur innocence est à couvert des foudres'.[41] But there is some confusion when he adds that such productions serve 'à former l'éloquence, à corriger les mœurs, à soulager l'esprit', and 'n'estant pas criminelles d'elles-mesmes, et estant si utiles au public, elles ne meritent pas les anathémes de l'Église'.[42] 'Former l'éloquence' does imply that Héliodore is talking of school drama, although in this case it is unlikely that he would condone profane subjects when they are strictly forbidden by the rules. The mention of such subjects at the same time as plays which are dangerous, the reference to the public, and later considerations regarding magistrates and professional actors all suggest that he is in fact speaking in a wider context.

Héliodore's acceptance of some forms of drama does not prevent him, in the case of plays he considers dangerous, from imposing strictures on the spectator similar to those found in the works of other religious moralists. He agrees that it is a far greater sin than people think to contribute 'à l'entretien des Acteurs de ces méchantes Pieces', and to authorize by their presence and 'bienveillance' people devoted to the corruption of morals.[43] Héliodore's leniency has its limits: although he distinguishes between different categories of plays, there cannot really be a distinction between types of actors since they perform all types of play,

[39] Ibid., 307.
[40] Ibid., 281.
[41] Ibid., 283.
[42] Ibid.
[43] Ibid., 284.

irrespective of their degree of decency.

It is in the question of the actor that it can most clearly be seen where Héliodore departs from other religious moralists on the question of civil and ecclesiastical responsibilities. As far as dangerous plays are concerned, he says, the ecclesiastical authorities have done as much as is in their power,[44] and in this context he mentions two Councils of Arles which forbid the sacraments to actors unless they renounce a profession which not only inspires crime, but is 'coupable de tous ceux qu'elle fait, et qu'elle peut faire commettre'.[45] But the great interest of Héliodore's work lies in his demand that the secular powers complete what is necessarily left undone by the Church, whose power in social matters is limited. The Church's sanctions against the actor are 'invisibles', by which he means that they have no effect on the actor's life on earth; they strike neither the body nor the purse, and as a result actors do not recant, and remain insensitive to the state of sin in which they find themselves; Héliodore continues:

les Puissances du monde ne sont pas excusables, si elles ne prêtent leur bras, et leurs forces à l'Église, pour reprimer ces ennemis declarez de Dieu, et des vertus, pour étouffer ces conspirations publiques, contre la majesté Souveraine de Dieu, contre la sainteté des peuples, et pour empescher qu'on ne represente sur les theatres quelque chose qui puisse offenser Dieu, et corrompre les hommes.[46]

Exemplary action is demanded from magistrates before whom, as things stand, actors are innocent because they commit no crime punishable by secular law. Héliodore, in this demand, makes no difference between civil and moral offence.

Héliodore now proceeds to justify his position. There is nothing, he tells us, which can excuse the toleration of plays that are evil, because they constitute blatant outrages against the divine majesty and are 'conspirations visibles contre les bonnes mœurs'.[47] That magistrates do not attend the theatre themselves does not excuse them from applying sanctions to it, for 'leur seule dissimulation, leur seule foiblesse' suffice to

[44] Ibid., 291.
[45] Ibid., 292.
[46] Ibid.
[47] Ibid., 290.

make them guilty.[48] The need for action on their part is the more urgent because of the very nature of drama; although reading plays is enough to corrupt one's morals, 'leur representation est beaucoup plus dangereuse, et attaque l'innocence avec une violence plus redoutable'.[49] Furthermore, and here we may note a more general application despite the distinctions between plays made earlier, 'Les Theatres portent le feu dans le cœur des hommes, les Theatres empoisonnent et tuent les ames.'[50]

Magistrates are not therefore limited by purely political considerations. They must act every time the Christian faith is attacked, even though things spiritual are in principle the domain of the Church:

La faveur du Ciel est si necessaire pour la conservation, et pour le bonheur mesme temporel des Estats, que les Magistrats pechent contre l'Estat, s'ils refusent leur protection à la Religion, et aux autres vertus qui entretiennent l'union du Ciel et des Estats, s'ils ne suppriment par des Édits constants et vigoureux, s'ils n'empeschent de representer sur les theatres ces Pieces criminelles qui corrompent les mœurs, et qui deviennent enfin les calamitez generales des Estats, comme elles sont l'horreur du Ciel.[51]

Thus moral corruption leads to the moral collapse of the State as a whole. Although Héliodore does indeed distinguish between the civil and ecclesiastical domains, the distinction concerns only the practical limitations of their respective powers; the difference is one of means not ends.

There is, however, a more telling reason for the sort of action demanded of magistrates: Héliodore writes:

Les Magistrats sont obligez d'empescher les desordres publics; les particuliers n'ont ny l'autorité ny la force d'en arrester le cours; *Dieu, qui en a donné le pouvoir aux Magistrats*, les oblige sans doute de s'en servir pour remedier à des maux qui luy déplaisent d'autant plus, qu'ils sont plus pernicieux que les pechez particuliers, à des maux qu'il veut étouffer, et qui sans miracle ne le peuvent estre que par la puissance qu'il a donnée aux Magistrats principalement pour ce sujet.[52]

The power of magistrates is not simply of a temporal nature;

[48] Ibid.
[49] Ibid., 286.
[50] Ibid., 290-1.
[51] Ibid., 296-7.
[52] Ibid., 291.

it emanates from God himself. Héliodore does not fail to draw the fullest conclusions from this argument. Having earlier stated the need for an alliance between the secular and ecclesiastical powers, he remarks that magistrates must be in no doubt that 'ils ne répondent à Dieu, et de ses propres outrages, et de la perte des ames, s'ils n'usent de toute leur autorité pour reprimer des insolences qui ne respectent ny le Ciel, ny la terre, et qui ne sont pas moins injurieuses à Dieu, que funestes aux peuples'.[53] If God has no pity on magistrates who pardon a murderer, what pity can they expect when they tolerate 'les sources d'un nombre presque infiny de crimes'?[54]

But while Héliodore proposes the suppression of plays which are morally harmful he does, as has been noted, accept drama as a fact in society: 'Quelque raison que nous alleguions, on nous demande des Comedies.'[55] Again, however, Héliodore is not absolutely clear on the nature of this theatre, for he adds:

on ne peut se resoudre de signer la condamnation des divertissemens que des personnes de sçavoir et de pieté font donner quelquefois au public dans les maisons les plus fameuses, où on élève la jeunesse aux lettres et aux vertus. Si tous les theatres estoient dressez avec ces intentions, conduits par les soins, et avec les precautions de ces hommes également sçavans et vertueux, il n'y auroit point de censure à craindre.[56]

Certainly the first part of this statement refers to school drama: but the significant point is that this is presented to us as an example for the public theatre to follow. Moreover, we are now introduced to the very important notion of an official censorship which would eliminate the moral danger incurred in attending plays in their existing form. Héliodore explains that because the pagans themselves have shown the way (and he specifically refers to the Roman institution of 'prefets de plaisir' whose task was to examine and correct plays)[57] there is no excuse if we do not follow their

[53] Ibid., 285.
[54] Ibid., 291.
[55] Ibid., 315.
[56] Ibid.
[57] Ibid., 317.

example.[58] Naturally, he is concerned not only with the performance of good plays but with the reform of those which fall into the category of 'pièces ambigues', whose performance would be banned until their examination 'par des personnes de sçavoir et de pieté'.[59]

In his mind there is no doubt as to those who should be responsible for such an initiative: magistrates, knowing that the plays referred to above are being performed, cannot in all conscience allow them to continue until they have been examined; 'ils ne doivent pas avoir moins soin des peuples, en tout ce qui regarde le bien public, que les peres et les meres doivent en avoir de leurs enfans'.[60] This is not simply a social duty: 'Dieu établit . . . les Magistrats pour estre les curateurs et les tuteurs des peuples et pour leur servir de peres.'[61] Indeed he points to the moral and political aspects of censorship in his comment that 'La seule consideration de l'honnesteté publique nous a portez à corriger et à prévenir la corruption et l'infamie que les Comedies peuvent causer à l'Estat.'[62] Héliodore envisages no greater difficulty in establishing censors in this century than in that of the pagans and heretics.[63] Héliodore sees it, therefore, as even more of a duty to introduce censorship in a century 'qui surpasse les precedens dans la Religion'.[64] If the Council of Trent allows for the examination of theological works, why should this not be the case for plays which are shorter and more dangerous?[65]

The responsibility for establishing some form of censorship, however, does not rest solely with the magistrature. The Church too has its part to play, and here Héliodore shows great originality in his view of ecclesiastical responsibility. It is important to remember that he considered the treatment

[58] Ibid., 315.
[59] Ibid., 283. D'Aubignac obviously saw himself as such in his demand for an *Intendant* to whom all plays would be submitted prior to performance (*Projet*, in *La Pratique du théâtre*, p. 396).
[60] Ibid., 306.
[61] Ibid., 306-7.
[62] Ibid., 323.
[63] Ibid., 325.
[64] Ibid.
[65] Ibid., 319.

of actors by the Church as just, since they were responsible for performing corrupt plays; he says now that:

Plusieurs Comediens m'ont témoigné bien de la passion pour cét établissement [i.e. censorship]: ce qu'ils entendent dire dans les chaires contre leur profession, et les difficultés que l'on fait de les absoudre leur donnent un juste sujet de s'étonner de ce que les Puissances de l'Église, et du monde ne conviennent point pour un établissement aussi necessaire à leur salut, qu'à celuy des Acteurs, et du peuple, et qu'au bien public dont elles sont responsables.[66]

This statement suggests that if magistrates perform their duty in banning evil plays and reforming others actors will no longer be open to the same accusations as before. Moreover, it is the Church (now responsible for the well-being of society) who, in conjunction with the civil authorities, must take the initiative in the establishment of a censorship which would improve the actor's status within the Church; he is no longer considered a soul lost forever and excluded from the sacraments by the ritual. Héliodore also implicitly rejects the notion that traditional authorities have said the last word on the problem. He is arguing that in the event of plays being reformed the actor's profession would gain respectability and the actor himself, *while still exercising his profession*, would become acceptable to the Church. It is the Church's duty to achieve this.

Héliodore was not alone in advocating censorship. But other writers did not share the positive aspects of his reforming spirit. The accent was on suppression rather than on change. Yves de Paris declares that magistrates are responsible for the suppression of plays which undermine sound moral principles and, moreover, it is God who demands this.[67] According to the anonymous preacher from Cologne, since magistrates cannot prevent actors from performing, especially when the King tolerates their existence, equally 'il est indubitable qu'ils sont obligés en conscience d'empécher les abus dans lesquels degenerent ces sortes de permissions'.[68] This, he continues, would include banishing them for performing plays where decency is openly shocked and which

[66] Ibid., 325.
[67] *L'Agent de Dieu*, p. 472.
[68] *Instructions morales et populaires*, p. 32.

is only too common in farce; such a policy does not mean that the laws may be violated in any other way, but this cannot be prevented unless one bans all performances.[69] Given that the preacher has already mentioned their acceptance by the King he can only say that 'les personnes publiques sont obligées, dans ces rencontres, de se servir de l'authorité que leur donne le Souverain, dont l'intention n'est pas qu'il y ait des écholes publiques du vice dans son état'.[70] He adds that magistrates and 'les personnes de qualité' must never attend 'ce qu'ils voyent bien que le Souverain ne permet que par tolerance'.[71] He is therefore more circumspect in his relation of the magistrature's powers to the divine order: magistrates here are little more than a last resort in the face of the prevailing social practice, sanctioned by the King himself.

Even Pégurier can conceive of at least the idea of a practical censorship of plays. Caffaro had proposed as an example to follow in this question an ordinance of St. Charles Borromeo, one of the great figures of the Italian Counter-Reformation, whereby the performance of plays was permitted only after their examination by the Vicar-General.[72] Pégurier's comment is that if a play contains sentiments which are not contrary to the laws of religion or good conduct, is well composed and well performed, 'elle plaira en émouvant les passions, sans pourtant faire du tort ni inspirer la corruption, parce que ce sont des passions innocentes'.[73] Such are the plays he wishes to see performed (concession enough in itself) and, he believes, those permitted in accordance with St. Thomas's pronouncements. Again there are no precise indications regarding the nature of these plays. Perhaps they exist purely on the level of hypothesis. They may portray the Christian virtues which religious moralists find so lacking in plays as they stand. Some idea of what he means, however, is seen in his statement that when the public theatre is on the same footing as school drama 'il n'y aura pas sans doute plus

---

[69] Ibid., pp. 32-3.
[70] Ibid., p. 33.
[71] Ibid., p. 34.
[72] *Lettre d'un théologien*, U/L, pp. 86-7.
[73] *Réfutation des sentiments relâchés*, pp. 108-9.

d'infamie dans la suite de monter sur l'un que sur l'autre'. Pégurier's concession to the idea of reform is, however, greatly qualified when he says resignedly that 'on ne s'attend pas à voir cette reforme, on se contente de la souhaiter'.[74]

Alas, Pégurier's pessimistic conclusion is typical of most religious moralists who oppose the existence of drama and the theatre. Vincent sees drama's corruption as an eternal fact of history and points to no solution for the future. Drama's apologists, he says in 1647, would have us believe that the theatre has already been reformed; but, he adds, places which have corrupted morals for two thousand years cannot have changed so suddenly; since they are the same theatres, the same actors, and the same general apparatus as before, 'C'est abus de penser qu'on croie qu'ils soient autres qu'ils n'avoient esté, et qu'au lieu du vice ils enseignent la vertu.'[75]

Bossuct too has history in mind but at least he offers the beginnings of a more empirical argument. He refers to a time when the Church hoped to render comedy decent or bearable, but soon realized that 'le plaisant et le facétieux touche de trop près au licencieux, pour en être entièrement séparé'.[76] Not, he adds, that in metaphysics this separation is impossible; 'on voit en effet des représentations innocentes',[77] this referring of course to school plays, for Bossuet proceeds to quote the *Ratio Studiorum*. He casts doubt, however, on the applicability of the latter's rules to the public theatre when he introduces a major obstacle to the reform of plays:

Les personnages de femmes, qu'on exclut absolument de la comédie pour plusieurs raisons, et entre autres pour éviter les déguisements que nous avons vu condamnés, . . . la réduisent à si peu de sujets, qui encore se trouveraient infiniment éloignés de l'esprit des comédies d'aujourd'hui, qu'elles tomberaient d'elles-mêmes, si on les renfermaient dans de telles règles.[78]

Even less encouraging is the view that plays which are to all appearances harmless and decent have the same or possibly

[74] Ibid., p. 127.
[75] *Traité des théâtres*, p. 26.
[76] *Maximes et réflexions*, U/L, p. 266.
[77] Ibid.
[78] Ibid., pp. 267-8.

worse effects than their patently evil counterparts. Conti tells us that even if plays contain nothing that is indecent, even if the passions are portrayed in all moderation, 'cette apparence d'honnesteté et le retranchement des choses immodestes le rend beaucoup plus à craindre'.[79] Voisin explains more fully that performing some plays which include nothing contrary to good morals is a trick of the Devil calculated to 'accoustumer les hommes par le plaisir qu'ils y prennent' and to 'se plaire insensiblement à celles qui sont sales et malhonnestes'.[80] But a quite categorical statement on this point comes in du Bois's reply to Racine, where he admits that sometimes the words of plays may be innocent in themselves, 'mais la volonté du poëte est toujours criminelle; les vers n'ont pas toujours assez de charmes pour empoisonner, mais le poëte veut toujours qu'ils empoison-nent: il veut toujours que l'action soit passionnée, et qu'elle excite du trouble dans le cœur des spectateurs'.[81] Therefore the original *intention* is seen as the major obstacle to the view that drama can be harmless, even in a state of 'reform'.

The most insuperable obstacle is that drama sets out to please and will use every means at its disposal to do so. As du Bois's statement suggests, dramatic pleasure is ineradicably associated with the experience of illicit passions. Bossuet has already advanced an argument which denies the legitimacy of sensual pleasure in drama (even in the service of virtue)[82] because 'on aura toujours une peine extrême à séparer le plaisant d'avec l'illicite et le licencieux'.[83] For Pégurier the reform of drama is especially meaningless in the eyes of spectators since it would remove the very thing they seek; most people want only the pleasure they find in immodest words and gestures; 'et les pieces purgées et châtiées par un Official ou par des Docteurs, ne seroient pas sans doute du goût de ces gens-là'.[84] It is not drama which first needs to be reformed but man.

[79] *Traité de la comédie et des spectacles*, pp. 30-1.
[80] *Défense*, p. 246.
[81] In Racine, *Œuvres*, iv, 302.
[82] *Maximes et réflexions*, U/L, p. 275.
[83] Ibid., p. 269.
[84] *Réfutation des sentiments relâchés*, pp. 60-1.

XI

RELIGIOUS DRAMA

If one species of drama cannot in any way be reformed is it possible to find another, free of corrupt elements such as passion and crime, which is acceptable in aim and content? Many writers believed that the performance of religious drama could contribute to the justification of actors and drama in general. There existed of course a strong tradition of religious plays in the seventeenth century. There were two main periods of activity: the first comes in the years following 1640 with performances of du Ryer's *Saül* (1640) and *Esther* (1642), of two plays about St. Genest by Desfontaines (1644) and Rotrou (1645-6), *Polyeucte* (1641-2), and many others; the second comes towards the end of the century with the performances of Racine's *Esther* (1689) and *Athalie* (1691), and of two plays by Boyer, *Jephté* (1691) and *Judith* (1695), the latter provoking a discourse on the acceptability of religious drama by Lebrun. How, then, in precise terms do dramatic theorists and playwrights envisage the notion of religious drama?

It is not surprising that the avowed aim of such plays is the edification of the spectator. Du Ryer regards his *Saül* as 'une instruction sans aigreur' and 'un divertissement sans scandale'.[1] Support for this view is found later in the century in Boyer's preface to his own *Jephté*. Interestingly, however, du Ryer's description of his plays suggests that the approach to religious drama is not essentially different from that of its secular counterpart; religious drama must not be overbearing in its message and must still entertain. At the same time there is pleasure but no offence.

Playwrights are indeed ever conscious of the most successful means by which they may bring about the spectator's pleasure. Racine writes that he was asked to produce a play

---

[1] Preface to *Saül*, Paris, 1642.

in *Esther* 'lié par une action qui rendit la chose plus vive et
moins capable d'ennuyer'.[2] Corneille remarks that although
the style of *Polyeucte* is not as 'majestueux' as that of *Cinna*
or *Pompée* it is more moving; furthermore, 'les tendresses de
l'amour humain y font un si agréable mélange avec la fermeté
du divin, que sa représentation a satisfait tout ensemble les
dévots et les gens du monde',[3] a conclusion based more on
optimism than fact. Boyer regards the dramatic qualities of
his *Judith* as particularly worthy of attention: where, he
asks, do we find 'une plus violente opposition d'intérêts et
de devoirs, et un plus grand contraste de sentimens et de
passions'?[4]

Equally theorists and playwrights are not blind to the
problems which arise from writing on pious subjects. A major
issue in discussions of religious drama is the poet's licence
to invent: is he allowed to change certain parts of a sacred
subject to suit his dramatic purpose? La Mesnardière is
categorical: if a poet used the 'Archives sacrées' as his source
he must keep faithfully to the text; it is moreover a crime
approaching sacrilege to 'renverser insolemment un ordre
mysterieux de qui mesme l'Esprit de Dieu s'est rendu le
Secretaire'.[5] Racine expresses a similar view in the preface
to *Esther* when he claims that without changing the slightest
circumstance in the Scriptures, which would be 'une espèce
de sacrilège', he could write a play 'avec les seules scènes que
Dieu lui-même . . . a préparées'.[6] He still leaves himself
enough room for manœuvre since presumably God has not
stipulated what form the dialogue should take. Du Ryer's
scruples stretch even to the title of his *Esther*; he comments
that although its principal theme is the deliverance of the
Jews the Bible has not supplied another title than the one his
play bears; 'il estoit plus raisonnable de suivre et de respecter
l'Escriture, que les regles du theatre'.[7]

---

[2] *Œuvres*, iii, 455.
[3] *Writings*, p. 118. On the reception of *Polyeucte* in the salons see Loukovitch,
K., *L'Évolution de la tragédie religieuse classique*, Paris, 1933, p. 270.
[4] Preface to *Judith*, Paris, 1695.
[5] *Poétique*, pp. 32–3.
[6] *Œuvres*, iii, 455.
[7] Preface to *Esther*, Paris, 1644. On this question as a whole see Loukovitch,
pp. 274–83.

Boyer is somewhat less rigorous in his approach to the problem. First of all his formulation in the matter of altering scriptural narrative is subtly different from the writers that have just been discussed: a biblical subject must be treated with the care demanded by 'une matière sacrée, dont *à peine il est permis de changer la moindre circonstance*'.[8] It is, then, a question of degree. But even strict adherence to what is written in the Scriptures does not preclude the addition of episodes which are the poet's own invention. Boyer, in order to give *Jephté* a new form, has inserted episodes which arise naturally from the subject and which are directly connected with the main action.[9] His stated authority for such a move is Racine, whom Boyer does not, however, mention by name. Indeed Racine's scruples did not prevent him in *Athalie* from adding to his source Joad's appeal to the Levites to attack the usurper queen on her throne. But Boyer explains that in a sacred subject the art of invention lies in the ability to 'parer la verité, non à la defigurer, à l'enrichir, non à la des-honorer'.[10] One is, then, permitted to add episodes which are according to the spirit of any particular passage. What Boyer in fact proposes comes dangerously near a subjective approach to the Scriptures.

Corneille approaches the problem of invention from the point of view of the spectator's attitude to the mixture of truth and fiction. He discerns two principal attitudes: there are spectators who are so convinced by what they see on the stage that, once they recognize in the play a few events which are true, they give equal credence to the motives behind these events and to the fictional circumstances which accompany them: others, however, because they are 'mieux avertis de nôtre artifice', suspect everything outside their knowledge to be false and impute the more obscure subjects (in themselves true) to the writer's imagination. Both attitudes, Corneille continues, would be dangerous in the case of Polyeucte because 'il y va de la gloire de Dieu, qui se plaît dans celle des saints', and the death of saints, so precious in the eyes of God, 'ne doit pas passer pour fabuleuse devant

---

[8] Preface to *Jephté*. My emphasis.
[9] Ibid.
[10] Preface to *Judith*, Paris, 1695.

ceux des hommes': thus, 'Au lieu de sanctifier notre théâtre
par sa représentation, nous y profanerions la sainteté de leurs
souffrances, si nous permettions que la crédulité des uns et la
défiance des autres, également abusées par ce mélange, se
méprissent également en la vénération qui leur est due, . . .'[11]
Corneille does not therefore question the validity of mixing
truth and fiction in religious drama: he merely points to the
need to warn the spectator of exactly what he must expect,
in order that the various degrees of theatrical belief should
not undermine religious belief. It is only right that the
spectator should be able to 'démêler la vérité d'avec ses
ornements', and to recognize 'ce qui lui doit imprimer du
respect comme saint, et ce qui le doit seulement divertir
comme industrieux'.[12] But it is the scholars who must judge
whether his additional incidents are 'selon l'art' or not;
his aim, he says, is not to justify them but simply to 'avertir
le lecteur de ce qu'il en peut croire'.[13] Any justification
would therefore be on artistic and not on moral grounds.[14]

Not all material, however, is to be treated in the same
way. Like Racine, Corneille argues in the *Examen* to
Polyeucte that nothing in the Bible must be changed;[15] but
because we owe only 'une croyance pieuse' to the lives of
saints, as opposed to 'une foi chrétienne et indispensable'
to the Bible, poets are entitled to exercise the same rights
as with other historical sources.[16] Accordingly, like other
writers, he allows the poet to invent additional material
provided he destroys 'rien de ces vérités dictées par le Saint-
Esprit'.[17] Corneille makes a more original point, however, in
his assertion that one must omit certain things contained in
biblical sources, which would be a source of displeasure to
the spectator, although nothing must be put in their place:
that would be to change history, something not allowed

[11] *Œuvres*, iii, 475.
[12] Ibid., 476.
[13] Ibid., 478.
[14] *Moral* in the context of this chapter applies to those considerations regarding
religious or theological issues as opposed to purely aesthetic problems.
[15] *Writings*, p. 118.
[16] Ibid., pp. 117–18.
[17] Ibid., p. 118.

on account of the respect we owe to the Scriptures.[18] He
cites as an example of possible omission the story of David
and Bethsheba, explaining that he would not describe how
David fell in love with her when he saw her bathing in a fount-
ain 'de peur que l'image de cette nudité ne fit une impression
trop chatouilleuse dans l'esprit de l'auditeur'.[19] One wonders
to what extent Corneille has his tongue in his cheek in
deliberately referring to a biblical source as dangerous.

There are certain things which Boyer too would not
include in religious plays; they must be free of 'tout ce qu'il
y a de plus vif, et de plus touchant dans les Tragedies
ordinaires, c'est-à-dire tous les emportements de l'amour
profane'.[20] While the latter is not wholly excluded it must
be dealt with wisely, and all expressions whose 'licence' and
'mollesse' would poison the mind must be banished.[21] So
even writers of religious drama cannot do without passion,
and it was remarked on earlier that Corneille is in fact proud
of the fusion in *Polyeucte* of the love intrigue with the
religious aspect of the tragedy. D'Aubignac, however, has
no time for the relationship of Pauline and Sévère.[22] He
proscribes altogether what he calls 'les galanteries du siècle'
and warns that 'des passions humaines . . . donnent de
mauvaises Idées aux spectateurs, et . . . les portent à des
pensées vicieuses'.[23] Moreover, such *galanteries* 'deviennent
odieuses par la saincteté du sujet' which is often 'méprisée
par la complaisance que plusieurs ont à cette coquetterie'.[24]

Just as there are limitations applied to the material used
for religious plays, so too are there limits regarding style.
A major dispute on precisely this issue arose in 1634 when
Guez de Balzac attacked Heinsius for including classical
allusions in his Latin play, *Herodes Infanticida*. The tone
of Balzac's *Dissertation* is at times most violent in its
condemnation and is by no means attenuated by Balzac's

[18] Ibid.
[19] Ibid.
[20] Preface to *Jephté*.
[21] Ibid.
[22] *Pratique*, p. 329.
[23] Ibid.
[24] Ibid.

belated praise of other aspects of the play.[25]

Balzac's principal complaint is that the Furies appear on stage to torment Herod. Is this legitimate? That Herod himself speaks Latin and uses words like Acheron, Styx, and Bacchus does not concern Balzac overmuch. He laboriously explains that, when such words lose their religious significance, they represent no more than 'choses vulgaires' and are easily integrated into ordinary speech; moreover, this language is well suited to Herod, for he is both a familiar of the Romans and a violator of his Father's religion.[26] Latin terms thus perform an aesthetic function in the play and are representative of Herod's treachery.

The question of the gods, however, is rather different. Balzac has difficulty in understanding how, in a poem where an angel delivers the prologue, Tisiphone and her sisters appear along with 'le terrible équipage que luy a donné le Paganisme'.[27] Balzac is therefore led to ask whether angels and the Furies are compatible in the same play, whether we are able to reconcile two religions which are natural enemies, and whether we are permitted to 'profaner un lieu sainct, par une marque d'Idolatrie'.[28]

Heinsius, Balzac tells us, argues in his defence that the Furies are representative of passion rather than bodily presences in their own right.[29] But Balzac is unimpressed and produces much evidence in an attempt to prove that they were in fact goddesses,[30] thereby reinforcing his point regarding their unsuitability as characters in a religious play. They cannot, he says later, be merely symbolical since they actually appear on the stage; he further retorts that if this idea were followed up one could introduce almost anything into a religious play.[31] Balzac denies, therefore, that the Furies perform an aesthetic function and implies that Heinsius, by making them appear before an audience, gives

[25] For the historical details of this dispute see Lebègue, 'L'*Herodes Infanticida* en France', in *Neophilologus*, vol. xxiii, Paris, 1938, pp. 148–54.
[26] *Œuvres*, ii, 532.
[27] Ibid., 533.
[28] Ibid.
[29] Ibid., 539.
[30] Ibid., 541.
[31] Ibid., 543–4.

them equal status with angels.

Balzac is also concerned with more general considerations. Firstly, the subject-matter in Heinsius's play 'est toute nostre et toute Chrestienne', and false gods may only be included 'par violence'.[32] Secondly, they must never appear in any form of drama, for Pan died at the birth of Christ's doctrine and must never be revived; 'Il est juste que le changement du style accompagne le renouvellement de l'esprit.'[33] Furthermore, a Christian poet must consider that 'par la Conversion de l'Empire Romain la Langue Latine s'est convertie';[34] he must be content with retaining the words and grammar 'sans s'obliger aux Dogmes et aux Opinions du premier temps':[35] if our compositions are Christian, this must be reflected in the form as well as in the subject-matter.[36]

Balzac does not, however, advise the use of Hebrew words; he wishes to preserve the language's integrity, and not to violate it with 'ces termes durs et sauvages' which destroy poetry's charm and which 'ne peuvent obeïr à aucune regle de la Grammaire'.[37] There is no need, he continues, to use the word 'Tisiphone'; why not 'mauvais Esprit' and other 'mots communs à toutes les Sectes, et receus de tous les Peuples'?[38] Aesthetic considerations are, then, just as much a part of Balzac's argument as religious zeal.

Heinsius replied in suitably vehement terms to Balzac's attack on his tragedy in a long treatise in Latin, which is mostly composed of counter-quotations from numerous erudite sources and of interpretations which attempt to invalidate Balzac's contentions. Most of his arguments are fortunately taken up in simpler form by Jean de Croÿ in his contribution to the dispute published in 1642.[39] Some of his criticisms of Balzac are based on aesthetic grounds: for example, he reiterates Heinsius's explanation that the Furies

---

[32] Ibid., 533.
[33] Ibid.
[34] Ibid., 534.
[35] Ibid.
[36] Ibid., 538. Corneille sees Heinsius's use of the Furies as an 'agrément' (*Writings*, p. 118).
[37] Ibid.
[38] Ibid.
[39] Loukovitch omits any mention of this work in his discussion of the dispute.

are representative of passion, adding that they are nothing more than examples of prosopopoeia which in no way offend the Christian religion;[40] furthermore, he justifies Heinsius's portrayal of Herod (about whom there is really no argument) by emphasizing the poet's need to create characters 'selon leur naissance, selon leur religion, avec leurs passions, avec leurs sentimens et avec leurs actions',[41] thus suggesting that one's religious sensitivity must yield to historical realism. Incidentally, this is thoroughly rejected as a justification by Voisin who is adamant that a Christian must never 'publier des maximes Payennes qui ne peuvent servir qu'à corrompre les mœurs, et à violer les loix'.[42] But for Jean de Croÿ a poet does not become a pagan merely because he introduces pagans on the stage.[43] His work inevitably deviates into historicism, his main concern being to point out that, since Christianity began only at the ascension of Christ into heaven and not at his birth, Balzac's description of Heinsius's material as Christian is based on erroneous premises; nobody has suggested that Herod was a Christian.[44]

The rigorist view of a Christian writer using pagan material, represented here by Balzac, was rejected later in the century by Rapin in his reply to a zealous clergyman who had attacked the common use of the legends of antiquity in the literature of the time. Rapin's point is simple enough: when a painter is dealing with a Christian subject his imagination must be appropriately Christian, and free of any intrusion of the profane or *fabuleux*.[45] On the other hand, Charles Le Brun painting Apollo must not include anything holy; 'quoy que l'imagination de l'un soit toute profane, et celle de l'autre toute sainte: on seroit ridicule de dire que l'un est moins chrestien que l'autre, parce que le Christianisme n'a aucun

[40] *Response à la lettre et au discours de Balzac sur une tragédie de Heinsius intitulée Herodes Infanticida*, n.p., 1642, pp. 120-1.
[41] Ibid., pp. 16-17.
[42] *Défense*, p. 352.
[43] *Réponse à la lettre et au discourse de Balzac*, p. 17.
[44] Ibid., pp. 42-4.
[45] Rapin, *La Défense des fables contre M.D.S., bachelier de Sorbonne*, n.p., n.d., p. 6.

rapport à la qualité de Peintre'.[46] What is true for the artist is also true for the playwright: when Buchanan writes *Jephté* he must be Jewish; when Corneille writes *Andromède* he must be pagan, and when Racine writes *Britannicus* he must be Roman; one may therefore conclude that the poet and the artist may each portray in his own way the story of Daphne, and each make a god of Apollo 'sans blesser le Christianisme, qui n'a rien de commun avec ces deux Arts'.[47] Rapin, of course, sees no objection to dealing with pagan material; he even condones the metamorphosis deemed necessary in the poet by La Mesnardière and Scudéry, and does not seem concerned that the poet must sometimes 'become' a pagan. But most important is Rapin's conception of art as autonomous for, although he is careful to separate the sacred from the profane in any single work, he suggests that there is an objective idea of artistic quality which is independent of any religious considerations.

But while some writers propose and defend the existence of a religous theatre, not all enthusiasts for drama were advocates of religious plays. Saint-Évremond devotes some time to the subject in *De la tragédie ancienne et moderne*, where his doubts are founded both on aesthetic grounds and on attitudes regarding religious belief. In the first place, Saint-Évremond asserts that 'de la doctrine la plus sainte, des actions les plus Chrétiennes et des véritez les plus utiles, on fera les Tragedies du monde qui plairont le moins'.[48] His reason is quite simply that the spirit of the Christian religion is directly opposed to that of tragedy; the patience and humility of saints are too contrary to the sort of heroic virtue demanded by the theatre.[49] This attitude is not surprising in one who upholds the more ambitious heroics of Cornelian characters. But even *Polyeucte* is not spared in Saint-Évremond's general doubts about religious tragedy: 'ce qui eût fait un beau Sermon faisait une misérable Tragédie, si les entretiens de Pauline et de Sévére, animés d'autres sentimens et d'autres passions n'eussent conservé à l'Auteur

[46] Ibid.
[47] Ibid.
[48] *Œuvres*, iv, 173.
[49] Ibid.

la réputation que les vertus Chrétiennes de nos Martirs lui eussent ôtée'.[50] Curiously Corneille himself adopts a similar stand when, despite his earlier enthusiasm for his *Polyeucte*, he describes his later creation, Théodore, as having a character 'entierement froid', adding that 'une vierge et martyre sur un théâtre n'est autre chose qu'un terme qui n'a ni jambes ni bras, et par conséquent point d'action'.[51] For these two writers, therefore, plays with religious subjects are a positive obstacle to dramatic quality.

Saint-Évremond, however, also turns his attention to the moral questions posed by religious plays in that 'les choses saintes perdent beaucoup de la religieuse opinion qu'on leur doit, quand on les représente sur le Théâtre'.[52] For example, miracles like the crossing of the Red Sea or Samson's defeat of an army using only an ass's jaw would not seem credible in a theatre 'parce qu'on y ajoute foi dans la Bible', but rather 'on en douteroit bien-tôt dans la Bible, parce qu'on n'en croiroit rien à la Comédie'.[53] In other words, the unconvincing portrayal of the miracles which form an essential part of our religious belief would lead to the undermining of biblical authority. Truth is, then, just as much an obstacle in religious drama as it is in secular drama. But whereas in the latter truth could be replaced by the more credible *vraisemblance* no such opportunity exists for the former. In order to preserve belief in biblical truth it is better for drama to do completely without it.

A much wider issue is, however, in the mind of Saint-Évremond. Referring to the Ancients' practice of portraying on the stage gods endowed with human passions he comments that if a contemporary author were to include saints and angels in his plays 'il scandaliseroit les Dévots comme profane et paroîtroit imbécile aux Libertins'.[54] He is therefore concerned with the attitudes of unbelievers and sceptics: exposing religious truth in public would be to the advantage of *libertins* who could ridicule in the theatre the very things

---

[50] Ibid., 173-4.
[51] *Writings*, pp. 128-9.
[52] *Œuvres*, iv, 174-5.
[53] Ibid., p. 175.
[54] Ibid., 172.

they accept in a church 'avec une apparente soûmission
et par le respect du lieu où elles sont dites, et par la révérence
des personnes qui les disent'.[55]

For Saint-Évremond the theatre clearly lacks the necessary
authority to convince or to convert. If religious truth is to be
believed (and this is a need in Saint-Évremond himself if he is
to remain 'soûmis') it is better that it should come from the
mouths of those ordained to preach. Once religious truth is
portrayed on the stage it is no longer only God's truth; it is
subject to the conditions of the stage and the demands of
actors. In a church there is a closer association with God
because it is God's house. In a theatre religion is exposed to
attack because it is no longer held in check by the necessary
authority.

Saint-Évremond's rejection of religious subjects as suitable
for drama is supported by l'Abbé d'Aubignac, who deals
with the matter at some length in the *Pratique*. One reason
for which he discourages writers from dealing in sacred
matters concerns the nature of theatre: drama is now only a
'divertissement public', and 'n'a plus de part aux choses
sainctes et ne peut souffrir ce meslange sans profanation'.[56]
Allied to this is the attitude of the spectator. D'Aubignac
urges the poet not to construct great discourses on Christian
morality with the rules and terms of theology because:

en exhortant le peuple à pratiquer les saints commandements de la
loy et à renoncer à la vie du siècle, cela sent trop la predication que le
temps et le lieu ne peuvent aysément souffrir. On ne sçauroit oster de
l'imagination des Spectateurs que la Comedie leur doit servir de
divertissement, et tout ce qu'ils ont present à leurs yeux les empesche
d'avoir une autre persuasion.[57]

In this frame of mind they cannot approve any condemnation of their pleasures or any exhortation to 'des pratiques
austeres et mal agreables aux sens et qu'on leur fasse un
reproche public de toute leur vie'.[58] He concludes that poets
in their moral teachings must avoid mention of '[les]
pratiques severes de la vie chrestienne'; they must be content

[55] Ibid., 173.
[56] *Pratique*, p. 324.
[57] Ibid., p. 328.
[58] Ibid.

with propagating 'une morale raisonnable et vertueuse, en se renfermant dans une belle et genereuse philosophie'.[59]

Indeed Boyer explains that authors are reluctant to undertake writing a religious play if, to find the necessary embellishments, 'il faut se remplir des grandes veritez de la Religion, et tirer de l'Écriture sainte ces riches expressions que nous fournit la divine Poësie du Psalmiste et des Prophetes'.[60] But, he continues, one must know how to choose and 'ménager les sentimens de pieté, qui sont amenez par la matiere';[61] one must increase their number only when such plays are performed in religious communities; on the public stage 'les instructions de pieté' must never be frequent or affected; they must be seen to come naturally from the characters and to be inspired by the action in hand.[62] The similarity of these statements with d'Aubignac's views on sententiae is obvious: it is, however, interesting that for one who is, unlike d'Aubignac, totally committed to religious drama there must still be a compromise with the nature of the audience.

For both writers, therefore, the spectator's enjoyment of the dramatic experience is the playwright's first priority. D'Aubignac seems to suggest that religious drama is far too similar to the direct moralizing which was rejected in the name of pleasure and that the spectator is in fact seeking an alternative to the religious experience found in a church, where he may have his fill of preaching from the pulpit. Religious drama is a positive obstacle to enjoyment in that it suggests an unpalatable alternative to the pleasure drama sets out to provide.

But D'Aubignac is, like Saint-Évremond, also worried lest religious plays should confirm certain types of spectators in their anti-religious prejudices; when the 'instructions' mentioned earlier are heard on stage, 'les esprits un peu libertins s'en raillent . . . et s'endurcissent dans les mauvais sentiments qui les leur font mepriser quand elles leur sont

[59] Ibid., pp. 328-9.
[60] Preface to *Judith*.
[61] Ibid.
[62] Ibid.

debitées par le Ministere des Histrions'.[63] Indeed d'Aubignac believes that a religious play is better read than performed because the reader does not hear the *histrions* who perform 'pour la necessité de leur mestier et dont peut-estre la croyance n'est pas moins deguisée que leur personne'.[64] The theatre is thus unfit to handle religious truth partly because of the actor whose status d'Aubignac is so much at pains to defend elsewhere.

But his first statement also questions the authority of the theatre as a place for the treatment of religious questions, since those who are already possessed of sincere piety revolt at seeing sacred words 'ainsy profanez dans un lieu où ils sçavent bien qu'ils sont entierement perdus, et mal à propos exposez au mepris de tout le peuple'.[65] D'Aubignac's more general reason for proposing that a religious play should only be read is that the reader suffers no disturbing influence 'qui porte sa pensée à la profanation des choses sainctes'[66] and is not surrounded by 'railleurs qui parlent contre le respect qu'ils doivent à ce qu'ils entendent'.[67] The suggestion in the works of both d'Aubignac and Saint-Évremond is that in the theatre, seen in terms of stage and audience, the spectator is subject to pressures which encourage conformity with others rather than identification with the spirit of the thing performed. Both authors in fact echo the religious moralists' apprehension before the dangers of drama as a collective experience in a place designed for that effect, and where the agent of this experience has no other authority than the material demands of his profession.

D'Aubignac's reluctance to see religious drama performed does not prevent him from offering extensive advice on its composition. Although the poet must include in his work

---

[63] *Pratique*, p. 328.

[64] Ibid., p. 331.

[65] Ibid., p. 328. *Le Tartuffe* was criticized for this very reason. The author of the *Lettre sur la comédie de l'Imposteur* replies, however, that Panulphe's use of sacred words contributes to showing up the character for what he is (iv, 541-2). He is in fact arguing that one cannot isolate a single item in a work and criticize it for the mere fact of its appearance. In other words one must consider its artistic function, which may very well lead to good.

[66] Ibid., p. 331.

[67] Ibid.

'des discours de religion qui donnent les idées de la grandeur de nos mysteres' and 'des sentiments et des paroles de devotion'[68] two things must be avoided: the first, which is the problem of reconciling religious sententiae with the spectator's *divertissement*, has already been discussed; the second concerns more directly the religious import of the propositions advanced.

One must, he declares, never contradict or proclaim against religion, nor 'traiter en controverse la verité de son établissement'.[69] This is because poets, not sufficiently competent in matters of doctrine, can neither fully reply to the attacks of uncomprehending or iniquitous men, nor satisfactorily explain the doctrinal difficulties raised by their plays.[70] The Christian religion, he continues, is raised above the 'commerce des sens' and is difficult to understand by natural reason alone, whereas pagans and unbelievers can oppose to these revealed truths only what is drawn 'des lumières de la Nature et de la corruption des sens'.[71] Thus the poet's lack of time or of knowledge in theological matters may lead to many dangerous impressions remaining in the spectator's mind, which may weaken the faith of some or foster the impiety of others.[72] In this context he criticizes *Polyeucte* on the grounds that Stratonice and others speak favourably of the pagan religion, and direct several insults against Christianity, while Corneille introduces no character capable of replying to this manifest falsehood.[73]

In the end result it must be assumed that d'Aubignac totally rejects religious drama as a justifiable dramatic form, since a criticism on intellectual grounds, namely that playwrights are not competent to deal with religious matters in the first place, has now been added to arguments based on moral and aesthetic grounds. Moreover, employing the senses as a means of moral instruction is far from desirable in sacred, as opposed to secular, subjects. Again it is evident

---

[68] Ibid., p. 326.
[69] Ibid.
[70] Ibid.
[71] Ibid.
[72] Ibid., pp. 326-7. It is not surprising that d'Aubignac should later express his disapproval of *Le Tartuffe* and *Dom Juan* (ibid., p. 330).
[73] Ibid., p. 327.

that truth in this context has a moral quality which renders it untouchable, especially since religious drama requires a specialized knowledge beyond the scope of most actors and writers. Jean–Marie Piemme's statement that 'les partisans du théâtre refusent la tragédie religieuse au nom de la drama-turgie' is therefore a gross understatement of the case.[74]

Some writers, however, advocate religious drama because they consider that it would contribute in no small measure to the rehabilitation of both the actor and the theatre in general. 'Les Comediens ont-ils un moyen plus seur et plus glorieux pour confondre ceux qui s'obstinent sans cesse à décrier leur profession?', Boyer asks in his preface to *Judith*. Other writers credit certain playwrights with the moral regeneration of the stage because they have introduced sacred subjects into their works. Saint-Amant, paying tribute to Corneille for his work as a writer and translator of religious works, urges him not to renounce the stage because 'Dieu qui te l'interdit/ Veut par le Sacré Bois le remettre en credit.'[75] Racine's attempts to 'donner un nouveau lustre à la Scene avilie' are praised in a work of Bardou, significantly entitled *Épistre sur la condemnation du theatre.*[76] But Bardou's principal theme is that the spectator of these plays is brought closer to God: he uses his leisure hours wisely since he is pleasurably instructed; moreover, the actor 'innocemment peut jouer son rôle', and the author exercises a talent given him by God, which is abused if spent purely on plays with secular subjects.[77]

Such an attempt to justify drama in general by religious plays is strongly resisted by many religious moralists. In the first place the actor's position within the Church itself is not to his own or to drama's advantage. Rivet categorically declares with Mariana that it is unfitting that the parts of saints should be performed by 'des hommes infames'.[78] Coustel remarks that instead of praising Corneille for his religious plays we should rather reproach him, for there is nothing more dishonourable for Christianity or so opposed

---

[74] Piemme, 'Le théâtre en face de la critique religieuse', p. 55.
[75] In *Œuvres*, ii, 103.
[76] *Épistre*, p. 5.
[77] Ibid., p. 6.
[78] *L'Instruction chrétienne*, p. 33.

to the sanctity of religion than seeing people excommunicated by the Church 'oser impudemment faire le personnage d'un Saint et d'en contrefaire les actions'.[79] Corneille is therefore guilty of having written for the public stage and of exposing religious truth to the peril of being uttered by actors.

The question of authority is also very much in the minds of religious moralists. For Voisin, there can be no possible justification of religious drama because: 'Dieu veut que [les mysteres du salut] soient publiés par ceux qu'il s'est consacrés pour estre sa bouche, et non pas qu'on les croïe de ces autres impurs, que Satan louë, pour dire des vanités ou des saletés.'[80] Moreover, religious drama is misplaced on the public stage because the actor earns his living from it (a motive also suspect to d'Aubignac): 'ceux qui pour le gain representent sur le Theatre les histoires des saints, ne laissent pas pour cela d'estre infames'.[81] Profit from something holy is unacceptable.

In the second place it makes no difference what the actor performs: the sins of his profession are entirely alien to any spiritual design; Yves de Paris, while conceding that if sacred subjects alone were performed on the stage 'les theatres seroient . . . plus que les predications', none the less adds that, 'parce que l'acteur a pour dessein d'exciter les passions; de tous les sujets il choisit ceux où elles se portent le plus, il passe ainsi pour fort adroit à mouvoir les cœurs en leur representant ce qu'ils ayment . . .'[82] According to Lebrun religious elements are present in plays merely to save appearances; actors insert 'ce que nous avons de plus saint dans leurs divertissemens profanes, pour nous empêcher de les faire passer pour mauvais'.[83]

How indeed could religious plays remain untainted when they are far from constituting the actor's main preoccupation? Lebrun writes: 'Sera-t-il dit que les adorables paroles soient le sujet d'un divertissement si profane; qu'on joüe indifferemment ou Moliere, ou l'Écriture; que des bouches si souvent

[79] *Sentiments de l'Église*, p. 56.
[80] *Défense*, p. 45.
[81] Ibid., p. 275.
[82] *L'Agent de Dieu*, p. 465.
[83] *3ième Discours*, pp. 334-5.

profanées par des chansons et des paroles lascives, prononcent les oracles de Dieu, et que les actions des Saints soient representées par des Acteurs de Sganarelle?'[84] The fact that the religious plays in themselves may be irreproachable is of no consequence: it would always be profanity if the Scriptures were uttered 'dans la bouche des Comediens et des Comediennes, pour être joüée dans un lieu destiné au divertissement'.[85]

Here indeed we are at the crux of the matter. For Rivet:

il n'est loisible de destourner la parole de Dieu de son droit usage, pour la faire servir aux jeux et aux plaisirs des sens; puisqu'en l'Église de Dieu, toutes choses doibvent estre raportées à la modestie et vraye pieté, afin que l'ame soit portée à la Religion, et à la contemplation respectueuse des choses divines.[86]

This cannot be so:

avec des clameurs, risées, et applaudissemens; moins encore par les histoires sainctes, destournées de leur droit usage, et profanées quand elles sont converties en fables. Car lors elles exposent en moquerie la Religion Chrestienne.[87]

He too, then, believes in the unsuitability of a theatre, where the restraint demanded by a holy place does not operate, for the propagation of religious values.

The view that religion has no place in the theatre was strongly challenged by the author of the *Lettre sur la comédie de l'Imposteur*. He contends that banishing religion from the stage is 'un des plus considérables effets de la corruption du siècle où nous vivons'; it is also a 'fausse bienséance' which relegates reason and truth to little-known and barbarous countries, and which confines these two qualities within schools and churches, where their power is useless 'parce qu'elles n'y sont cherchées que de ceux qui les aiment et qui les connoissent'.[88] The author thus rejects the notion of preaching to the converted. He goes on to accuse the *dévots* of fear and cowardice when he remarks that by prohibiting the mention of religion in drama they

[84] Ibid., p. 340.
[85] Ibid., p. 342.
[86] *L'Instruction chrétienne*, p. 34.
[87] Ibid., pp. 34-5.
[88] *Œuvres*, iv, 555.

give the impression of mistrusting the strength and authority
of truth and reason, since they do not expose them in places
where they may encounter their enemies.[89] This, he adds,
is precisely where they should be; they are not reason and
truth unless they convince and pursue error, since their
essence is in action; reason and truth are destroyed in some
way if reduced to appearing only before their advocates.[90]
Why should not religion like reason (the former indeed being
described as 'une raison plus parfaite') be everywhere just as
God is in everything, 'dans les lieux du monde les plus
infâmes que dans les plus augustes et les plus sacrés'?[91] It is
no Christian soul who by 'ces indignes ménagements et ces
cruelles bienséances' wishes to prevent us from working for
'la sanctification de nos frères partout où nous le pouvons'.[92]
The author thus claims for his idea of theatre the virtue
of charity.

There is, on the other hand, a lack of charity on the part
of those who oppose the presence of religion on the stage,
for religion itself knows no bounds: 'elle n'a point d'égard à
sa dignité, quand il y va de son intérêt; et comment pourroit-
elle en avoir, puisque cet interêt consistant . . . à convertir
les méchants, il faut qu'elle les cherche pour les combattre,
et qu'elle ne peut les trouver, pour l'ordinaire, que dans les
lieux indignes d'elle?'[93] The author is quick to add, however,
that the theatre cannot become a church, the latter being
consecrated for the various ceremonies and rites of religion:
but its truths are of all times and all places 'parce que le
parler étant nécessaire en tout et partout, il est toujours plus
utile et plus saint de l'employer à publier la vérité et à
prêcher la vertu qu'à quelque autre sujet que ce soit'.[94]
Thus a distinction is drawn between the priest who performs
functions confined to the church and others who are free
to carry the word to their brothers. He continues by saying
that truth cannot be heard too often, and that indeed the
theatre is better suited for the propagation of the Word
because 'l'agréable manière de l'insinuer au théâtre est un
avantage si grand par-dessus les lieux où elle paroît avec toute

[89] Ibid.   [92] Ibid., 556.
[90] Ibid.   [93] Ibid.
[91] Ibid., 555-6.   [94] Ibid., 557.

son austérité, qu'il n'y a pas lieu de douter . . . dans lequel des deux elle fait plus d'impression'.[95]

But it is precisely the fact of entertainment that moves the religious moralists to indignation at the idea of a religious theatre. The two things are just not compatible. Lebrun, replying in his *Discours*, prompted by the performance of *Judith*, to the hypothetical objection that the same Scriptures that contain 'instructions mortifiantes pour ceux qui aiment le monde' also contain admirable stories capable of pleasing all sorts of people, retorts that this is undoubtedly true; but these stories are not destined for performance by actors on the stage and before people 'qui voulant s'en divertir, seroient semblables au malheureux Herode, qui vouloit que Jesus-Christ contentât sa curiosité par quelques miracles'.[96] Indeed the nature of drama as *divertissement* gives rise in religious plays to what Lebrun calls *altération* of the Scriptures, which, in his *Discours*, he discusses at some length.

In the first place the spirit of the Scriptures is entirely opposed to what we seek in drama, which is to say that those who attend plays 'ne sçauroient souffrir qu'on y exposât la fin pour laquelle tout est écrit, et qu'on y developpât les maximes qui sont comme la clef de l'Écriture'.[97] The aim of the Scriptures, he continues, is to establish the need to 'renoncer à soi-même, mépriser les richesses, et n'aimer et ne craindre que Dieu'.[98] Earlier in the century Lamy too explains that men are reluctant to receive these biblical truths (which indeed d'Aubignac advises playwrights to avoid) and want nothing of a spiritual God who does not correspond to their morals and inclinations;[99] since the Holy Scriptures are not to their liking they prefer the pagan gods with their human passions.[100] Both authors, then, echo d'Aubignac's implication that drama is an alternative to religious truth.

Another cause of *altération* involves what most religious moralists consider the prime aim of drama, the excitation of passion. For this purpose playwrights select 'des endroits que l'Église ne permettoit autrefois de lire qu'avec des

[95] Ibid.
[96] *3ième Discours*, p. 318.
[97] Ibid., p. 310.
[98] Ibid.
[99] *Nouvelles Réflexions*, p. 126.
[100] Ibid.

précautions qui ne sçauroient s'observer à la Comédie'.[101]
Such, he adds, are those which deal with beautiful but
adulterous women.[102] Stories which may be edifying when
accompanied by intelligent comment, 'proposées à des
hommes charnels par des Auteurs peu versés dans l'Écriture et
peu instruits dans la science des Saints', make a completely
different impression.[103] Thus Lebrun finds no difference
between secular and religious drama as it stands, because
passion is still an essential feature of the latter.

Inevitably, love is the particular passion which is most
discussed. A third cause of *altération* is that in whatever sort
of subject one will always find a love element.[104] Lebrun
attacks Boyer's *Judith* because, instead of the words and
sentiments showing that God had warned Judith in advance
of her fate, she is portrayed as a woman racked with doubt,
'occupée de pensées toutes charnelles, et partagée entre la
honte, la complaisance, la vaine gloire, et la vûë affreuse des
derniers désordres'.[105]

Lebrun was not the first to attack the presence of love
in religious drama. Voisin feels that the author's need to
satisfy worldly people means that the devotion of theatrical
saints is always 'un peu galante'; indeed 'la galanterie' is used
by the Devil to destroy the idea of 'la generosité et ... la
charité chrétienne' found in the actions of saints, and to
'relever d'éclat de l'amour prophane pour en donner de
l'estime et pour en exciter les flammes dans les cœurs des
spectateurs'.[106] Coustel explains the introduction of a love
element into *Polyeucte* (where Pauline is considered to give
a fine lesson in flirtation by her explanation to Stratonice of
her relationship with Sévère) by the fact that without love
drama is too boring.[107] Conti's view is that *Polyeucte* has
nothing 'de plus sec et de moins agreable que ce qui est de
saint', and nothing 'de plus delicat et de plus passionné que

[101] *3ième Discours*, pp. 320–1.
[102] Ibid., p. 321.
[103] Ibid., p. 322.
[104] Ibid., pp. 325–6.
[105] Ibid., p. 324.
[106] *Défense*, p. 276.
[107] *Sentiments de l'Église*, p. 63.

ce qu'il y a de prophane'.[108] What better person to corroborate this opinion than Saint-Évremond!

Varet chooses to attack Corneille's *Théodore* on the grounds that love is overwhelmingly present in such a play: whatever the intentions of playwrights, the saints they portray have such a weakness for love that instead of drama being sanctified by the acts of martyrs, 'on . . . profane la sainteté de leurs souffrances par les fictions amoureuses que l'on y mesle'.[109] In *Théodore*, at the same time as the triumph of faith over the infliction of the most humiliating suffering, one sees the triumph of a profane love which pursues 'une sainte Vierge et genereux martyr' to the death; furthermore, the Christian charity which obliges Didyme to endanger his own life for the sake of Théodore is so obscured by 'la passion feinte que l'auteur met dans ses paroles et celles de la Sainte' that it is impossible to tell whether it is 'zele d'amant' or 'fureur de Chrestien'.[110] Although, he continues, the Saint himself declares it to be Christian generosity there are spoken so many tender and passionate words that the impression gained is rather of a lover's ardour.[111]

The most controversial element of *Théodore*, however, was the question of the heroine appearing as a prostitute,[112] a point on which Corneille offered a spirited and barbed defence to his detractors. He does not, he explains, observe without some satisfaction that most of his critics attack the idea of prostitution 'qu'on n'a pu souffrir, bien qu'on sût assez qu'elle n'aurait point d'effet', and when all in his power had been done to attenuate the horror of such a thing.[113] There is, he says, even reason to congratulate the French stage on its purity, since a story which constitutes the finest adornment of St. Ambrose's second book of the *Virgins* is found to be too licentious for it.[114] What, he continues,

---

[108] *Traité de la comédie et des spectacles*, p. 36.
[109] *L'Éducation chrétienne*, pp. 252-3.
[110] Ibid., pp. 254-5.
[111] Ibid., p. 255.
[112] See Coustel, *Sentiments de l'Église*, p. 64. In the *Pratique* d'Aubignac remarks that *Théodore* failed, despite its many good points, because the idea of prostitution is forever in one's mind with the result that 'les idées n'y peuvent estre sans degoust' (pp. 66-7).
[113] *Writings*, p. 128.
[114] Ibid.

would have been said if, like St. Ambrose, I had shown Théodore in the brothel itself, and if I had portrayed her disturbed mind at the sight of Didyme in the same place?[115] However, he remarks, I refrained and 'la modestie de nôtre théâtre a désavoué ce peu que la nécessité de mon sujet m'a forcé d'en faire connaître'.[116] Thus, again, Corneille proclaims himself the guardian of the stage's purity, especially where it concerns religious subjects. This is not the opinion of Nicole, who argues that the very fact that *Théodore* can be performed at all shows to what extent audiences will accept horrible events on the stage.[117]

Once again drama, even in its form as religious tragedy, is incompatible with Christianity. The appearance of martyrs on the stage is devalued because of their portrayal by actors and because of their depiction as slaves of profane love. They rarely act as servants of God, and in any case religious moralists complain that there is no Christian virtue which would appeal to the majority of spectators. Nicole finds that 'il faut quelque chose de grand et d'élevé selon les hommes ou du moins quelque chose de vif et d'animé'.[118] One consequence of this is that playwrights have been obliged to portray their saints as 'fiers' and to give them lines more suited to a hero of Ancient Rome.[119] Nicole cites Théodore as being guilty in this respect. Lebrun implies that martyrs, in this case Judith, always represent the strength and attraction of the human personality alone; there is no subject 'où Dieu ne paroisse seul grand, seul aimable, seul digne de nos attentions, où les plaisirs de ce monde ne soient condamnez, et la Penitence loüée'.[120] God has been banished even from supposedly religious plays.

---

[115] Ibid.
[116] Ibid.
[117] *Traité de la comédie*, p. 51.
[118] Ibid., p. 53.
[119] Ibid.
[120] *3ième Discours*, pp. 319–20.

CONCLUSION

Clearly, the *querelle du théâtre* provides an excellent focus for many fundamental artistic and moral problems confronting seventeenth-century writers, as the wide range of issues arising from the controversy testifies. A major issue is the way in which theorists and moralists at this time viewed the responsibility of the artist towards society, and the moral consequences of the practice of a particular art form. Dramatic theorists considered that moral and artistic concerns were inseparable, and the didactic aim with which all playwrights should invest their works eliminated any case for the complete autonomy of the artist. But they were still very much concerned with the dramatist's art since moral instruction itself could not be effective unless certain artistic conditions were fulfilled. In this connection, they insisted on the importance of the concept of imitation, being in the vanguard of discussions of a topic which was to preoccupy French painters and art theorists as well as literary theorists so much in the seventeenth and eighteenth centuries.

The application of the principle of imitation, and more especially of *vraisemblance*, to problems of theatre is important in that the Aristotelian definition of art as the imitation of an action becomes indissolubly linked with the theorists' concern with didacticism. In their view no moral instruction is possible when the action on stage is not *vraisemblable*, for, if the message is to be clearly understood by an audience, the characters' actions illustrating it must be convincing according to that audience's experience of reality. For d'Aubignac and others, to be convincing, a play must conform to the customs and beliefs of the modern spectator, rather than display strict historical accuracy, (one reason perhaps why, as opposed to art theorists, their dramatic counterparts do not insist on historical accuracy of costume and decor). But, just as those who write on painting believe that the spectator's own visual field is the criterion governing the presentation of space in a picture, so dramatic theorists emphasize the importance of the perspective set in creating a convincing illusion in the theatre. Hence, the spectator's apprehension of the moral value of the spectacle is dependent on the success with which the theatre can reproduce our everyday perception of reality.

But seventeenth-century theories of imitation do not require that reality should be imitated exactly in all its circumstances. Playwrights must select from reality that which best suits the didactic purpose, re-ordering reality where necessary by rewarding the virtuous and punishing the evil. Thus what happens on the stage is what 'ought to' happen, as long as the action and characters are in themselves credible. Thus even events attested as having happened may be deemed 'incredible' and hence 'unconvincing' because they 'ought not' to have happened. The right choice for a dramatic subject was at the centre of the *querelle du Cid*. For Scudéry, the historical fact of Chimène's marriage to Rodrigue was not *vraisemblable* because it shocked 'la raison et les bonnes mœurs'.[1] What is *invraisemblable* in this instance is clearly what is also morally undesirable, and gives (or should give) a jolt to our moral beliefs. For the stage imitation to be convincing, then, it must embody those beliefs. A play is not the imitation of reality as such, but the imitation of a commonly held interpretation of that reality. *Vraisemblance* has a moral as well as a technical function. Significantly, Corneille rejects both the orthodox concepts of moral instruction and of *vraisemblance*.

This analysis of moral instruction leads us to ask what exactly moral instruction is when, if the message of a play can only convince by conforming to 'la raison et les bonnes mœurs', no new moral truths are given. One answer is that a play becomes a celebration of those values the audience ought already to know and love, and which are corroborated in the examples portrayed. More importantly, however, the spectators, through their affective involvement in the action (itself dependent on the quality of imitation), are

---

[1] Gasté, p. 77.

offered a dynamic experience of their values in operation. In this sense, a play has not only a moral aim, conceived as a necessary pre-condition to composition, but also provides a process which increases the moral awareness of the spectator.

The religious moralists were not persuaded by the dramatic theorists' claims regarding didacticism in the theatre. The *querelle du théâtre* is indeed in many ways a good illustration of the clash between two fundamentally opposing views of human nature in Christian spirituality of the period. The dramatic theorists, while accepting as a fact man's reluctance to be taught moral truths in any direct way, none the less believe that he can be morally improved by a compromise with his reluctance. The means adopted to persuade spectators of the morally good is the art of gentle deceit where they are offered instruction under the guise of a pleasurable experience. It is also clear from the writings of many theorists that the pleasure of tragedy in particular derives from our affective involvement in a play, a point which a practical dramatist like Racine and a critic such as Boileau insist, in their coupling of *plaire* and *toucher*, is at the heart of the dramatist's achievement. Rapin could not have put it better when he writes that 'La Tragédie ne devient agréable au spectateur, que parce qu'il devient luy-même sensible à tout ce qu'on luy represente, qu'il entre dans tous les differens sentimens des Acteurs.'[2] Dramatic theorists obviously share in that tradition of Christian morals which views the passions with some indulgence, holding that it is unrealistic to hope to eradicate them and that it is even possible to use them to good effect. Catharsis itself rests on the optimistic assumption that, by arousing passions in the spectators and by showing them the consequences of acts arising from irrational behaviour, man can be led to some form of emotional control.

The capacity of man to control the irrationalities of his conduct and to achieve moral enlightenment by means of a pleasurable theatrical experience is, for the religious moralists who condemn theatre, a contradiction in terms, especially when, in order to show men what is morally good, you have

---

[2] *Réflexions*, xviii, p. 143.

at the same time to show them the morally bad. At the basis of their criticism of moral instruction in drama is their utter rejection of the positive view of man asserted by Christian humanists and shared by dramatic theorists. In the growing climate of austerity fostered by the influence of radical Augustinianism they emphasize rather the concupiscent nature of man whose basic instincts are more frequently victorious over his moral effort. An essential feature of his concupiscence is the pleasure he derives from harmful passions, the very sort of pleasure sought by spectators in the theatre, and provided by actors and playwrights. In these circumstances moral instruction stands no chance. Even d'Aubignac admits that the nature of the moral instruction should not be such as to blunt the spectator's pleasure. The dramatic theorists' compromise with man's nature is, therefore, a calamitous error, allowing only for the aggravation and exploitation of an already dangerous tendency in humanity. Plays lead spectators further into error and deny them the possibility of contributing to their own salvation.

Drama's ability to influence the behaviour of spectators concerned dramatic theorists as well as religious moralists. Indeed the question of influence still constitutes part of the present-day debate on the arts and pornography. The dramatic theorists' position is a good example of the difficulties inherent in the assertion that drama can lead to good, because they must also envisage that it may lead to evil. Here the parallel with modern preoccupations on the same subject is clear. Seventeenth-century religious moralists and their twentieth-century counterparts argue that we are led to re-enact in actuality what we experience pleasurably in a play or a film. Violence is, it can be argued, encouraged by the media which present it as entertaining or exhilarating. A further problem for religious moralists and the critics of our own time is the frequent portrayal of those who commit reprehensible acts as eminently likeable.

Some seventeenth-century critics who write in favour of drama are very conscious of those elements of theatre which can harm their own cause. D'Aubignac is unhappy at the reintroduction of farce on to the French stage and Chappuzeau disapproves of comedies which contain 'sales équivoques' and 'méchantes idées'. The most remarkable admission of the pernicious influence plays can exert comes from Chapelain in his *Sentiments de l'Académie sur le Cid* where he describes Corneille as having enslaved the minds of his audience by involving them emotionally with his characters, particularly Chimène. He argues further in the same context that 'les mauvais exemples sont contagieux, mesme sur les theatres', although, admittedly, he is referring to the lower elements of society, generally considered more easily swayed than their more cultivated fellow citizens.[3]

But the mere fact that such an admission is possible highlights the importance of seventeenth-century dramatic theorists' attempts to impose some form of control on the dramatic experience. The case of *Le Cid* illustrates the need both to choose a suitable subject in the first place and to ensure that the behaviour of a character whom we look up to is beyond reproach. Corneille is severely reprimanded for allowing Chimène to receive Rodrigue after he has killed her father. In other cases playwrights must leave no ambiguity regarding the models which spectators are to follow; if an evil character is not punished or a virtuous character not rewarded, another character is required to apportion blame or praise accordingly. L'Abbé d'Aubignac, in his *Projet pour le rétablissement du théâtre*, even proposes that all plays should be submitted to an official censor before their performance.[4] Boileau takes a more liberal, but none the less morally serious, attitude and places the responsibility squarely on the writer who must ensure that his own behaviour is beyond reproach; otherwise his dissoluteness would inevitably be reflected in his works. While, however, it is true that many seventeenth-century writers were obviously aware of their own responsibilities and those of playwrights to society, their very concern, in a sense, played right into the religious moralists' hands.

Religious moralists are also aware of another aspect of the power of the theatrical world and that is its hold on our imagination to the extent that we leave reality behind us.

---

[3] Gasté, p. 360.
[4] *Pratique*, p. 396.

Suspicion of the imagination is not new to the seventeenth century, but yet again it seems that problems arising from the illusionist theatre serve to give new life to a long-standing tradition. Allied to religious moralists' and theologians' attitudes to the imagination is their disapproval of the irrational inclination to know which they call curiosity (in his *Summa* St. Thomas devotes to it *Question 167* of the *Second Part of the Second Part*). In the theatre the spectator's desire to experience an unknown imaginary world, beyond his normal realm of experience, is all the more dangerous both for his failure to weigh the consequences and his willing acceptance of it.

There are of course many other moral and religious implications behind the theatre's power to involve us in an imaginary world. Firstly, the religious moralists come close to Brecht's position on empathy when they argue that our total absorption in the actions and emotions of the characters seriously impairs our moral and critical senses, leading us to accept as good characters we like. Secondly, continuing the tradition of suspicion held from the primitive Church onwards towards any imaginative interference with reality, they argue that the theatre offers spectators no less than an alternative creation, governed by its own laws and with its own objects of worship. We become involved, then, in a world which is not ours, where, worse still, we exchange our own personalities for those of the fictional beings in whose lives we become absorbed. This would be especially the case for actors who spend the whole of their lives portraying the lives of others.

But the world offered by the theatre is of even less consequence than the real one, particularly when we waste real tears on fictional objects or on heroes who have been dead for centuries. The religious moralists' stress on the futility of drama's imaginary world demonstrates how great an influence the Platonist tradition of the *Republic* still exerted in the seventeenth century. Since all things temporal are mere shadows, plays can only portray shadows of shadows, offering nothing but vanity and falsehood. For Lamy, whose Oratorian theology is heavily Platonist in inspiration, theatre induces a love of creatures for their own sake, whereas we ought to see them rather as reflections of a higher order, to which our natural inclination should be more properly directed.

The major importance of the *querelle du théâtre* in the seventeenth century lies in the picture it presents of a church jealous of its own powers of attraction over men's hearts and sensitive to any threat to its grip on their minds, particularly if it comes from a secular source. The public theatre, in its powerful appeal to the spectators' emotions, enhanced by the combination of verse, voice, gesture, costume, decor, and, in some cases, music constitutes an intolerable rival to what the Church has to offer, providing an experience which escapes its control and which many writers regard as irresistible. Indeed the threat posed by drama to the Church, coming as it does from outside the latter's sphere of influence, may well resemble in moralists' minds the threat posed by witchcraft, still very much regarded as a danger in seventeeth-century France. In many ways the assimilation is easy to make: both seduce men's minds by casting a spell (in the context of drama *charmer* and *enchanter* retain very much of their literal meaning) and both possess individuals with specialized skills able to conjure up an alternative world. As far as drama is concerned, in the words of Pierre-Aimé Touchard, '[le] miracle se laïcise'.[5]

The rivalry of Church and theatre in the quest for souls is suggested in other ways. The theatre offers an alternative place of worship (many religious moralists, as has been seen, assimilated certain aspects of drama to idolatry), and according to La Grange, seems to 'dresser Autel contre Autel, et avoir des palais fixes, qui sont comme les Temples du prince des tenebres, dont il se sert pour faire insulte à Dieu'.[6] The theatre even claims to instruct, thus challenging the Church as the sole authority in questions of morals. Baillet, for example, attacks d'Aubignac as 'un Ecclesiastique qui a pretendu transporter les droits et les privileges de la Chaire au Theatre'.[7]

It is indeed clear that, in their critique of the values

[5] *Dionysos: apologie pour le théâtre*, Paris, 1938, p. 18.
[6] *Réfutation d'un écrit*, p. 78.
[7] *Jugement des sçavans*, iii, 305.

embodied in plays, religious moralists fear most of all an increasing secularization of values which would seriously undermine the Church's own moral teaching. The most harmful passions are regarded as socially acceptable virtues; sexual love between man and woman is considered praiseworthy, its pernicious influence extending even to plays with religious subjects. The *querelle du théâtre* thus illustrates the wider consequences of the tension between secular and religious views of social life which, Raymond Picard convincingly argues, lies at the root of the Church's attitude to *Le Tartuffe*, Cléante being the representative of a more wordly and less evangelical religion, in opposition to those who preach the abandonment of worldly life.[8] For rigorist theologians and religious moralists of the seventeenth century no division exists between secular and religious life. The notion of *scandale* here plays a crucial role in that a Christian's conduct in society must be exemplary in every way. The slightest deviation from the path of righteousness is sufficient to bring the reputation of the Church into disrepute and sets a bad example to others. Hence, the regular attendance of such prominent laymen as magistrates at theatrical performances lowers the Church's status as a legislative moral force, and threatens the homogeneity of religious and social life. All this applies in a sense to other forms of imaginative literature. What distinguishes the theatre is, on the one hand, its nature as a visible institution and as a public gathering, where the individual will is subject to collective influence, and, on the other hand, the persuasive nature of the performance of a play embodying corrupt values.

It is a tribute to the French theatre in the seventeenth century that it managed to provoke such a violent and worried response from its critics for whom, obviously, the dramatic illusion works far too well. While dramatic theorists emphasized the need for the artist to be aware of his responsibility, the religious moralists regard the moral awareness required as entirely opposed to playwrights' real motives in satisfying the spectators' corrupt inclinations. Equally the

---

[8] *'Tartuffe*, "production impie"', in *De Racine au Parthénon*, Paris, 1977, pp. 171-3.

religious moralists show no confidence in the audience's ability to evaluate what they see and to reject what they find as morally harmful or ambiguous. Whatever the merits of either side of the case the *querelle du théâtre* exemplifies the chasm separating those who believe the individual capable of making the right moral choices, and those who believe he must be protected from himself at all costs.

APPENDIX

LE VÉRITABLE SAINT GENEST

This appendix deals with the special problems raised by Rotrou's *Véritable Saint Genest*. The importance of this religious tragedy lies not only in its sustained view of the relationship of reality and fiction on the stage, but also in its portrayal of an actor in a particularly dramatic relation to his role. The tragedy therefore raises the questions of illusionism and the nature of acting which have been discussed in earlier chapters. However, the order of arguments chosen for the study as a whole would not in my view have done justice either to the play's aesthetic coherence or to its specific importance as a contribution to the problem of the actor. Moreover, any discussion of the play has been complicated by Robert Nelson's view that Rotrou's tragedy is a form of auto-criticism on his part for having composed any sort of play and therefore represents an anti-aesthetic. It therefore seemed more appropriate, especially since the appendix replies directly and at length to Nelson's views on the play, to deal with *Le Véritable Saint Genest* separately from the main study.

Nelson believes that when Genest is converted to Christianity he rejects worldly values completely, which means that he may no longer play saints in derision. This conclusion, which is a plausible interpretation of the text, is now extended by Nelson to Genest's not performing any play at all 'even in praise of the Saints'.[1] The actor must renounce the theatre. He goes on: 'The worldly theatre is a fiction, a make-believe, a lie. Though perhaps not sinful in themselves, the plays of the theatre distract us from taking a full and serious part in the infinitely more important play whose rewards are not ephemeral applause and mortal happiness but eternal

[1] Nelson, Robert J., *Play Within a Play: The Dramatist's Conception of his Art: Shakespeare to Anouilh*, New Haven, 1958, p. 43.

salvation and everlasting glory. The esthetic of the *Véritable Saint Genest* is anti-esthetic.'[2] Nelson suggests that according to Genest's insights Rotrou should not have dallied with his secular plays, nor even with *Le Véritable Saint Genest*. Nelson admits that the view of theatre suggested by Rotrou's play can be reconciled to the *fact* of the play, that is, to Rotrou's having written it at all. But the solution to the problem is, he continues, to be found in the play's inspiration rather than in its form: 'if the form of *Le Véritable Saint Genest* is that of French Classical tragedy, its inspiration lies in the religious theatre of the Middle Ages'.[3] In fact, according to Nelson, Rotrou denies that a play is only a play conceived to astound and amuse. He concludes that: 'In rejecting the illusoriness of art through the "lesson" of Genest, Rotrou rejects the very form in which the lesson is presented to us; a play which is a work of art. Art is illusion and to cultivate the illusory, Genest tells us, is sinful.'[4]

To what extent can Nelson's views be substantiated by a careful reading of the play? The worldly aspects of theatre are by no means neglected in Rotrou's tragedy, nor are they presented in such a way as to suggest that we are not to enjoy them. We are shown some of the difficulties of the *décorateur* who makes some quite original remarks on the shortcomings of a backdrop in perspective.[5] The play does not lack good humour: Marcelline's complaints about her pestering admirers are good-naturedly dismissed by Genest.[6] There is even an implicit plea on behalf of actors when Marcelline says:

Notre métier surtout, quoique tant admiré,
Est l'art où le mérite est moins considéré.[7]

But the most important of all is the fulsome praise accorded to Pierre Corneille.[8] All this does not encourage us to think that Rotrou wants nothing to do with the worldly theatre.

What is the attitude towards acting and the dramatic

---

[2] Ibid., pp. 43–4.
[3] Ibid., p. 44.
[4] Ibid., p. 45.
[5] *Le Véritable Saint Genest*, II, i, 326-33.
[6] Ibid., iii, 361-8.
[7] V, ii, 1529-30.
[8] I, v, 278-9.

illusion in the play? Dioclétien gives us some idea of what an audience regards as good acting when he says to Genest:

Par ton art les héros, plutôt ressuscités
Qu'imités en effet et que representés,
Des cent et des mille ans après leur funérailles,
Font encor des progrès, et gagnent des batailles.[9]

Genest's attitude is slightly different: he is initially astounded at the transformation working within him and remarks that:

Il s'agit d'imiter et non de devenir.[10]

This runs counter to all prevailing dramatic theory where metamorphosis is deemed essential in acting. There is of course an aesthetic reason for Genest's statement, since some difference between fiction and reality must exist if Genest's conversion is to have the appropriate effect. This would explain the reactions of Marcelle and Lentule,[11] and the various interventions of Valérie who is astounded that such a fine spectacle is possible when there is chaos behind the scenes.[12]

Genest's conversion does, then, take place; he becomes the part he is playing to the extent that he, Genest, welcomes martyrdom in the cause of Christianity. Does this mean that acting is in itself a sinful activity? At no point in the play is this implied. It is true that Genest refers to the members of his troupe as 'chers compagnons de la basse fortune' (l. 1287), but this is a statement of fact in line with Marcelle's plea in ll. 1529-30. Moreover, he refers to his new situation in terms of acting, hardly appropriate if acting is to be renounced altogether. He says, for example:

J'ai pleuré mes pechés, le Ciel a vu mes larmes;
Dedans cette action il a trouvé des charmes,
M'a départi sa grâce, est mon approbateur,
Me propose des prix, et m'a fait son acteur.[13]

Genest merely rejects one form of acting, that which consists in the persecution of saints. He himself says 'J'ai corrigé mon rôle . . .'[14]

[9] Ibid., 239-42.
[10] II, iv, 420.
[11] IV, vii, 1296-8.
[12] III, i, 671-2.
[13] IV, vii, 1311-14.
[14] Ibid., 1309.

What then, of Nelson's view that 'In rejecting the illusoriness of art through the "lesson" of Genest, Rotrou rejects
the very form in which the lesson is presented to us; a play
which is a work of art"? In the first place, as Nelson himself
points out, we must bear in mind that Rotrou has indeed
written a play, moreover, it should be added, a play which
uses the dramatic illusion as its vehicle. The answer to
Nelson's problem lies not in the fact of illusion itself but
in the attitude towards it. In the play it is never implied
that the dramatic illusion — or art — is responsible for the
pagan spectator's derision of Christian martyrs. At no point
in the play is it suggested that Genest consciously satirizes
saints, as both Nelson and J. D. Hubert imply.[15] Apart from
the obvious conviction of Adrien's lines Valérie says to Genest:

Mais on vante surtout l'inimitable adresse
Dont tu feins d'un chrétien le zèle et l'allégresse,
Quand le voyant marcher du baptême au trépas,
Il semble que les feux soient des fleurs sous tes pas.[16]

The opposite of mockery is suggested here. The mockery
comes rather from the spectators in whose eyes any Christian
martyr is an object of derision. Such a situation does not
arise before a Christian audience where the roles are reversed
and the pagans become the object of derision. The dramatic
illusion, seen by Rotrou as the most effective means of
convincing us of Genest's value as a model of Christian virtue,
in no way departs from, and does not misrepresent, the
Christian truth which the audience possesses. In this sense the
dramatic illusion and the play as art form (bearing in mind
the point that art for dramatic theorists is an acceptable way
to men's souls in that it persuades more easily) are wholly
acceptable to a Christian audience. The illusory is not
devalued for Genest himself since it is precisely by its culti-
vation that his conversion has been achieved. Art is not
rejected but proposed as the servant of a higher cause. *Le
Véritable Saint Genest* is a celebration of theatre.

---

[15] For the latter see 'Le Réel et l'illusoire dans le théâtre de Corneille et dans
celui de Rotrou', *Revue des sciences humaines*, 1958, pp. 333-50, pp. 343-4.
Genest is seen as a mocker of Christians, however, in Desfontaine's version of the
play.
[16] I, v, 293-6.

BIBLIOGRAPHY

PRIMARY SOURCES

ANDREINI, Giovanni Battista. *Lo Specchio, composizione sacra e poetica, nella quale si rappresenta al vivo l'imagine della commedia, quanto vaga e deforme sia, alhor che da comici virtuosi o viziosi rappresenta viene*, Paris, 1625.

— — *Teatro celeste, nel quale si rappresenta comme la divina bontà, habbia chiamato al grado di beatitudine e di santità comici penitenti e martiri*, Paris, 1624.

ARGENSON, le comte René de Voyer d'. *Annales de la Compagnie du Saint-Sacrement*, ed. le R. P. Dom H. Beauchet-Filleau, Marseilles, 1900.

ARISTOTLE. *Aristotle on the Art of Poetry*, ed. I. Bywater, Oxford, 1909.

— — *Nichomachean Ethics* in *The Works of Aristotle Translated into English*, vol. ix, Oxford, 1925.

— — *Poétique*, ed. J. Hardy, Paris, 1952.

AUBIGNAC, Fr. H., Abbé d'. *La Pratique du théâtre*, ed. P. Martino, Paris, 1927.

— — *Dissertation sur la condamnation des théâtres*, Paris, 1666.

BAILLET, A. *Jugements des sçavans sur les principaux ouvrages des auteurs*, 7 vols., Paris, 1722.

BALZAC, J. L. Guez de. *Œuvres*, 2 vols., Paris, 1665.

BARBIER D'AUCOURT, J. *Réponse à la lettre adressée à l'auteur des Hérésies imaginaires*, in Racine, *Œuvres*, vol. iv, pp. 306–22.

BARDOU, P. *Épistre sur la condamnation du théâtre. A. M. Racine*, Paris, 1694.

BAYLE, P. *Œuvres diverses*, 4 vols., The Hague, 1725–7.

BEAULIEU, Mlle de. *La Première Atteinte contre ceux qui accusent les comédies par une demoiselle françoise*, Paris, 1603.

BOILEAU, l'Abbé J. *De l'abus des nuditez de gorge*, Paris, 1677.

BOILEAU-DESPRÉAUX, N. *Œuvres complètes.* Introduction par A. Adam. Textes établis et annotés par Françoise Escal, Paris, 1966.

BORDELON, l'Abbé L. *La Belle Éducation*, Paris, 1694.

BOSSUET, J.-B. Letter to le P. Caffaro, 9 May 1694, in Urbain and Levesque, *L'Église et le théâtre*, pp. 121–41.

— — *Maximes et réflexions sur la comédie*, ibid., pp. 169–306.

BOURDALOUE, le Père L. 'Sermon pour le troisième dimanche après Pâques: sur les divertissements du monde', in *Sermons . . . pour les dimanches*, 4 vols., Paris, 1716, vol. ii, pp. 64–121.

— — 'Sermon pour le septième dimanche après la Pentecoste: sur l'hypocrisie', ibid., vol. iii, pp. 50–94.

BOYER, l'Abbé C. Preface to *Jephté*, Paris, 1692.

— — Preface to *Judith*, Paris, 1695.

BRÉCOURT, G. M. de. *Les Comédiens françois à Monsieur le Curé de Saint-Sulpice, prêchant contre eux, à Paris*, in *Le Voyage de Bachaumont et de La Chapelle avec un mélange de pièces fugitives tirées du cabinet de M. de Saint-Évremond*, Utrecht, 1697.

CAFFARO, le Père Th. *Lettre d'un théologien illustre par sa qualité et par son mérite, consulté par l'auteur pour savoir si la comédie peut être permise, ou doit être absolument défendue*, in Urbain and Levesque, *L'Église et le théâtre*, pp. 67–119.

— — Letter in reply to Bossuet, 11 May 1694, ibid., pp. 143–7.

— — Letter to the Archbishop of Paris, 11 May 1694, ibid., pp. 149–56.

CAMUS, J.-P. *Les Leçons exemplaires*, Paris, 1632.

CERNAY, L'Abbé. *Le Pédagogue des familles chrétiennes, recueilly par un prêtre du seminaire de Chardonnet*, Paris, 1662.

CHAPELAIN, J. *Opuscules critiques*, ed. Alfred C. Hunter, Paris, 1936.

— — *Correspondance*, ed. Ph. Tamizey de Laroque, 2 vols., 1880–3.

— — *Lettere inedite a corrispondenti italiani*, ed. P. Ciureanu, Geneva, 1964.

CHAPPUZEAU, S. *Le Théâtre françois*, Lyons, 1674.
— — *Le Théâtre françois*, ed. G. Monval, Paris, 1875.
CHARLES BORROMEO, Saint. *Opusculum de choreis et spectaculis in festis diebus non exhibendis*, Toulouse, 1662.
— — *Traité contre les danses et les comédies*, Paris, 1664.
CHARPENTIER, Fr. *Carpentariana, ou remarques d'histoire, de morale, de critique, d'érudition et de bons mots de M. Charpentier*, Paris, 1724.
CHEMINAIS DE MONTAIGU, le Père T. 'Sermon sur l'Immaculée Conception de la sainte Vierge', in *Sermons*, 5 vols., Paris, 1737–64, vol. ii, pp. 43–78.
CONTI, Armand de Bourbon, Prince de. *Traité de la comédie et des spectacles*, Paris, 1666.
— — *Traité de la comédie et des spectacles*, ed. K. Vollmöller, Henninger, 1881.
CORNEILLE, P. *Œuvres*, ed. Marty-Laveaux, 12 vols., Paris, 1862–8.
— — *Writings on the Theatre*, ed. H. T. Barnwell, Oxford, 1965.
— — *Trois discours sur le poème dramatique*, ed. L. Forestier, Paris, 1963.
COSNARD, Mlle M. Preface to *Les Chastes Martirs*, Paris, 1651.
COURTIN, A. de. *Traité de la paresse ou l'art de bien employer le temps, en forme d'entretiens*, Paris, 1673.
COUSTEL, P. *Les Règles de l'éducation des enfants*, 2 vols., Paris, 1687.
— — *Sentiments de l'Église et des saints Pères pour servir de décision sur la comédie et les comédiens, opposés à ceux de la lettre qui a paru à ce sujet depuis quelques mois*, Paris, 1694.
CROY, J. de. *Response à la lettre et au discours de Balzac sur une tragédie de Heinsius intitulée Herodes Infanticida*, n.p., 1642.
CYPRIAN, Saint. *Des spectacles*, trans. A. Deschaussé, Paris, 1640.
DACIER, A. *Dissertation critique sur l'Art poétique d'Horace*, Paris, 1681.
— — *La Poétique d'Aristote*, Paris, 1692.
— — *Remarques critiques sur les œuvres d'Horace*, 10 vols., Paris, 1709.

DESFONTAINES. *L'Illustre Comédien*, Paris, 1645.

DU BOIS, Ph. G. *Réponse à l'auteur de la lettre contre les Hérésies imaginaires et les Visionnaires*, in Racine, *Œuvres*, vol. iv, pp. 290–305.

DURVAL, J.-G. Preface to *Agarite*, Paris, 1636.

— — Preface to *Panthée*, Paris, 1639.

DU RYER, P. Preface to *Saül*, Paris, 1642.

— — Preface to *Esther*, Paris, 1644.

FÉNELON. *L'Éducation des filles*, Paris, 1687.

FLEURY, L'Abbé C. *Mœurs des chrétiens*, Paris, 1682.

FONTAINE, N. *Mémoires pour servir à l'histoire de Port-Royal*, 2 vols., Cologne, 1738.

FRAIN DU TREMBLAY, J. *Conversations morales sur les jeux et les divertissements*, Paris, 1685.

— — *Nouveaux Essais de morale*, Paris, 1691.

FRANÇOIS DE SALES, Saint. *Introduction à la vie dévote*, ed. F. Henrion, Tours, 1939.

GACON, Fr. *Le Poéte sans fard*, Paris, 1698.

GASTÉ, A. *La Querelle du Cid, pièces et pamphlets publiés d'après les originaux*, Paris, 1898.

GERBAIS, J. *Lettre d'un docteur de Sorbonne à une personne de qualité, sur le sujet de la comédie*, Paris, 1694.

GERBERON, Dom Gabriel. *Jugement de la comédie, du bal et de la danse*, Paris, 1688.

GIROUST, le Père J. 'Sermon sur la vie inutile du monde', *Les Faux Prétextes du pécheur ou le pécheur sans excuse: Avent*, 2 vols., Paris, 1700, vol. i, pp. 346–86.

— — 'Sermon sur la coutume', ibid., vol. i, pp. 204–50.

— — 'Sermon sur la fuite des occasions', ibid., vol. ii, pp. 253–301.

GODEAU, A. *Œuvres chrétiennes*, Paris, 1633.

— — *Poésies chrétiennes*, Paris, 1654.

GOMBAULD, J. Ogier de. Preface to *L'Amaranthe*, Paris, 1631.

GOUGENOT. *La Comédie des comédiens*, Paris, 1633.

GRANET, l'Abbé Fr. *Recueil de dissertations sur plusieurs tragédies de Corneille et de Racine*, 2 vols., Paris, 1739.

GRENAILLE, Fr. de. Preface to *L'Innocent malheureux ou la Mort de Crispe*, Paris, 1639.

GUÉRET, G. *Le Parnasse réformé*, Paris, 1669.

HEINSIUS, D. *D. Heinsii epistola, qua dissertatione D. Balsaci ad Heroden Infanticidam respondetur*, Leiden, 1636.

HÉLIODORE DE PARIS, le R.P. *Discours sur les sujets les plus ordinaires des désordres du monde*, 4 vols., Paris, 1684-6.

HORACE. *Satires, Epistles and Ars Poetica*, ed. H. Rushton Fairclough, London, 1966.

HOUDRY, le R.P. Vincent. *La Bibliothèque des prédicateurs*, ed. l'Abbé V. Postel, 18 vols., Paris, 1865-9.

L'IDÉE des solides recréations, par un missionaire de saint François, Lyons, 1661.

INSTRUCTIONS morales et populaires sur les spectacles et les dances recueillies de quelques sermons prêchés par un missionnaire, Cologne, n.d.

JOLY, C. (Chantre et chanoine de l'Église de Paris). *Avis chrétiens et moraux pour l'institution des enfants*, Paris, 1675.

JOLY, C. (Évêque et Comte d'Agen). 'Prône pour le dimanche de la Quinquagésime: sur les débauches du Carnaval, et les prières de quarante heures', in *Prônes de Messire Claude Joly*, 4 vols., 1692–4, vol. ii, pp. 1–32.

— — 'De la manière de vivre saintement au temps du Carnaval et du Carême', in *Œuvres mêlées*, Paris, 1696, pp. 264-309.

LA BRUYÈRE. *Les Caractères*, ed. R. Garapon, Paris, 1962.

LA CALPRENÈDE, G. de Coste de. *Épistre* in *La Mort des enfants d'Herodes ou La Suite de Mariane*, Paris, 1639.

LA CHÉTARDIE, Ch. Trotti de. *Instructions pour une jeune princesse, ou l'Idée d'une honnête femme*, Paris, 1684.

LA COLOMBIÈRE, le Père C. de. 'Sermons pour les derniers jours du Carnaval', in Migne, *Collection intégrale*, vol. vii, col. 990-1058.

LA GRANGE, Ch. de. *Réfutation d'un écrit favorisant la comédie*, Paris, 1694.

LALOUETTE, A. *Histoire et abrégé des ouvrages latins, italiens et françois pour et contre la comédie*, Paris, 1697.

LA MESNARDIÈRE, H.-J. Pilet de. *La Poétique*, Paris, 1640.

LAMY, B. *Nouvelles Réflexions sur l'art poétique*, Paris, 1678.

LAWTON, H. *Handbook of French Renaissance Dramatic Theory*, Manchester, 1949.

LEBRUN, le Père P. *Discours sur la comédie, où l'on voit la réponse au théologien qui la défend, avec l'histoire du théâtre*, Paris, 1694.

— — *Lettre où l'auteur des discours précédens répond à quelques difficultés qu'on lui avoit proposées*, Paris, 1694.

— — *Discours sur la comédie: ou Traité historique et dogmatique des jeux du théâtre et des autres divertissements comiques soufferts ou condamnés depuis le premier siècle de l'Église jusqu'à présent. Avec un discours sur les pièces de théâtre tirées de l'écriture sainte*, Paris, 1731.

LE GENDRE, l'Abbé L. *Mémoires*, ed. M. Roux, Paris, 1865.

LEIBNIZ, Gottfried W. von. *Correspondance avec l'Électrice Sophie de Brunswick-Lunebourg*, ed. O. Klopp, 3 vols., Hanover, 1874.

LEJEUNE, le Père J. 'Sermon LXII contre les bals, les danses, ou comedies et autres divertissements mondains qui sont les allumettes de luxure', *Le Missionnaire de l'Oratoire ou Sermons pour les Avents, Carêmes et fêtes de l'année*, 10 vols., Toulouse, 1688–9, vol. ii, pp. 467–91.

— — 'Sermon XLVIII: de l'observation du dimanche', ibid., vol. ii, pp. 151–73.

— — 'Sermon XLIV: de bon usage du temps', ibid., vol. x, pp. 269–93.

— — 'Sermon LII: des mocqueries', ibid., vol. x, pp. 502–22.

LELEVEL, H. *Entretiens sur ce qui forme l'honnête homme et le vray sçavant*, Paris, 1690.

— — *Réponse à la lettre du théologien défenseur de la comédie*, Paris, 1694.

LE MOYNE, le Père P. *La Dévotion aisée*, Paris, 1652.

LETTRE à l'auteur de la réponse aux Hérésies imaginaires et aux deux Visionnaires, in Racine, *Œuvres*, vol. iv, pp. 323–6.

LETTRE sur la comédie de l'Imposteur, in Molière, *Œuvres*, vol. iv, pp. 529–66.

LETTRE sur les Observations d'une comédie du Sieur Molière intitulée Le Festin de Pierre, ibid., vol. v, pp. 240–55.

MAIRET, J. de. Preface to *Silvanire*, Paris, 1631.

— — Preface to *Sophonisbe*, Paris, 1635.

— — Preface to *La Virginie*, Paris, 1635.

MARESCHAL, A. Preface to the *Seconde Journée* of *La Généreuse Allemande*, Paris, 1631.

MASSILLON, J.-B. 'Sermon XVIII sur l'inconstance dans les voies du salut', in Migne, *Collection intégrale*, vol. xlii, col. 688-704.

— — 'Sermon XXVIII sur l'injustice du monde envers les gens de bien', ibid., vol. xlii, col. 881-903.

MÉNESTRIER, le Père C.-F. *Des représentations en musique anciennes et modernes*, Paris, 1681.

— — *Des ballets anciens et modernes selon les règles du théâtre*, Paris, 1682.

MIGNE, l'Abbé J.-P. *Collection intégrale et universelle des orateurs sacrés du premier et du second ordre ... et Collection intégrale des orateurs du troisième ordre ...*, 99 vols., Paris, 1844-55.

— — *Patrologiae cursus completus, sive Bibliotheca universalis, integra, uniformis, commoda, oeconomica omnium ss. Patrum, doctorum scriptorumque ecclesiasticorum qui ab aevo apostolico ad usque Innocenti III tempora floruerunt ...*, 221 vols., Paris, 1844-64.

MOLIÈRE. *Œuvres*, ed. E. Despois and P. Mesnard, 13 vols. and album, Paris, 1873-1900.

MOREAU, Chanoine Bertrand. *De l'aumosne, ou des devoirs des riches envers les pauvres*, Liège, 1673.

MOTTEVILLE, Mlle de. *Mémoires pour servir à l'histoire d'Anne d'Autriche*, 5 vols., Amsterdam, 1723.

NICOLE, P. *Les Imaginaires*, 2 vols., Liège, 1667.

— — *Traité de la comédie*, ed. G. Couton, Paris, 1961.

NORVILLE, De. Preface to *La Poétique d'Aristote*, Paris, 1671.

OUVILLE, A. d'. Prologue to *Les Trahisons d'Arbiran*, Paris, 1638.

PANÉGYRIQUE de l'École des femmes ou Conversation comique sur les œuvres de M. de Molière, Paris, 1663.

PASCAL, B. *Pensées*, ed. L. Lafuma, 3 vols., Paris, 1947.

PÉGURIER, l'Abbé L. *Décision faite en Sorbonne touchant la comédie, du 20 mai 1694, avec la réfutation des sentiments relâchés d'un nouveau théologien*, Paris, 1694.

PERRAULT, Ch. *Épistre à Bossuet* in *Saint Paulin, évesque de Nole*, Paris, 1686.

— — *Parallèle des anciens et des modernes*, 4 vols., Paris, 1688-97.

PURE, l'Abbé M. de. *Idée des spectacles anciens et nouveaux*, Paris, 1668.

QUARRÉ, le R.P. *Le Riche charitable, ou de l'obligation que les riches ont d'assister les pauvres, et de la manière qu'il faut faire l'aumosne*, Brussels, 1653.

QUESNEL, le Père P. *Correspondance*, ed. Mme A. Leroy, 2 vols., Paris, 1900.

RACINE, J. *Œuvres*, ed. P. Mesnard, 9 vols., Paris, 1865–73.

— — *Principes de la tragédie*, ed. E. Vinaver, Manchester, 1944.

RAPIN, le Père R. *Les Réflexions sur l'éloquence, la poétique, l'histoire, et la philosophie*, Paris, 1684.

— — *La Défense des fables contre M.D.S., bachelier de Sorbonne*, n.p., n.d.

RATIO *et institutio studiorum Societatis Jesu superiorum permissu*, Tournon, 1603.

RÉPONSE *aux Observations sur le Festin de Pierre de M. Molière*, Molière, *Œuvres*, vol. v, pp. 232–40.

RIVET, A. *L'Instruction chrétienne touchant les spectacles publics*, The Hague, 1639.

ROCHEMONT, B. A., Sieur de. *Observations sur la comédie de Molière intitulée le Festin de Pierre*, in Molière, *Œuvres*, vol. v, pp. 217–32.

ROTROU, J. de. *Le Véritable Saint Genest*, ed. R. W. Ladborough, Cambridge, 1954.

ROULLÉ, l'Abbé P. *Le Roy glorieux au monde, ou Louis XIV le plus glorieux de tous les roys au monde*, n.p., 1664.

SAINT-ÉVREMOND, Ch. de. *Œuvres en prose*, ed. R. Ternois, 4 vols., Paris, 1962–9.

SARRASIN, J.-F. *Discours de la tragédie ou Remarques sur l'Amour tyrannique de M. de Scudéry*, n.p., 1683.

SAUMAISE, C. *Ad Aegidium Menagium epistola super Herode Infanticida Heinsii tragedia et censura Balzacii*, Paris, 1644.

SAVARON, J. *Traité contre les masques*, Paris, 1608.

SCUDÉRY, G. de. *La Comédie des comédiens*, Paris, 1635.

— — Preface to *La Mort de César*, Paris, 1636.

— — Preface to *Didon*, Paris, 1637.

— — Preface to *L'Amour tyrannique*, Paris, 1639.

— — *L'Apologie du théâtre*, Paris, 1639.

SENAULT, le Père J.-F. *De l'usage des passions*, Paris, 1641.

– – *L'Homme criminel ou la corruption de la nature par le péché selon les sentiments de saint Augustin*, Paris, 1644.

– – *Le Monarque, ou les devoirs du souverain*, Paris, 1661.

SIMON DE LA VIERGE, le Père. 'Sermon VI, pour le second dimanche de l'Avent: sur le scandale', in Migne, *Collection intégrale*, vol. x, col. 578-93.

SOANEN, Mgr J. 'Sermon pour le Ier dimanche de Carême: sur les spectacles', in *Sermons sur les différents sujets prêchés devant le roy*, 2 vols., Lyons, 1767, vol. i, pp. 42-85.

SOREL, Ch. *De la connoissance des bons livres*, Paris, 1671.

SOUCANYE. *In pestem theatralem, carmen*, n.p., n.d.

SUFFREN, le R.P. Jean. *L'Année chrestienne ou le sainct et profitable employ du temps pour gaigner l'éternité*, 2 vols., 1640-1.

TERTULLIAN. *Traité des spectacles*, trans. P. de Labriolle, Paris, 1937.

THIERS, J.-B. *Traité des jeux et des divertissements*, Paris, 1686.

THOMAS AQUINAS, Saint. *Summa Theologica*. Literally translated by the Fathers of the English Dominican Province, 22 vols., London, 1937.

THOMASSIN, le Père L. *La Méthode d'étudier et d'enseigner chrétiennement les lettres humaines*, 3 vols., Paris, 1681-2.

URBAIN, Ch. and LEVESQUE, E. *L'Église et le théâtre*, Paris, 1930.

URFÉ, H. de. Preface to *La Sylvanire ou La Morte vive*, Paris, 1627.

VARET, A.-L. *De l'éducation chrétienne des enfants selon les maximes de l'écriture sainte et les instructions des saints Pères*, Paris, 1666.

VINCENT, Ph. *Traité des théâtres*, La Rochelle, 1647.

– – *Recherches sur les commencements et les premiers progrès de la Réformation en la ville de La Rochelle*, La Rochelle, 1693.

VOISIN, J. de. *La Défense du traitté de Monseigneur le prince de Conti touchant la comédie et les spectacles, ou la Réfutation d'un livre intitulé: Dissertation sur la condamnation des théâtres*, Paris, 1671.

YVES DE PARIS. *L'Agent de Dieu dans le monde*, Paris, 1656.

— — *Les Vaines Excuses du pécheur en ses passions*, 2 vols., Paris, 1662-4.

SECONDARY SOURCES

ADAM, A. *Histoire de la littérature française au dix-septième siècle*, 5 vols., Paris, 1948-56.

ARNAUD, Ch. *Étude sur la vie et les œuvres de l'Abbé d'Aubignac et sur les théories dramatiques au dix-septième siècle*, Paris, 1888.

ARRÉAT, L. *La Morale dans le drame, l'épopée et le roman: étude philosophique et littéraire*, Paris, 1884.

AUERBACH, E. *Scenes from the Drama of European Literature*, New York, 1959.

BALSDON, J. P. V. D. *Life and Leisure in Ancient Rome*, London, 1969.

BARISH, Jonas A. 'The Antitheatrical Prejudice', *Critical Quarterly*, vol. 8, 1966, pp. 329-48.

BARNWELL, H. T. *Les Idées morales et critiques de Saint-Évremond*, Paris, 1957.

— — 'Saint-Évremond and Pascal: a Note on the Question of *Le Divertissement*', *Studies in Philology*, vol. 53, 1956, pp. 35-50.

— — 'Some Reflexions on Corneille's Theory of Vraisemblance as formulated in the *Discours*', *Forum for Modern Language Studies*, 1 (1965), pp. 295-310.

BARRAS, M. *The Stage Controversy in France from Corneille to Rousseau*, New York, 1933.

BAUMAL, F. *La Genèse du Tartuffe: Molière et les dévots*, Paris, 1919.

BÉNICHOU, P. *Morales du Grand Siècle*, Paris, 1948.

BERGSON, H. *Le Rire: essai sur la signification du comique*, Paris, 1940.

BORGERHOFF, E. B. O. *The Freedom of French Classicism*, Princeton, 1950.

BOURQUIN, L. 'La Controverse sur la comédie au XVIIe siècle et la Lettre à D'Alembert sur les spectacles', *Revue d'histoire littéraire de la France*, vol. 26, 1919, pp. 43-86 and 556-76; vol. 27, 1920, pp. 548-70; vol. 28, 1921, pp. 549-74.

BOYSSE, E. *Le Théâtre des Jésuites*, Paris, 1880.

BRAY, R. *La Tragédie cornélienne devant la critique classique, d'après la querelle de Sophonisbe*, Paris, 1927.

– – *La Formation de la doctrine classique en France*, Paris, 1951.

BUTLER, Ph. '*Tartuffe* et la direction spirituelle au XVIIe siècle', *Modern Miscellany presented to Eugène Vinaver*, ed. T. E. Lawrenson *et al.*, Manchester, 1969, pp. 48–65.

CARRÉ, le R.P. A. M. *L'Église s'est-elle réconcilée avec le théâtre?*, Paris, 1956.

– – 'De Molière à Louis Jouvet. L'Église, le théâtre et les comédiens', *Annales du Centre Universitaire Méditerranéen*, vol. 9, 1955-6, pp. 167–80.

CHRISTOFIDES, C. G. 'Bossuet on Dramatic Theory', *Symposium*, vol. 16, 1962, pp. 225-7.

COUBÉ, le P. 'Le Tricentenaire de Molière et la moralité de son théâtre', *Revue des objections*, 15 January 1922, pp. 3–9.

– – '*Le Tartuffe*, contraire à la religion et à la morale?', ibid., pp. 9–16.

– – 'La Mort de Molière. Mort en bon chrétien', ibid., pp. 16–22.

COUTON, G. *La Vieillesse de Corneille* (1658-84), Paris, 1949.

– – 'Réflexions sur "Tartuffe" et le péché d'hypocrisie, "cas réservé" ', *Revue d'histoire littéraire de la France*, vol. 69, 1969, pp. 404–13.

CRITIQUE et création littéraires en France au XVIIe siècle, Colloques internationaux du CNRS., no. 557, Paris, 1977.

DAINVILLE, F. de. 'Les Comédiens et le clergé: une pièce au dossier de Tartuffe', *Revue d'histoire du théâtre*, vol. 1, 1948-9, pp. 263–4.

DAVIDSON, H. M. *Audience, Words and Art*, Ohio, 1965.

DAWSON, F. K. 'La Mesnardière's Theory of Tragedy', *French Studies*, vol. 8, 1954, pp. 132–9.

DEFFOUX, L. 'L'Hypocrisie et *Tartuffe*', *Mercure de France*, 1 October 1923, pp. 222–5.

DEIERKAUF-HOLSBOER, S. Wilma. *Le Théâtre du Marais*, 2 vols., Paris 1954-8.

– – *Le Théâtre de l'Hôtel de Bourgogne*, 2 vols., Paris, 1968-70.

DELAPORTE, P. V. *Du merveilleux dans la littérature française sous le règne de Louis XIV*, Paris, 1891.

DELAVIGNE, F. *La Tragédie chrétienne au XVIIe siècle*, Toulouse, 1847.

DESLANDRES, P. 'L'Église et le théâtre', *Revue des études historiques*, vol. 16, 1925, pp. 131-6.

DUBU, J. 'La Condition sociale de l'écrivain de théâtre au XVIIe siècle', *XVIIe siècle*, vol. 39, 1958, pp. 149-83.

— — 'De quelques rituels des diocèses de France au XVIIe siècle et du théâtre', Part I in *Année canonique*, vol. v, 1958, pp. 95-124; Part II, ibid., vol. vi, 1959, pp. 99-116.

— — 'Pour une étude canonique des rituels', ibid., vol. vii, 1960, pp. 27-32.

— — 'L'Église et le théâtre', *Les Amis de saint François*, 1960, pp. 84-9.

— — 'Racine et le rituel d'Aleth: méditation devant un acte de baptême', *Studi in onore di Vittorio Lugli e Diego Valeri*, Venice, 1967, pp. 347-62.

— — 'L'Église catholique et la condamnation du théâtre en France', *Quaderni francesi*, Naples, vol. 1, 1970, pp. 319-49.

DUMAINE, F. 'Bossuet et le théâtre', *La Vie catholique en France et à l'étranger*, 13 September 1930.

DUSSANNE, B. 'Molière et Bourdaloue', *Revue universelle*, 16 September 1929, pp. 641-56.

DUTERTRE, E. 'Scudéry et la querelle du Cid', *XVIIe siècle*, vols. 84-5, 1969, pp. 61-74.

DUVIGNAUD, J. *L'Acteur: esquisse d'une sociologie du comédien*, Paris, 1965.

ÉRIAU, J.-B. *Pourquoi les Pères de l'Église ont condamné le théâtre de leur temps*, Paris, 1914.

FAGE, R. 'Étienne Baluze et *le Tartuffe*', *Bulletin de la Société des Lettres, Sciences et Arts de la Corrèze*, vol. 34, 1912, pp. 297-315.

FUMAROLI, M. 'Rhétorique et dramaturgie dans l'*Illusion comique* de Corneille', *XVIIe siècle*, vols. 80-1, 1968, pp. 107-32.

— — 'La Querelle de la moralité du théâtre avant Nicole et Bossuet', *Revue d'histoire littéraire de la France*, vol. 70, 1970, pp. 1007-30.

GAQUÈRE, Fr. *Le Théâtre devant la conscience chrétienne*, Paris, 1965.

GASTÉ, A. *Jean Racine et Pierre Bardou*, Paris, 1901.

GAZIER, A. *Mélanges de littérature et d'histoire*, Paris, 1904.

— — 'Les Comédiens et le clergé', *Revue critique*, vol. 2, 1884, pp. 377–9.

GENETTE, G. *Figures II*, Paris, 1969.

GIRBAL, F. *Bernard Lamy*, Paris, 1964.

GOFFLOT, L.-V. *Le Théâtre au collège du moyen âge à nos jours*, Paris, 1907.

HALEY, Sister M. P. *Racine and the Art Poétique of Boileau*, Baltimore, 1938.

HALL, H. G. 'Desmarets de Saint-Sorlin and the *Querelle des Imaginaires*', *Modern Language Review*, vol. 55, 1960, pp. 181–5.

HERLAND, L. 'Les Qualités du personnage de tragédie', in *Mélanges de la Société toulousaine d'Études classiques*, Toulouse, vol. 2, 1946, pp. 205–22.

HOPE, Quentin M. 'Molière et Saint-Évremond', *Publications of the Modern Language Association of America*, vol. 76, 1961, pp. 200–4.

HORVILLE, R. *Dom Juan de Molière: une dramaturgie de rupture*, Paris, 1972.

HOUSE, H. *Aristotle's Poetics: a Course of Eight Lectures*, London, 1956.

HUBERT, J. D. 'Le Réel et l'illusoire dans le théâtre de Corneille et dans celui de Rotrou', *Revue des sciences humaines*, 1958, pp. 333–50.

JUSSELIN, M. 'Gilles Marie, curé de Saint Saturin de Chartres', *Revue d'histoire du théâtre*, vol. 1, 1948–9, pp. 269–70.

KELLY, J. *La Querelle du théâtre en France de 1657–1700* (Thèse pour le Doctorat de l'Université de Paris), 1952.

KERN, E. G. *The Influence of Heinsius and Vossius upon French Dramatic Theory*, Baltimore, 1949.

KNIGHT, R. C. *Racine et la Grèce*, Paris, 1951.

LANCASTER, H. C. *A History of French Dramatic Literature in the Seventeenth Century*, 9 vols., Baltimore, 1929–42.

LAPOMMERAYE, H. de. *Molière et Bossuet, réponse à M. Louis Veuillot*, Paris, 1877.

LARROUMET. 'Le Théâtre et la morale', *Revue bleue*, 22 October 1887, pp. 513-23.

LAWRENSON, T. E. *The French Stage in the Seventeenth Century*, Manchester, 1957.

LEBÈGUE, R. 'L'Herodes Infanticida en France', *Neophilologus*, vol. 23, 1938, pp. 148-54.

LE BIDOIS, G. *De Comoedia et de nostratibus scenicis poetis quid judicaverit Bossuetius*, Thesis fac. litt. in univ. Parisiensi, Paris (Macon pr.) 1900.

LEDRÉ, Ch. 'Théâtre et "exercices publics" dans les collèges lyonnais du XVIIᵉ et du XVIIIᵉ siècles', *Bulletin de la Société lyonnaise*, vol. 16, 1940-4, pp. 1-29; ibid., vol. 17, 1945-9, pp. 1-19.

LOUGH, J. *Paris Theatre Audiences in the Seventeenth and Eighteenth Centuries*, Oxford, 1957.

LOUKOVITCH, K. *L'Évolution de la tragédie religieuse classique*, Paris, 1933.

MACCHIA, G. *Il paradiso della ragione*, Bari, 1960.

MANTÉRO. *Corneille critique et son temps*, Paris, 1964.

MAUGRAS, G. *Les Comédiens hors la loi*, Paris, 1887.

MÉLÈSE, P. *Le Théâtre et le public à Paris sous Louis XIV, 1659-1715*, Paris, 1934.

MESNARD, J. 'De la *diversion* au divertissement', *Mémorial du 1er Congrès international des Études montaignistes*, Bordeaux, 1964, pp. 123-8.

MICHAUT, G. *Les Luttes de Molière*, Paris, 1925.

MOFFAT, Margaret M. *Rousseau et la querelle du théâtre au XVIIIᵉ siècle*, Paris, 1930.

MONGRÉDIEN, G. *Les Grands Comédiens du XVIIᵉ siècle*, Paris, 1927.

— — *Dictionnaire biographique des comédiens français, suivi d'un inventaire des troupes (1590-1710), d'après des documents inédits*, Paris, 1961.

— — *La Vie quotidienne des comédiens au temps de Molière*, Paris, 1966.

— — 'La querelle du théâtre à la fin du règne de Louis XIV', *Revue d'histoire du théâtre*, vol. 2, 1978, pp. 103-19.

MOORE, W. G. 'Molière's Theory of Comedy', *Esprit créateur*, vol. 6, 1966, pp. 137-44.

MORAMBERT, Tribout de. 'A Château Thierry en 1670', *Revue d'histoire du théâtre*, vol. 1, 1948-9, pp. 266-8.

MOREL, J. *Jean Rotrou, dramaturge de l'ambiguité*, Paris, 1968.

MORNET, D. *Histoire de la littérature française classique 1660-1700*, Paris, 1942.

NADAL, O. *Le Sentiment de l'amour dans l'œuvre de Pierre Corneille*, Paris, 1948.

NELSON, Robert J. *Play Within a Play. The Dramatist's Conception of his Art: Shakespeare to Anouilh*, New Haven, 1958.

— — *Immanence and Transcendence: the Theatre of Jean Rotrou 1609-50*, Ohio, 1969.

— — 'Pierre Corneille's *L'Illusion comique*: the Play as Magic', *Publications of the Modern Language Association of America*, vol. 71, 1956, pp. 1127-40.

— — 'Art and Salvation in Rotrou's *Le Véritable Saint Genest*', *French Review*, 1956-7, pp. 451-8.

NURSE, P. 'Essai de définition du comique moliéresque', *Revue des sciences humaines*, 1964, pp. 9-24.

PALMER, J. N. J. 'The Function of "le Vraisemblable" in French Classical Aesthetic Theory', *French Studies*, vol. 19, 1975, pp. 15-26.

PASCOE, Margaret E. *Les Drames religieux du milieu du XVIIe siècle, 1636-50*, Paris, 1932.

PEYRE, H. *Qu'est-ce que le classicisme?*, Paris, 1933.

PHILLIPS, H. 'Vraisemblance and Moral Instruction in Seventeenth-Century Dramatic Theory', *Modern Language Review*, vol. 73, 1978, pp. 267-77.

PICARD, R. *La Carrière de Jean Racine*, Paris, 1961.

— — *Racine polémiste*, Paris, 1967.

— — 'Tartuffe, "production impie"?', *De Racine au Parthénon*, Paris, 1977, pp. 159-73.

PIEMME, J.-M. 'L'Utile dulci ou la convergence des nécessités: recherches historiques sur les causes de l'adoption de la règle scaligérienne de l'utilité par les théoriciens de 1630', *Revue d'histoire du théâtre*, vol. 2, 1969, pp. 118-33.

— — 'Le Théâtre en face de la critique religieuse: un exemple, Pierre Nicole', *XVIIe siècle*, vol. 88, 1970, pp. 49-59.

POMMIER, J. *Aspects de Racine*, Paris, 1954.

REESE, Helen R. *La Mesnardière's Poétique (1639): Sources and Dramatic Theories*, Baltimore, 1937.

REISS, T. J. *Toward Dramatic Illusion: Theatrical Technique and Meaning*, New Haven and London, 1971.

REYNIER, G. 'Un Épisode du conflit de l'Église et du théâtre au XVIIe siècle', *Revue d'histoire littéraire de la France*, vol. 32, 1925, pp. 576-9.

REYVAL, A. *L'Église et le théâtre, essai historique*, Paris, 1924.

— — *L'Église, la comédie et les comédiens*, Paris, 1953.

— — 'L'Église et le théâtre', *XVIIe siècle*, vol. 39, 1958, pp. 218-27.

ROBERT, R. 'Des commentaires de première main sur les chefs-d'œuvre les plus discutés de Molière', *Revue des sciences humaines*, 1956, pp. 19-49.

ROUSSET, J. *La Littérature de l'âge baroque en France*, Paris, 1953.

— — *L'Intérieur et l'extérieur: essais sur la poésie et sur le théâtre au XVIIe siècle*, Paris, 1968.

SAISSELIN, R. *The Rule of Reason and the Heart: A Philosophical Dictionary of Classical French Criticism, Critics and Aesthetic Issues*, Cleveland and London, 1970.

SALOMON, H. P. *Tartuffe devant l'opinion française*, Paris, 1962.

SCHERER, J. *La Dramaturgie classique en France*, Paris, 1950.

— — *Structures de Tartuffe*, 2ième, édition revue et augmentée, Paris, 1974.

— — 'Une Scène inédite de *Saint Genest*', *Revue d'histoire littéraire de la France*, vol. 50, 1950, pp. 395-403.

SEILLIÈRE, E. 'Esthétique et morale au XVIIe siècle', *Journal des Débats*, 8 September 1935.

SNYDERS, G. *La Pédagogie en France au XVIIe et XVIIIe siècles*, Paris, 1965.

SOREIL, A. *Introduction à l'histoire de l'esthétique française: contribution à l'étude des théories littéraires et plastiques en France de la Pléiade au XVIIe siècle*, Brussels, 1955.

STONE, D. *French Humanist Tragedy: A Reassessment*, Manchester, 1974.

SWEETSER, Marie-Odile. *Les Conceptions dramatiques de Corneille d'après ses écrits théoriques*, Paris, 1962.

THOMAS, le R. P. 'Bossuet et le théâtre', *Revue des jeunes*, 10 November 1927, pp. 423–45.

TOUCHARD, P.-A. *Dionysos, apologie pour le théâtre*, Paris, 1938.

VÉDIER, G. *Origine et évolution de la dramaturgie néo-classique*, Paris, 1955.

VEUILLOT, L. *Molière et Bourdaloue*, Paris, 1877.

VILLIERS, A. 'Illusion dramatique et dramaturgie classique', *XVIIe siècle*, vol. 73, 1966, pp. 3–35.

WEINBERG, B. *History of Literary Criticism in the Italian Renaissance*, 2 vols., Chicago, 1961.

WILEY, W. L. *The Early Public Theatre in France*, Harvard, 1960.

WOSHINSKY, B. *La Princesse de Clèves: The Tension of Elegance*, The Hague, 1973.

INDEX

Actors,
  Church tradition, 179-82
  Edict of 1641, 4, 9, 11, 193, 193-6, 197-8
  Religious status, 212-3, 216-7
  Roman theatre, 175-9
  School theatre, 199-202
  Social status, 189-93
  Women on stage, 187-8
Admiration, *see under* Catharsis
Ambrose, St., 160, 169, 241
Anne of Austria, 16
Aristotle, 17, 18, 21, 36, 38, 39, 40, 41, 42, 43, 44, 46, 52, 53, 58, 61, 65, 69, 82, 167, 169, 170
  Poetics, 6
Aubignac, Fr. H., Abbé d', 5, 14, 20, 22, 25, 27, 34-5, 62, 63-4, 71, 72, 73-4, 106, 115, 137-8, 151, 152, 174, 175-7, 178, 188 n. 68, 199, 210, 216n.59, 225, 231-4, 236, 239, 241n.112, 243, 246, 247, 249
Augustine, St., 74, 158, 177

Baillet, A., 103, 249
Balzac, J. L. Guez de, 12, 32, 33, 225-7, 228
Bardou, P., 235
Baron, 15, 16
Basil, St., 149
Beaulieu, Mlle de, 12
Beni, P., 57, 63
Boileau-Despréaux, N., 32, 36, 37-8, 40, 90, 90-1, 96, 108 n. 116, 245, 247
Bossuet, J.-B., 2, 10, 11, 14, 73, 80-1, 82, 92-3, 94, 97, 104, 105, 108-9, 112-13, 121-2, 123, 124, 126, 127, 128-9, 133, 141-2, 149, 159, 164-5, 165, 165-6, 166-7, 168-70, 180-2, 186, 188, 195, 199, 219, 220
Bourdaloue, le Père L., 2, 147-9,
150, 154
Boursault, E., 14
Boyer, l'Abbé C., 15, 220, 222, 223, 225, 232, 235, 240
Brecht, B., 248
Brécourt, G. M. de, 15

Caffaro, le Père Th., 4, 14, 72-3, 74-6, 80, 85, 119, 120, 121, 122-3, 125, 158-61, 165, 166, 167-8, 170, 171, 180, 189-90, 192, 194, 199, 204-5, 206-7, 210, 218
Camus, J.-P., 3
Castelvetro, 23, 50, 56, 57
Catharsis, 7, 36, 91, 245
  Admiration, 54, 67-8, 69, 70
  Aesthetic catharsis, 40-1
  Characters' qualities and attitudes, 53-6
  Definition of terms, 38-9, 41-3, 45-6
  Identification of hero and spectator, 56-60
  Moeurs, 17, 52-3, 60
  Moralistic function, 37-46
  Separation of tragic emotions, 60-6
  Tragic error, 47-52, 55
Censorship, 7, 211-20
Chapelain, J., 5, 7, 18, 22, 26, 27, 30, 37, 38, 53, 100-1, 103, 104, 247
Chappuzeau, S., 14, 74, 77, 89, 127 n. 78, 161, 183, 190-2, 193-4, 196, 200-1, 210-11, 246-7
Charles Borromeo, St., 73 n. 4, 79, 218
Charpentier, Fr., 182-3
Cheminais de Montaigu, le Père T., 2
Clement of Alexandria, St., 2
Cologne, anonymous preacher from, 127, 153, 202, 217-18
Comedy, 131, 136-8, 138-41, 141-5, 149-50
Conti, Armand de Bourbon, Prince de, 2, 13, 85-6, 87-8, 94, 112, 113,

Q.2